AYUB KHAN DIN

Ayub Khan Din's play *East is East* (1996) was originally staged at the Royal Court Theatre and adapted into a feature film. The play and film have won a Writers' Guild Award for Best New Writer and a British Academy Award. Other plays include *Last Dance at Dum Dum* (1999), *Notes on Falling Leaves* (2004) and *Rafta, Rafta...* (2007), which won a Laurence Olivier Award for Best New Comedy. A film adaptation, *All in Good Time*, was released in 2012, a year after his sequel to *East is East*, named *West is West*. His most recent plays have been *All the Way Home*, directed by Mark Babych at the Lowry Theatre in Salford, musical comedy *Bunty Berman Presents*, produced on Broadway by The New Group, and an adaptation of E.R. Braithwaite's *To Sir, With Love*.

AYUB KHAN DIN

Plays: One

East is East
Notes on Falling Leaves
All the Way Home
To Sir, With Love

with a Foreword by the author

NICK HERN BOOKS
London
www.nickhernbooks.co.uk

A Nick Hern Book

Ayub Khan Din Plays: One first published in Great Britain as a paperback original
in 2014 by Nick Hern Books Limited, The Glasshouse, 49a Goldhawk Road,
London W12 8QP

Cover image: Ayub Khan Din's father holding his elder brother with relatives in
Salford

Designed and typeset by Nick Hern Books, London
Printed in Great Britain by Mimeo Ltd, Huntingdon, Cambridgeshire PE29 6XX

ISBN   978 1 84842 424 1

For Paul Bhattacharjee
4 May 1960 – 12 July 2013

Contents

Foreword

East is East

I began writing *East is East* in 1982 in my first year in drama school. It had never occurred to me that I might ever end up becoming a playwright but realising early on that there were so few parts for Asian actors, plus a dramatic turn of events at home, pushed me to start writing what eventually would become *East is East*.

Jobs for Asian actors at that time were few and far between and mostly consisted of race-crime victims and corner-shop owners, even then only as backdrops to the main event. The only real storylines that interested the programme-makers always centred on arranged marriages, where the girl was being forced into a relationship not of her choosing. Though this was an important issue, and still is today, in my case, it was my brothers who were the victims and the perpetrator was my father, who himself had chosen to marry an Englishwoman.

The dramatic event on the home front was that my mother had been diagnosed with Alzheimer's at the age of fifty-five. It seemed that every time I returned home to Salford, the disease had progressed and huge chunks of our lives were being eaten away and lost for ever. She was the only common denominator between my father and his estranged children, so even more reason to start writing things down before it was too late. I don't think I ever asked either of my parents any pertinent questions about their relationship. Why they did the things they did? Why they married? Why did he decide to marry an Englishwoman, even though he already had a wife and two daughters in Pakistan, whom he always considered his family?

A million questions any writer should have asked for research. But I wasn't and I didn't. It's not what we talked about in my family. In fact, we really didn't talk about anything. We never questioned my father or any of the decisions he made. The TV blared loudly in the corner, and we did as we were told.

As my older siblings decided that my father's way of life wasn't the life they wanted, there would be conflicts and banishments. My mother always defended our right to make choices and would be on the receiving end of my father's physical abuse, all of which I witnessed. It wasn't all doom and gloom: you learn to live the life you have, because it's the only life you know and it's actually perfectly normal to you. We knew what buttons not to press with my father, but inevitably they did get pressed.

Writing *East is East* took place over a number of years, through drama school and my first acting job with the Tara Arts Theatre Company, an Asian theatre group, where I spent some of my most formative years as an actor. Tara was an ensemble group that devised all its own shows, then toured them up and down the country, playing to diverse audiences. I didn't know it but I was learning my craft, and how to formulate arguments and develop characters, all of which would add to *East is East*. It went through a couple of drafts and then got slung in the back of a drawer. I was too busy being a celluloid tart to think about writing.

It was always something I did as a hobby in between acting jobs. Never ever something I showed to anybody. It had a play-reading in 1986 at the Albany Empire purely because I was taking part in a playwriting competition as an actor. I mentioned it to the director and he got me to bring it in. When I got the title role in *Sammy and Rosie Get Laid* by Hanif Kureishi, which was being directed by Stephen Frears, once again my whore's eyes turned to dreams of Hollywood and stardom. *East is East* went back in the drawer.

Cut to: 1995 and my friends had set up Tamasha Theatre. Sudha Bhuchar and Kristine Langdon-Smith had been approached by the Royal Court to do a joint production. Kristine and Sudha suggested a two-week workshop to look for and develop new Asian writers. Sudha asked me if I still had *East is East*.

I did. We did the workshop. I fell in love with writing. The play was chosen. It opened at Birmingham Repertory studio on the 8th October 1996 and the Royal Court Theatre Upstairs on the 19th November 1996. Eventually we were allowed downstairs at the Royal Court in March 1997.

Notes on Falling Leaves

I don't know why I choose the subjects I write about, I think they choose me. I never set out to write plays with messages, I'm not interested in telling an audience what to think. I prefer my characters to present the truth according to the world they inhabit. I don't always agree with what they say, but it's important that they say it. Sometimes they may say things we'd rather not hear, that may be offensive to some, but that's life. For me the most enjoyable drama should attempt to stimulate argument, thought and debate.

Notes on Falling Leaves took me out of my comfort zone. It became a much more abstract play than I had originally intended. As I mentioned earlier, my mother was diagnosed with Alzheimer's at an early age and eventually the disease claimed her life after three years. I always found it difficult during the family visits to see her. In my mind, I was never quite sure what it was I was actually visiting... It sounds a harsh and unfeeling statement, but it was made from a place of safety, that I could observe from. I never saw any sign of recognition and really didn't want to be around her, as I found it too upsetting. I didn't know how to engage with her on this level.

The first draft of the play started in a very conventional manner. Set on a ward similar to my mother's, about a group of women all suffering from Alzheimer's. What struck me about the ward was that the women had led full and active lives. One had been a concert pianist, another a high-ranking official in the Salvation Army, and one woman had been head of Manchester libraries. Then, of course, there was my mother and all she had been through in her life (see *East is East*).

The idea was always to discover what happened to the women they were. Was there anything left of their personalities? I had the idea that they came alive at night, when no one was around. A magic hour when they became themselves once again. The pianist would play, the Salvation Army officer would talk about God and her faith, the librarian would read, and my mother – my mother would make tea and talk about her children.

It was all very nice and lovely and magical. But was also a lie. It said nothing of what they were going through and felt totally dishonest about the disease that was slowly destroying them. After about thirty pages of this Hans Christian Alzheimer's nonsense, I frustratedly deleted it – but was left with a small passage of dialogue. The dialogue was the character of the Mother. There was something in what she said that struck home. I felt that she suddenly had a voice that had expression from wherever her personality had retreated to.

Here was a woman who still had feeling, who was still being affected by the world that was increasingly fading around her, striving to communicate. From that point on I realised that it could be only about her. Her understanding of the world she lived in and what was happening to her through what was left of her personality. And me. About my feelings towards her. About a journey we took together, that altered both our lives for ever.

The play had to be raw, ugly and visceral. I remembered that journey we took. To the doctor's, when we were told she had Alzheimer's. How our world suddenly changed. The tables turned and I wasn't a child any more. She was asked to wait outside. And then they told me. I was nineteen and felt completely useless, alone with this awful knowledge. Outside the world was light and sunny, but the walk back home was dark and would continue to get darker.

In the play, the Mother and son make the same journey, which is seared into both their minds. And heard from both their perspectives. For the Man, it becomes a journey he recreates, the night he returns to the family home for the last time, with a girlfriend he barely knows. Back to a house that is completely familiar to him, nothing changed, everything in its place. But untouched, it sits empty in the shadows, silently waiting the return of the family that will never return.

All the Way Home

Yet another piece inspired by family tragedy!

My eldest brother had been diagnosed with cancer and was dying. In his last months we'd all try to make it back to Salford to visit him. It was strange, as it was the first time all ten siblings had been together since childhood. Some of us had been estranged for many years. The Salford we knew had changed. The last bits we recognised were literally being pulled down around our ears. It was no longer the place we grew up in, and, for most of us, escaped from. I say escape, because that is what it felt like. It didn't mean that we hated Salford, quite the opposite, we all carry a certain nostalgia for the time we lived there. But it would be wrong to think we have the same kind of relationship now. We all change and look at things differently. Particularly with the relationships we have with our past. The Salford we knew was gone, particularly so for the people who left. Not so for the people who stayed behind.

There was such a sense of heightened reality at this time. Everything seemed so vivid, to me. Colours, what people said and the way that they said it. The clichés of death and dying that haunted that environment. The wet dreary weather, the endless stillness as I stood and watched the gush of water from a tap that overflowed into the kettle. The sound of a washing machine, as it filled the silence of a sombre conversation. I felt that I was waiting, not for a death, but a judgement. People asked if I'd spoken to my brother, as if he were going to impart some great critique of my life to date. Had something happened that I wasn't aware of? Had I said something untoward? Even complete strangers were looking at me knowingly, as if saying, 'You'd better go and get it off your chest.'

One man had the gall to tell me he hadn't spoken to my brother, his best friend, since they fell out over *East is East*! He said it in such a way that it was obvious he held me responsible for this rift. The accusation was left hanging in the air between us. Time stood still, yet again, as I registered the fresh shaving-cut on his chin, the smell of tobacco on his breath and the death's-head earring hanging from a hairy lobe. The mind boggles as to what their argument was about. Nonetheless, he stood there taking the moral high ground, idiot-like in his expectation, waiting for some kind of apology. Now, here was his big chance to face the creator of the film that initiated the argument, that had destroyed an obviously much-cherished friendship.

'Oh,' I said, 'that was a bit fucking stupid,' and walked away.

I can only hope that brought him some kind of closure.

All the Way Home is about the clash of the past and present. How the past is always a major contributor to our present and our future. How it informs who we are, the paths we choose to follow and the mistakes we make. It's a play about a family and their struggle to come to terms with each other. How, inevitably, while facing the death of one of their own, they are compelled to confront their own lives and those of their siblings. Forced to evaluate each other through their own disappointments. What is it that brings them together? What are the things that remain unsaid, boiling below the surface, as they move through the rituals of death? What is it that makes these things eventually erupt?

To Sir, With Love

I was asked, quite by chance, if I'd be interested in adapting this wonderful book. What really resonated for me was the subject of education, of how we teach our children – not just the basics of reading and writing, but how we send them out into the world to become part of society. Something I believe is sadly lacking in today's world. So many of the theories we have about education today can trace their DNA back to the work of Alex Bloom, the Headmaster of St George-in-the-East, the school on which *To Sir, With Love* is based.

Some of Bloom's ideas were revolutionary, but, like most geniuses, Alex Bloom was largely ignored by his own education authorities. However, many of his theories were put into practice by educationalists across post-war Europe.

To Sir, With Love is also about our history, the history of Empire and Commonwealth, subjects so many of our young people know little about. It's the key to understanding who we are and what our place is in today's Britain.

E.R. Braithwaite understands this: it's why his story has such relevance to young people of immigrant backgrounds at a time when the Government is telling us how to be British citizens.

It's important for young white Britain to know that black and Asian Britain has been part of the make-up of this country for centuries. That we are descendants of races who have fought and died for the freedoms that this country now enjoys. We are an essential part of British history and an indivisible part of the fabric of her society, not just as former subjects from across the seas, but as active participants of this nation's history.

This is one of the lessons Braithwaite used to fight the racism he found in the classroom and which was levelled at him. It was important for him that his kids knew they had a useful place in society, and that their participation in that society was imperative if it was to continue to grow and flourish.

We all have to understand each other's histories and stories, because it's only when we do, that we discover that there is so much more that binds us than divides us.

Ayub Khan Din
Cortijo Cabeza Baja, 2014

EAST IS EAST

To Hilda, Charlie, and all at 63

This version of *East is East* was first performed at the Trafalgar Studios, London, as part of the Trafalgar Transformed season, on 15 October 2014 (previews from 4 October). The cast was as follows:

GEORGE KHAN	Ayub Khan Din
ELLA KHAN	Jane Horrocks
ABDUL KHAN	Amit Shah
TARIQ KHAN	Ashley Kumar
MANEER KHAN	Darren Kuppan
SALEEM KHAN	Nathan Clarke
MEENAH KHAN	Taj Atwal
SAJIT KHAN	Michael Karim
AUNTIE ANNIE	Sally Bankes
DOCTOR/MR SHAH	Hassani Shapi
MRS SHAH	Rani Moorthy

Director	Sam Yates
Set and Costume Designer	Tom Scutt
Lighting Designer	Richard Howell
Composer & Sound Designer	Alex Baranowski
Associate Director	Kimberley Sykes
Costume Supervisor	Jackie Orton
Dialect and Voice Coach	Edda Sharpe
Movement and Choreography	Georgina Lamb
Fight Director	Philip d'Orléans

An earlier version of *East is East* was first produced by Tamasha Theatre Company, the Royal Court Theatre Company and Birmingham Repertory Company. It was first performed at Birmingham Repertory Studio Theatre on 8 October 1996, at the Royal Court Theatre Upstairs on 19 November 1996, and the Royal Court Theatre Downstairs on 26 March 1997. The cast was as follows:

GEORGE KHAN	Nasser Memarzia
ELLA KHAN	Linda Bassett
ABDUL KHAN	Paul Bazely
TARIQ KHAN	Jimi Mistry
MANEER KHAN	Emil Marwa
SALEEM KHAN	Chris Bisson
MEENAH KHAN	Zita Sattar
SAJIT KHAN	Imran Ali
AUNTIE ANNIE	Gillian Hanna
DOCTOR/MR SHAH	Kriss Dosanjh
Director	Kristine Landon-Smith
Designer	Sue Mayes
Lighting Designer	Paul Taylor

Characters

GEORGE KHAN, *father, fifty-five*

ELLA KHAN, *mother, forty-six*

ABDUL KHAN, *son, twenty-three*

TARIQ KHAN, *son, twenty-one*

MANEER KHAN, *son, nineteen*

SALEEM KHAN, *son, eighteen*

MEENAH KHAN, *daughter, sixteen*

SAJIT KHAN, *son, twelve*

AUNTIE ANNIE, *fifty*

MR SHAH, *fifty-two*

MRS SHAH, *forty-eight*

ACT ONE

Scene One

Saturday. The action takes place in Salford in 1971, prior to the outbreak of war between India and Pakistan over the independence of East Pakistan. The KHANS are an Anglo-Pakistani family of eight. The contrast of cultures should come out in the set dressing, wallpaper, oilcloth, a coffee table with a picture of the Taj Mahal, a lazy Susan which is always full of washing.

The set is made up of a fish and chip shop, a parlour, living room, and a kitchen with a shed attached. The parlour should be more upmarket as it's used for entertaining. When the play begins we find ELLA and ANNIE sat in the living room talking, drinking tea and smoking. They're very good friends who go back a long way. ANNIE is like a second mother to the kids.

GEORGE (*off*). Come here you dirty little baster...

ELLA. Hey, hey, hey... What the bleeding hell has he done now?

GEORGE. Done? I tell you what he bloody done, missus. He bloody make a show of me. All a time. All your family alway make a bloody show of me. Four year I been going that mosque, now I can't look mullah in bloody face now! Because he – (*Points to* SAJIT.) got bloody... tickle-tackle.

SAJIT *goes over to* ANNIE.

ANNIE. What's to do, cock?

ELLA. What are you going on about you big daft get? What bleeding tickle-tackle?

GEORGE. I tell you, stupy why you no listen. Your son bloody got it... (*Indicates his crotch.*) here, tickle-tackle.

ELLA *looks over to* ANNIE, ANNIE *looks at* ELLA, *they both know something.*

MEENAH. The mullah saw it, Mam. He went bleeding barmy!

ELLA. Less of the bleeding you.

GEORGE (*to* MEENAH). Oi, you, who bloody asking your bloody 'pinion? What you doing looking boys in the first bloody place, don't trouble with me 'cause I bloody fix you!

ELLA. Just what did he see, George?

GEORGE. Bloody everything, how he can go mosque again, when he got bloody tickle-tackle?

ELLA. Are you saying he's not been circumcised?

MEENAH. What's circumcised, Mam?

ELLA. You shop, now!

Exit MEENAH.

GEORGE. Why you not bloody fix this thing when he was baby, same as others?

ELLA. Well someone's got it wrong somewhere 'cause they were all done, all six of them.

ANNIE (*backing* ELLA *up*). I'm sure she's right George, he was in the same ward as our Clifford in Hope Hospital when he had shingles.

GEORGE (*exasperated*). Look, I know what I bloody talking about, I see you sees, mullah see, all bloody all mosque seeing. You no believe me, you bloody looking.

ELLA. Sajit, come here.

SAJIT (*starts to cry*). No, you're gonna hurt me.

ELLA. I'm not gonna hurt you, I just want a little look, that's all.

SAJIT. Get stuffed!

ANNIE. Oi! – language.

GEORGE. Take bloody off!

ELLA. I'll stuff you in a minute you cheeky little bleeder, now get here and get 'em off!

SAJIT. I don't want to.

GEORGE. Hey baster, I bloody fix you, you talk to you mam like that. You already cause me enough bloody troubles today.

ANNIE. Come Saj, let me have a look, I've seen it all before. Go on, I'll be dead quick.

SAJIT. Orrrr.

ANNIE. Come on, I've wiped your shitty arse before now.

ELLA. Let Auntie Annie have a look.

SAJIT. Alright, but you've got to be quick.

He opens his pants for her, she has a quick look.

ANNIE. He's right you know, Ella, it's still there. (*To* SAJIT.) This is one little fish that got through the net.

GEORGE. You see, is your bloody fault.

ELLA. How the hell was I supposed to keep count, you could have remembered.

ANNIE. Nowt to worry about, George, you can still get him done.

ELLA. I know who I'd like to get done.

ELLA *and* ANNIE *laugh.*

GEORGE. Is not bloody funny you knows, you just bloody fix. This tickle-tackle very embarrassing you see, Annie. I have important arrangement to make, and I can't now see, 'cause of this. All men think I bad my son having this thing, has to be cutting.

ELLA. What arrangements?

GEORGE. You not need to know my bloody business, missus.

SAJIT. I'm not going to the doctor!

GEORGE. You can't have this thing puther, it no belong to you, not our religion see, is very dirty. No worry about it, I buy you nice watch.

ELLA. Look cock, it's just a little operation, it'll be over in a day.

ANNIE. You won't feel a thing.

SAJIT *runs out*.

GEORGE. Come here, baster…

ELLA. Leave it, he'll only get more upset.

ANNIE. I'll go and talk to him.

ANNIE *goes out through the kitchen to the shed, where* SAJIT *has locked himself in*.

ELLA. Why bother with all this now at his age?

GEORGE. What you talking about? You know nothing about my religion, no try a understand. You no bloody care your children have no God. Your son no Muslim with this thing, when he die he go straight to hell.

ELLA. He's not gonna be sent to hell, just because he's got a foreskin.

GEORGE. You see, I try to explain to you, but you no bloody listen.

ELLA *sits back and lights a fag, she's heard this lecture before*.

ELLA. I'm always bleeding listening, can't get a word in edgeways with you.

GEORGE. All your bloody children run a wild, but I telling you, missus, no more, because I'm fixing them. I bloody show them.

ELLA. You tried that with Nazir and look what happened.

GEORGE. I tell you, if I see that boy Nazir in my house, I bloody kill him baster.

ELLA. Your house? Whose frigging name's on the rent book!

GEORGE. Maybe your name, missus, but my shop money pay bloody rent, in't it?

ELLA. Oh yeah, and what do you think I do in that chippy from eight thirty in the morning till twelve thirty at night, count the mushy fucking peas!

GEORGE *grins slightly, these arguments happen all the time, and this one has reached its point.*

GEORGE. How bloody hell I know what you do all day, every time I look, you sit with Annie, talking, smoking, drink a tea, smoking, drink a tea, talking. Nobody serve my bloody chips.

ELLA. We work hard in that shop, and as for being sat around well you're a fine one to talk, ever since this trouble started in Pakistan, you're never away from the telly.

GEORGE. I have to take interest you sees, family in Azad Kashmir, near bloody border. Bloody make me worry, in't it?

ELLA. The answer's no.

GEORGE. What you bloody talking about 'no'. (*Grins.*) I not bloody ask anything.

ELLA. You don't need to, I can read your bleeding mind like the back of me hand, so you can piss off if you think you're bringing her over here.

GEORGE. I not understand why you talk to me like this my darling.

ELLA *smiles.*

ELLA. Never mind darling, if she steps foot in this country, I'm off, and I'll take the bleeding kids with me.

GEORGE. Why is big problem, first wife always treat second wife like sister. All live together happy.

ELLA. You think you're funny don't you? Well, she'll have nowt to be happy about if she walks in here, 'cause I'll wipe the smile right off her friggin' face!

GEORGE (*smiles*). I just joke with you, you my only wife in England.

Enter ANNIE.

ANNIE. He's locked himself in the coal shed again.

GEORGE. I tell you, this boy bloody stupy I think, no full shilling. Every time I walk in street with him, he talking to bloody self. Every time he turn corner, he bloody cutting, cutting. (*Makes a scissor-cutting motion.*) Bloody mentals.

ANNIE. Has he had the coat off yet?

ELLA. No. Won't let anyone go near it, it'll have to come off soon, though, 'cause it bleeding stinks.

GEORGE. I thought bloody dog shitting in house. No, it bloody Sajit. I rip baster thing off him soon.

ANNIE. Leave it, he'll come out of it, it's just a phase. Our Clifford had one with a bit of plasticine and a pumice stone.

GEORGE. Why he alway go hide in bloody coal shed? Kid in a Pakistan no like this.

ELLA. No, you're all so perfect over there aren't you.

GEORGE (*wags his finger at* ELLA). You not bloody start with me again missus or I send bloody invitation to Mrs Khan number one, in a Pakistan. I say, 'Come bloody quick, second wife give me bloody troubles.'

ELLA (*taking it in good humour*). Piss off.

GEORGE. I go butcher now, buy some chicken, you and Annie open up, I be back 'bout five.

ELLA. If you go past the shop, tell our Abdul to come and get Sajit out of the shed, we've a delivery at two and it took us half an hour to dig him out last time.

GEORGE *goes out*.

ANNIE (*checks to see* GEORGE *has gone*). You bleeding knew about Sajit didn't you?

ELLA. I did, but it had gone right out of me mind, he was supposed to be done, but the hospital cancelled it 'cause he got flu. George never found out, and what he didn't know wouldn't hurt him.

ANNIE. You knew he'd find out sooner or later, you daft sod.

ELLA. Oh yeah, and when was the last time you saw George washing a baby or wiping a shitty arse? You know Saleem had such a hard time of it when he was done, I don't think I could have listened to another one of 'em screaming in pain.

ANNIE. Mm. Now you're gonna have to.

Beat.

ELLA. That bastard's up to something, I don't know what yet, but I can feel it in me bones.

ANNIE. Has he started buying material?

ELLA. Every time he comes back from the market he's got another six yards.

ANNIE. What does he do with it?

ELLA. Presents. He sends it to Pakistan for them to make clothes, then they send us Sinbad waistcoats and he puts them in the trunk in the attic. He bought some silk the other week, bloody nice stuff as well, yards of it, must have cost a bomb.

ANNIE. It don't come cheap Ella.

ELLA. He's a bastard, sends silk to her in Pakistan and I'm lucky if I can afford a bit of net curtain for the bleeding parlour!

They both laugh.

Chip-shop door opens.

Scene Two

The boys and MEENAH *run into the chip shop, throwing* MANEER's *skull cap between them.* TARIQ *jumps onto the counter with it.* SALEEM *starts to mop the floor,* MEENAH *follows him round with a couple of old rags on her feet drying it off.* TARIQ *tosses the cap back to* MANEER *and stretches out on the counter.*

TARIQ. The thing is Maneer, even if your cap is religious, people round here just think you've got a tea cosy on your head.

All laugh except MANEER.

SALEEM. Where's that little twitching twat, he should be here doing this. I've got a still life that's got to be handed in by Monday.

TARIQ (*posh voice*). Oh have you Saleem, what a bleeding shame. And you've still the fish to cut and batter.

MEENAH. Me dad's going ape shit over there.

MANEER. He looked dead embarrassed in the mosque, I thought he were gonna cry.

TARIQ. Tough. Look, whatever happened with Twitch, it got us out of that place quick, and that's alright in my book.

SALEEM. You only go once a week, you ought to try it every night, and do project work for college.

TARIQ. You sit on your arse drawing all day with felt-tip pens. You don't know the meaning of hard work yet, just wait till Genghis finds out you're doing an art course, and not the engineering he thinks you're doing. I tell you mate, you'll be behind this counter servin' chips before the paint's dried on your palette.

SALEEM. Yeah, well he won't find out unless someone tells him, will he Tariq?

TARIQ. Don't look at me, it's Maneer you've got to watch, he's the one sharing hat tips with old Genghis, aren't you, Gandhi?

MANEER (*heard the same old jokes before*). Yeah right Tariq, funny, now will you get off the counter so I can clean it.

Enter ABDUL *carrying two baskets of potatoes.*

ABDUL. Tariq, do as you're told and let him clean it. You can start chipping these spuds. (*To* SALEEM *and* MEENAH.) Haven't you two finished yet?

SALEEM. Yeah, alright Abdul, we're doing it, God you're beginning to sound just like me dad.

MEENAH. He'll be kicking our heads in, in a minute.

The others start to laugh.

(*Mimicking* GEORGE.) 'Hey you move baster, I bloody kill you!'

ABDUL. Just get it done alright, Meenah?

TARIQ (*to* ABDUL). What time are we supposed to be going to Bradford tomorrow?

ABDUL. Poppah Sadeq's gonna pick us up at nine.

MEENAH. Are we all going?

ABDUL. No, just us two.

MANEER. But it's a first Sunday, we always all go to Bradford on a first Sunday.

ABDUL. Well, not this time.

TARIQ. Ask me dad if you can go instead of me, Gandhi. Last place I want to be this weekend is Bradistan.

ABDUL. The spuds, Tariq.

TARIQ. I don't see why I should go and meet more relatives, I'm related to half of Bradford as it is.

We hear knocking at the door, TARIQ *pulls aside the net curtain on it.*

Me dad!!

Everyone starts to panic. SALEEM *picks up the mop and bucket and runs around the other side of the counter where he starts to batter the fish.* TARIQ *leaps over the counter and chips potatoes in the chipper at an alarming rate.* MEENAH *shuffles around maniacally trying to dry the floor, while* MANEER *wipes everything in sight.*

Enter GEORGE.

GEORGE. Abdul, go over to house, Sajit in a coal shed.

MANEER. Dad, can I go to Bradford tomorrow as well?

GEORGE. No. You coming with me to mosque here, we go to see mullah, you come as well Saleem, and you, Meenah.

SALEEM. I've got college work to do, Dad.

GEORGE. This more important. (*Looks at* TARIQ's *hair.*) Why you not cutting you bloody hair when I tell you? You looking like bloody pansy. Get bloody cut.

TARIQ. Right Dad.

GEORGE. Short back-a-side. (*To* SALEEM.) And why you wear this stupy clothes? Where suit I buy you in market for you wear a college? I not made-a bloody money you know mister.

The others can barely hold in their laughter.

SALEEM. Me mam took it to the cleaner's, dad.

GEORGE. You bloody lucky go a college. I come to this country with nothing. Now what I got?

MEENAH. You've got a chip shop Dad.

GEORGE. I got own business see. You better chance than me see, go a college. So you sees, if you hair is tidy, and you looking smart, teacher looking see. Maybe help find job after. Always plenty job for engineer. Lotta job in a Pakistan, do good business there. Build house in Islamabad, very nice bungalow there.

SALEEM. Yeah, erm, long way off that though Dad.

GEORGE. You never know. Life change all a time, never know what bloody happening sees. When I first come a this country, in 1930, I here one year maybe and I make bloody film.

MEENAH, TARIQ and MANEER *can barely keep straight faces.* ABDUL *has to get away.*

MEENAH. What film was that Dad?

GEORGE. Maybe is name was *Sabu Elephant* or *The Drum.* Alexander Korda make film or maybe he brother.

TARIQ. Were you the star Dad?

GEORGE. No bloody star stupy, I shouting in crowd. 'I kill bloody English.' One day my friend say come make film, they wanting Indian. So I go. Mr Korda, very good man, one day, we all sit down eating, and he come in with woman who play actor. She say not want to eating with these people. He say, then you bloody get lost, 'cause I wanting to eat with them. Then he send her bloody away.

MEENAH. He sounds alright him Dad.

GEORGE. He very good man, look after see. No many people treat like this, 'cause we Indian.

MEENAH. I thought you're a Pakistani, Dad?

GEORGE. I Indian when I come here, stupy? Then I Pakistani. After English leave a India. Then it India and a Pakistan. Half a half, see. Why you laughing?

MEENAH. We're not laughing Dad, are we?

TARIQ. No Dad.

MANEER. No.

Beat.

GEORGE. I very strong when I young, very fit, I use bend a bars. People say you looking same as Errol Flynn! I go now, Tariq do two basket potatoes.

GEORGE *exits.*

TARIQ. Errol Flynn? More like Charlie bleeding Chaplin!

They all start to laugh.

Scene Three

Some days later. It's early morning at the KHANS' *house.* ELLA *comes from the kitchen with a tray full of cups and three packets of chocolate biscuits. She picks up a letter, opens it and lights a fag. Enter* GEORGE *carrying a plastic bucket, his head to one side, it's the piss bucket.* ELLA *winces at the smell.* GEORGE *goes out to empty it.*

GEORGE. I bloody tell Tariq empty this. I bloody kill him, baster.

ELLA. Letter here from the doctor, said he can get Sajit into Salford Royal on Tuesday. He's got to have a check-up later today. So you'll have to open up.

GEORGE. Good.

ELLA. Your tea's here, do you want biscuits or I can make you some toast?

GEORGE. Just half a cup, and biscuit. (*Exits.*)

ELLA *pours tea from one of the cups into her own. She picks up a paper and reads. Re-enter* GEORGE.

Any news about war in a Pakistan?

ELLA. Yeah, I've just read something here: 'There has been further unrest in Dacca, capital of East Pakistan, since the arrest of Sheik Mujib. West Pakistan has now declared martial law.'

GEORGE. More problem now I think, these people no good. Bloody India stir up trouble for a Pakistan.

ELLA. Well they only want their democratic rights, it's not much to ask for is it.

GEORGE. They bloody ask a India to come, maybe take Azad Kashmir. Kashmir, belong to Pakistan, whole country Muslim see. Mountbatten and bloody Nehru fixing it basters.

ELLA. If you're going to the fish market, we need some more plaice, we ran out last night.

GEORGE. I tell you, we go be lose half bloody country now.

ELLA. Only the east side. You said yourself they weren't proper Pakistanis, so I don't know what you're so bothered about. Better get some more cod as well while you're at it.

GEORGE. Of course I bloody worry, family in Azad Kashmir, on border. They be in danger.

She goes over to the door and opens it.

ELLA. Well you're not, so think yourself lucky. (*Shouting*.) Abdul, Tariq, Maneer, Saleem, Meenah, Sajit, get up, your breakfast's ready!

Pause.

GEORGE. Mr Shah be coming Sunday week, for visit.

ELLA. Oh aye, I thought you didn't like him?

GEORGE. Stupy, I never say I no like him, his family live near my village, nearly like family see. He been here twenty year, got double extension.

ELLA. How many are coming?

GEORGE. Mr Shah and a wife... He have two daughters you know, same age as Abdul and Tariq.

ELLA *is instantly suspicious.*

ELLA. Oh yeah.

GEORGE. That's why they coming here, we celebrate engagement.

ELLA. Bloody hell, George! I knew you were up to something, why didn't you tell me, for that matter, why haven't you told them?

GEORGE. Why I need to tell you my bloody business. Is my decision, no yours. Or bloody kid. I their bloody father, they do as I say. Anyway, we sort out on Sunday. I go now, tell Tariq do five basket potatoes.

ELLA. You're gonna have to say something before then.

GEORGE *exits*. ELLA *is by the door, she shouts*.

Abdul, Tariq, Maneer, Saleem, Meenah, Sajit get up now!

ELLA *sits down and lights a fag. Enter* ABDUL. *She is not sure if she should say something*.

ABDUL. What time is it Mam?

ELLA. Five past seven, you'd better hurry or you'll be late for work.

ABDUL. It's alright, Steve's giving us a lift on his bike.

ELLA. Oh be careful on that thing, he's like a bloody madman on it. Did your dad say anything the other day about Bradford?

ABDUL. No, just asked who was at Jahan Khan's.

ELLA. Did he mention anything about Mr Shah?

ABDUL. No. Nothing. They don't live in Bradford.

ELLA. I know.

Beat.

Did anyone there mention the Shahs?

ABDUL *is growing suspicious*.

ABDUL. Why? What's going on, Mam?

ELLA (*reluctant to say anything*). He's just told me he's gonna get you and Tariq engaged.

ABDUL. You what!

ELLA. To the Shahs' daughters.

ABDUL. Why didn't he said owt to me?

ELLA. He's only just told me.

ABDUL. All he talked about last night was being a good Muslim and the trouble in East Pakistan! He said nothing about getting me bloody married.

ELLA. I don't know, perhaps he thought you might do a runner like Nazir.

ABDUL. Why is it always Nazir! I'm not Nazir. Why does he never trust me, Mam? He makes decisions about my life as if he owned it.

ELLA. He thinks he does.

ABDUL. Why didn't you say something to him!

ELLA. What makes you think he's gonna start listening to me?

Pause.

ABDUL. I don't want to talk about this now, I'm going to work!

He storms out slamming the door.

ELLA. Abdul! I don't bleeding believe this family. (*Goes over to the door.*) Tariq, Maneer, Saleem, Meenah, Sajit, get up!

Beat.

If you're not up in five minutes, you're dead!

She sits down and lights a fag. MEENAH *enters.*

MEENAH. Morning. (*Takes a cup and biscuits.*)

ELLA. About bleeding time too.

MEENAH. You're bright and cheerful this morning, Mam.

ELLA. Less of the cheek as well, gobby.

MEENAH. What's wrong with our Abdul?

ELLA (*taps her nose*). Mind that. Drink your tea and get over to the shop, the floors need mopping.

MEENAH. Can I go to the school club tonight with Judy and Mary? Mary's mam said she'd take us and bring us back?

ELLA. I don't know why you're asking, 'cause you know you're going to the mosque later.

MEENAH. Oh, Mam it's not fair.

ELLA. And you can put that bleeding lip away as well, lady.

MEENAH. But these Pakistani girls always get me into trouble in the van.

ELLA. Well if you stopped to think before you hit them, you'd save yourself a lot of bother. Now get your breakfast eaten and look sharp.

Enter MANEER.

MANEER. Mam, Tariq came in through the window last night and left it open.

ELLA. Was he out again?

MANEER. He's never in.

MEENAH. You've got a right gob on you, you.

ELLA. I'll have that bleeder when he comes down.

Enter SALEEM.

SALEEM. Mam, Sajit had his coat on again last night.

MEENAH. He's a mong, him, Mam.

MANEER. I've got a scratch right down me back from the zip.

ELLA. Well tell him to take it off before he gets into bed.

MANEER. He won't listen to us, he just tells us to get stuffed and gets into bed.

ELLA. Well take it off him.

SALEEM. No way, I'm not touching him!

MEENAH. Have you felt that coat, it's all greasy, he's hanging.

Enter SAJIT*, takes a cup and a whole packet of biscuits.*

Hey, one at a time, Twitch.

SAJIT. Get stuffed, you.

ELLA. Sajit you've got an appointment with the doctor later on.

SAJIT jumps up and runs out.

That boy'll be the death of me. Right, I'm going over to the shop. Meenah, Maneer, don't take for ever over your breakfasts. As soon as Tariq comes down tell him to phone Holland's and put the pie order in. Then come over to the shop and help me change the oil in the fryers. Saleem, the money for your model's on the mantelpiece.

She exits.

MANEER. What's Twitch got to go to the doctor's for?

SALEEM goes to the mantelpiece to get his money.

SALEEM. Don't know, there's a letter here.

MEENAH. What's it say?

SALEEM (*reading*). Says it can get him into Salford Royal on Tuesday.

MANEER. What's all that about then?

SALEEM. Must be because he's a bit daft.

MEENAH. Daft? He's a fucking idiot, he wears a parka twenty-four hours a day. He doesn't need a doctor, he wants locking up.

Enter TARIQ.

TARIQ. Who wants locking up?

MEENAH. Twitch, me mam's having him put away. And Maneer told me mam that you came in through the window last night, didn't you, gobshite?

MANEER. It was freezing cold when I got up to pray this morning.

TARIQ goes over to MANEER and starts to ruffle his hair.

TARIQ. Ohh, did Gandhi have to pray in the coldy-poldy. Ohhh, what a shame.

ELLA *has entered behind* TARIQ, *she slaps him across the head.*

Ouch! What was that for?

ELLA. Where the bleeding hell were you last night?

TARIQ. In bed.

ELLA. Whose bleeding bed, that's what I want to know?

TARIQ. Me own.

ELLA. That's not what I heard. From now on I want to know your every move, lad. You go nowhere this week, without me or your dad knowing. Now get your tea drunk, and get over to the shop and change the frigging oil in the ovens.

TARIQ. But Mam...

ELLA. No bleeding 'buts', you've been warned, now shift it. Where are me fags? (*Sees* SALEEM *with the letter.*) What are you doing reading my bleeding letter? Give it here; and that's another thing, one of you make sure Sajit's here, washed and scrubbed at five o'clock for the doctor's. Use the Swarfega on him, I'm not having him looking riffy and showing me up.

MANEER. What's he going to the hospital for Mam?

ELLA. He's going to be circumcised if you must know.

MANEER (*over*). You what?

ELLA. So don't go taking the mickey out of him.

ELLA *exits.*

MEENAH. Is that what the chop is then?

TARIQ. The jammy little bastard, how's he got away with that for so long? God, what I wouldn't give to have a foreskin.

MEENAH. I've never seen one.

SALEEM. We draw them all the time at college, it's nothing special.

MEENAH. What, people stand there naked and you draw them?

MANEER. Better not let me mam find out.

SALEEM. It's part of the course, dickhead.

MANEER. Doesn't sound like art to me.

SALEEM. What fucking art do you know about, Gandhi?

MEENAH. Draw us a foreskin then.

SALEEM. You what?

MEENAH. Draw us a foreskin.

SALEEM. Give us that pen off the fireplace then.

> SALEEM *takes some paper from his bag and begins to draw a foreskin. The others look on.*
>
> (*Drawing.*) It's that bit there, it protects the end of the penis.

MEENAH. Hey that's dead good that, Saleem, innit, Tariq? Looks just like a real bloke. I didn't know you could draw that good.

SALEEM. I wouldn't be on a foundation art course if I couldn't draw, Meenah, there'd be no point in it.

MEENAH. Yeah, I know, am just saying that this is the first time I've seen you do it – God, do a Bamber Gascoigne on me or what!

MANEER. Foreskins are dirty.

TARIQ. If they're dirty, what are they doing there in the first place?

MEENAH. What are they gonna do with it after they cut it off?

TARIQ. Make it into a kebab for him. They throw it away, you divhead.

MEENAH. What do they cut it off for?

MANEER. Because you have to.

SALEEM. It lessens the feeling on your knob.

MANEER. No it doesn't.

TARIQ. How would you know, you haven't used it yet.

SALEEM. He's been trying, he were after Katy Jones the other day.

MEENAH. Katy Jones the bag of bones, everyone's snogged her.

MANEER. No I wasn't.

TARIQ. What'll me dad say about that, Gandhi, caught trying to snog the bag of bones.

MEENAH. Even Twitch has snogged her.

Enter SAJIT, *he goes for the biscuit packet.*

Hey Twitch, you see this. (*Shows him the picture.*) You're not gonna have it next week. Me dad's having your knob cut off.

The others laugh.

SAJIT. Get stuffed.

MEENAH. Don't frigging start, you little pleb, or I'll drop you.

TARIQ. Come on, we better get over the shop. Sajit, be here at four o'clock or I'll burn that coat off your back.

TARIQ, MANEER *and* SALEEM *make to go,* SALEEM *pulls a portfolio from behind the couch where it's been hidden.* MEENAH *gives* SAJIT *a clip across the head.*

MEENAH. Five, you mong. Don't forget.

They exit.

SAJIT *takes the drawing, looks at it, then pulls his pants forward to compare it with his own. He looks puzzled.*

Scene Four

TARIQ *sits on the counter mopping up curry from a plate.*
MEENAH *and* MANEER *are doing odd jobs around the shop,
there is Indian film music playing which* MANEER *and*
MEENAH *dance around to as they go about their jobs.
Someone knocks at the door.* MEENAH *bops over and opens it.
It's* SAJIT.

MEENAH. We said five, you mong, now scram.

SAJIT. Me mam said to put some more peas on. And that I can
have some mineral.

TARIQ. One bottle, Twitch, and that's all you're getting.

SAJIT *sees what* TARIQ*'s eating.*

SAJIT. Me dad said you're not to eat the chicken curry, until the
spinach is gone.

MANEER. Tariq, I told you that!

TARIQ. Oh fuck off, Gandhi, since when have you been curry
inspector?

SAJIT. I'm gonna tell me dad. (*Climbs on the counter.*)

TARIQ (*knows he has to pay the price*). One bottle of pop,
Twitch, and that's all you're getting.

SAJIT. Is there any cold chips left?

MEENAH (*gives him a can and knocks him off the counter*). No
there isn't.

MANEER. It's not fair, Tariq, I got blamed last time.

TARIQ. Will you stop whinging. And turn that crap off, it's
giving me a headache.

MANEER *doesn't do anything,* TARIQ *jumps over the
counter, switches the music off and returns to his position.*

MEENAH. Oi, I was listening to that as well.

TARIQ. Tough. I hate Paki music, go and make us some
chappatis.

MEENAH. Paki enough when you want feeding, aren't you?
Well you can fuck off if you think I'm gonna wait on you!

SAJIT. I'll make 'em if I can have some cold chips.

MEENAH *and* MANEER *laugh.*

TARIQ. Do you think I'm gonna put owt in my mouth that's been in your hands?

SAJIT. I'll wash 'em.

TARIQ (*laughing*). I don't care if you soaked them in Dettol for a week, I still wouldn't eat them.

SAJIT. Orrr, go on, I'm dead good.

TARIQ (*to* SAJIT). Come here, shuuuut, uuuup!

TARIQ *shakes vinegar onto* SAJIT *from the bottle on the counter.* MEENAH *and* MANEER *look on laughing.*

SAJIT. Get stuffed you. (*Retreats to a corner and mopes.*)

MEENAH. So who were you with last night?

TARIQ. Wouldn't you like to know?

MEENAH. Come on, I told you that Maneer grassed on you.

TARIQ. Alright... it was June Higgins.

SAJIT (*from his corner*). She's a slag, her!!

TARIQ. Button it, Twitch, you don't even know her.

SAJIT. Yeah I do, they live down Markindale Street, her mam goes out with that bloke with the limp who comes in here every Tuesday for fish and chips twice.

MANEER. Auntie Annie said the mother was a tart, and if the daughter wasn't reined in she'd go the same way as well.

SAJIT. She's shag bandy.

MEENAH. Take no notice Tariq, he knows fuck-all.

SAJIT. I know more about what goes on in this house than you do!

MEENAH. Bollocks!

SAJIT. I know all about the engagem...

MANEER *cuts him off, but it's too late, the cat's out of the bag.*

MANEER. Sajit!

TARIQ. What engagement?

> SAJIT *knows he's in trouble and bolts for the door, but is held by* MEENAH. *She and* TARIQ *pin him up against the wall.*

> Out with it, Twitch!

SAJIT. Maneer knows more about it than I do, me dad took him with him 'cause I smelt. Didn't he, Maneer?

TARIQ. Well Maneer, what's been going on?

MANEER. I can't tell you, me dad'll kill me. No one's supposed to know, I'm not supposed to know.

TARIQ. Maneer!

MANEER. It might not be true.

MEENAH. Come on Maneer, we've got a right to know if it's about us.

MANEER. Alright, but you haven't got it from me if it is. The other week when you went to Bradford with Abdul, me and Twitch went to a meeting about East Pakistan, Mr Shah was there and he came over and started talking to me dad. Then some blokes made a joke about getting his daughters married off.

SAJIT. That's when Mr Shah said it was being arranged. Then me dad smelt me and sent me home and took Gandhi with him.

TARIQ. What happened there?

MANEER. I don't know, they were talking in Pakistani.

MEENAH. Come on, Maneer, you must have picked something up?

MANEER. Look, all I could understand, was Mr Shah mentioned his daughters' names, Tariq's and Abdul's and me dad agreed to something.

MEENAH. Fucking hell!

The door bursts open, they all jump, it's ANNIE. *She has some white sheets under her arm.*

ANNIE. Is your mam not in?

MEENAH. No, Auntie Annie, she's at the house.

ANNIE. Right. What are you lot up to?

MANEER. Nothing.

TARIQ. Just doing the cleaning.

ANNIE. And butter wouldn't melt in your mouth, Tariq Ali Khan. Are they picking on you, Saj?

SAJIT. No, Auntie Annie. (*Doesn't sound convincing.*)

ANNIE. I bleeding bet, come on with me, I'm gonna see your mam.

They exit.

TARIQ. Meenah, lock that door in case me dad comes. I knew he was up to something when he didn't come to Bradford.

MEENAH. He's a right crafty old bastard, you can't afford to let your guard down with him.

MANEER. Just wait and see.

TARIQ. You wait and frigging see!

Lights up on the living room of the house as SAJIT *and* ANNIE *enter.* ELLA *is folding washing off the lazy Susan.*

ANNIE. It's only me!

ELLA. Hiya.

ANNIE. Do you want to give us a hand with old Sara Mack, they've just brought her home.

ELLA. Bleeding hell, that was quick, she was only in the wash-house the other day.

ANNIE. Ella, I was stood talking to her in the dockers' club last Sunday, and now I'm laying the poor bleeder out.

ELLA. You know, there's no telling is there?

ANNIE. It were a brain clot that did it, Ethel Shorrocks was in the shop when it happened. She said she came in, said 'I'll have a quarter of rodey bacon' and before she could say owt else, she were flat on her back, dead as a doornail. Funeral's on Friday, they're having salmon.

ELLA. Least it was quick, she deserved that, after putting up with that get of a husband. Do you want a cup of tea, it's just brewed?

ANNIE. Go on, I'll have a quick one, she's not going anywhere.

ELLA. Sajit go and get us another cup from the kitchen.

He goes.

ANNIE (*putting her sheets down carefully*). God forgive me for speaking ill of the dead... but he were an evil bastard that one, from top to bleeding toe. He knocked her about something chronic.

ELLA. Didn't you do him when he died?

ANNIE. What was left of him, he was crushed on the docks by a crate of West Indian bananas. Served him right for being a bigot I say.

ELLA. Bless her. Do you think she felt owt?

ANNIE. It was all over in seconds according to Ethel but that's Ethel Shorrocks for you.

ELLA. And she's not long for this world by the looks of her.

ANNIE. Well I laid Ethel's mother out as well, and she were no older than Ethel is now. In fact she looked better dead than Ethel does alive. Her dad said so at the time.

ELLA. He didn't?

ANNIE. He bleeding did. Good sense of humour he had, well he'd have to with Ethel's mother, oh she was depressing, Ella, you couldn't stick her for more than five minutes. A right miserable bleeder. Some say he committed suicide, you know.

ELLA. No!

ANNIE. Well it must have been tablets 'cause there wasn't a mark on her, we looked. It's funny, you don't get many suicides nowadays. Time was, it was every other week. Remember Mad Arthur in Monmouth Street, hung himself with a pair of braces.

ELLA. Did you do him?

ANNIE. No, undertakers down Ordsall Lane had him, I didn't mind really, he'd been up there two weeks before they found him. Thing is about suicides now, Ella, is all these bleedin' pills. They take so long, someone's found you before they start to work. Next thing you know you're in Salford Royal having your stomach pumped.

ELLA. They used to go t'ship canal up by Throstle's Nest, no messing see. A bag of coal and a bit of a jump and you were gone.

ANNIE. Or gas. There were them two blokes who ran that pub on't end of Regent Road, gassed themselves.

ELLA. That's right..

ANNIE. They call it the Gas Tavern now. They used to serve cucumber butties on paper doilys, in the afternoons. Nice lads they were, but very fussy. Hey have you seen these?

ANNIE *pulls out a pair of candlesticks from her holdall.*

ELLA. They're belting them, how much?

ANNIE. Fifteen bob a pair. Knock-offs from the docks. I got four, one for each corner of the coffin, I'll use the old ones for me altarpiece. It'll look nice won't it?

SAJIT. I'm going in the yard, Mam. (*Exits.*)

ELLA. Stay out of that shed!

ANNIE. Have you sorted him out yet?

ELLA. He's going to the doctor's later, if all's well, he gets the chop next week.

Enter GEORGE *with an old barber's chair.*

You're not bringing that bleeding thing in here.

ANNIE. Where've you got that from George?

GEORGE *puts it down and tries it out for comfort.*

GEORGE. I buy on market, is very good, very comfortable.

ELLA. It's an old barber's chair, you daft tute – the amount of bleeding rubbish he brings in here, Annie. How much did you pay for it?

GEORGE. Why you bloody complain, I buy for you my love, is no expenses, four pound, no rubbish, bloody bargain, in't it?

ELLA. You want your head feeling, spending four bob on that, never mind four pound, you daft sod. It's bleeding junk.

GEORGE. Oi stupy, is no junk, you think I spend-a-money buy-a-junk. You bloody daft I thinks, in't it?

ANNIE *picks up her sheets and holdall.*

ANNIE. Right I'm off to sort her out, I'll see you later. Ta-raa George.

She exits.

ELLA *gives up, it's obvious the chair is here to stay.*

ELLA. Do you want some tea, it's still warm?

GEORGE. I have half a cup. Kids no in yet?

ELLA. Saleem's still at college, Sajit's in the yard, the others are at the shop.

GEORGE. Come try this, you sees for self.

GEORGE *takes* ELLA'*s arm and tries to sit her in the chair.* ELLA *laughs.*

ELLA. Get off, you daft bleeder, I'm trying to pour your tea.

GEORGE. Try, very comfortable.

ELLA. Will you give over!

She sits in the chair.

GEORGE. See, very nice, make you relaxing.

GEORGE *sings a few lines from a Hindi film song.* ELLA *smiles and cuts him off.*

ELLA. Yeah, very bloody nice, now do you want your tea or what?

GEORGE. I think it good, got arms, swivel, everything.

ELLA. It'll take more than a bloody swivel to make me relax around you.

SAJIT *is in the kitchen getting a biscuit, he listens by the door.*

GEORGE. I buying nice material in a market.

ELLA. Oh aye.

GEORGE. Send some to Pakistan, celebrate engagement, and five suits for Shah's family.

ELLA. What do they need to celebrate for in Pakistan. Haven't they got enough to worry about with this war on?

GEORGE. What you bloody talking about stupy. You not understand my mind.

ELLA. Well amongst all this buying of presents and celebration, are you gonna tell Abdul and Tariq what's going on?

GEORGE. If I want telling Abdul and Tariq, I speak when I want bloody speaking, is not your bloody business. I fixing everything see.

ELLA (*under her breath, but audible enough for* GEORGE *to hear*). Yeah, just like you fixed our Nazir and look how well that went.

GEORGE. I bloody hear what you saying, missus, I no bloody daft. Why you alway mention this pucker baster name to me, how many time I tell you he dead.

ELLA. No he's not, he's living in Eccles, he might be dead to you, but he's still my son.

GEORGE. He no my bloody son. He should be here working in my bloody shop. Oh no, not like my shop, no like chip shop, he want be bloody hairdresser.

ELLA. He had a right to know what was happening.

GEORGE. Right, what you mean right, Pakistani believe if father ask son doing something, son follow father instructions, has respect see. Nazir follow bloody pansy hairdresser instructions, but I tell you, this no happen again, 'cause I bloody teach others respecting me.

ELLA. Not by force you won't, George.

GEORGE. I should have sent all bloody kids to Pakistan, when young, other wife teach bloody respect.

ELLA. Over my dead body you would have done.

GEORGE. Your bloody son bloody mad! Your daughter walking round in bloody short skirt like bloody prostitute!

ELLA. It's her school uniform! What more can the girl do to please you? The moment she finishes school she's back here and changed into trousers. She never moves off the bleeding doorstep unless I say so or she's in the shop.

GEORGE. I tell you my family in Pakistan show me bloody respect, she listen what I tell her doing.

ELLA. Alright George, bring her over here and send us over there. Let her graft in that shop while I sit around on me arse and wait for money to be sent over. But I'll tell you one thing, she'll find it hard serving fish and chips wrapped up from head to toe in a bleeding bedsheet. Hiding her beauty? If she's that frigging beautiful, why haven't you been back in twenty years!

GEORGE jumps up, for a moment we don't know what his reaction will be as he looks at ELLA. *He turns and storms out of the room, slamming the door as he goes.* SAJIT *runs out and goes to the shop, he'll get there ahead of* GEORGE.

That door'll be off its hinges by the end of the week.

Lights up in the shop. TARIQ, MEENAH, MANEER *and* SALEEM. *His portfolio leans against the counter. Same day and time.*

TARIQ. I don't fucking believe this, he can't do this to me, I'm not gonna marry a Paki.

MEENAH. What you gonna do Tariq?

SALEEM. Now you're sure he didn't say owt about me?

MANEER. No Saleem, you weren't even mentioned.

SALEEM. So, it's just you and Abdul, Tariq.

TARIQ. There's no need to sound so pleased about it Saleem!

SALEEM. I'm not, honest, I'm just saying, you know, thank God it's not me 'cause I'd miss out on going to university.

MEENAH. Shut it Saleem, alright.

There's banging at the door. MEENAH *looks through the curtain.*

SAJIT. It's me dad!

MEENAH. Me dad's coming! (*Lets him in.*)

SAJIT. Quick, Genghis is coming, and he's just had an argument with me mam.

They all run out, MANEER *grabbing what's left of* TARIQ*'s curry.* SALEEM *runs out then remembers his portfolio, returns and gets it. Enter* GEORGE. *He's upset, he goes over to the counter, leans against it and sobs into his hands. He does not see* SAJIT *watching him from the doorway.*

Scene Five

Tuesday a week later. SAJIT *is sat on a wheelchair.* GEORGE *is trying to strap a wristwatch to his wrist.*

ELLA. I told you, stop playing with that.

GEORGE. You see puther, I tell you I buy you watch, is very special watch it tell you when to pray see, in Arabic. When you learn reading Arabic, you know when to pray.

ELLA *looks at* GEORGE, *bemused.*

ELLA. The last thing he wants to be doing, is squatting down on his knees in his condition.

GEORGE. I know this stupy.

SAJIT. What did they cut off Dad? Meenah said they'd cut me balls off as well.

GEORGE *does not know what to say.*

GEORGE. You no need bloody worry about that.

ELLA. Take no notice of her.

A DOCTOR *comes over to them.*

DOCTOR. Excuse me, it's Mr and Mrs Khan, isn't it?

ELLA. Yes.

DOCTOR. I'm Dr Krishna Mehta. Do you think I can have a word with you?

ELLA. Erm, of course, doctor... George.

GEORGE. You Indian?

DOCTOR. I'm sorry?

ELLA. Shut up George. It's nothing serious is it, doctor, I mean with our Sajit? 'Cause we'd like to know straight away.

GEORGE. Everything okay, doctor? Tickle-tackle all gone?

DOCTOR. The what?

ELLA. Oh for Christ's sake, George, do you have to keep saying that. Sorry doctor, but he'd make a bloody saint swear.

GEORGE. What you know, missus, what you want me to say?

DOCTOR. I think you both ought to know, that the circumcision was absolutely fine. No, it's not that I want to talk about.

ELLA. Oh.

DOCTOR. We are concerned about him though.

ELLA. He's not said anything to anyone has he, swore at you or something?

DOCTOR. No, nothing like that, I was wondering Mrs Khan, how long has he had his coat?

A beat, the penny drops.

ELLA. You've noticed that then doctor?

DOCTOR. One could hardly fail to.

ELLA. Well you know what kids are like with new fashions, they never want to take them off.

DOCTOR. Mrs Khan, it wasn't until he was under the anaesthetic that we could get it off him.

ELLA *looks at* GEORGE.

ELLA. It's the coat.

GEORGE. Well you baster buy for him, now baster never come out. You see in my country these things never happen. I been this country forty year...

ELLA. Aye, and you still know nowt.

GEORGE. How many time I tell you, boy bloody stupy. He bloody pogle, doctor, this boy always bloody belkuf. You Indian, you know what I mean, in't it?

DOCTOR. Well I don't think he's mad, but there are a couple of things we'd like to look into.

ELLA. He just has his little quirks, I mean we all do.

DOCTOR. What other quirks are they?

ELLA (*almost regretting she mentioned it*). Well I don't know if you've noticed, when he walks about, especially round corners.

DOCTOR. Yes! What is that?

ELLA. He cuts a piece of string attached to his back... it's not actually there, he just believes it to be, and he cuts it off as he goes round corners.

DOCTOR. I'm sorry, could you explain that again?

ELLA. He thinks he has a piece of string coming out of his back, which he has to cut with a pair of imaginary scissors, as he goes round corners.

DOCTOR. Anything else?

ELLA. Not really, well he did jump head-first into a cast-iron paddling pool in Rhyl, but I think he thought it was deeper. Either that or he was just being clever.

DOCTOR. Was he injured?

ELLA. Oh aye, back of his head were like jelly, came up as big as a Mills grenade.

DOCTOR. Did he see a doctor?

ELLA. Yeah, they're very good like that at Sunny Vale, they brought a specialist in to see him. He tested his eyes with his fingers and a pendulum, that sort of thing.

DOCTOR. And?

ELLA. Well, he's never been able to keep his eyes still at the best of times, he's got a bit of a twitch if you've noticed.

DOCTOR. Would you mind if I asked Sajit if he'd like to come back and see me again, Mrs Khan?

ELLA. If you think it'll help, doctor.

DOCTOR. What about you Mr Khan?

GEORGE. No problem with that.

DOCTOR. Well, if you don't mind waiting here, I'll just go and have a little chat with him before you go.

The DOCTOR *goes over to* SAJIT.

GEORGE. You know he bloody Indian doctor?

ELLA. Well he's hardly likely to blame Sajit for the partition of India, is he, you daft tute.

GEORGE. I not bloody trust these peoples.

ELLA. He's a bleeding doctor, not some Indian spy.

Lights up on SAJIT *and the* DOCTOR.

DOCTOR. Nearly ready to go Sajit?

SAJIT. Yeah.

DOCTOR. Sajit, we were wondering if you would like to come back and see us again.

SAJIT (*worried*). Are you gonna cut more off?

DOCTOR. No, no, just to talk.

SAJIT. What about?

DOCTOR. Anything you want to talk about, school, your family, anything.

SAJIT. Are you Pakistani?

DOCTOR. No, my family's from India, why?

SAJIT. You talk different. I know about East Pakistan.

DOCTOR. Then we can talk about that if you like.

SAJIT. Me dad says there's gonna be a war with India, and they're gonna nick the rest of Kashmir. Are you gonna do that?

DOCTOR. I'm not going to do anything, I live here and I'm a doctor, not a politician. Besides, there are ways other than war to get what you want.

SAJIT *thinks*.

SAJIT. Me and me brothers hope the Indians win, 'cept we don't want them to take Azad Kashmir, 'cause that's Pakistan's, but they can win other things, 'cause me dad'll be dead pissed off.

The DOCTOR *smiles*.

DOCTOR. Do you like it when he gets angry?

SAJIT. Me brothers do, I'm not bothered.

He beckons to ELLA *and* GEORGE. *They come over.*

DOCTOR. What are you gonna do when you get home, go out and play with your friends?

SAJIT. I can't do that, I've just had an operation.

DOCTOR. I mean after, do you play football?

SAJIT. Naa, it's boring that. I sit in our coal shed, it's dead quiet.

ELLA *has come over, followed by* GEORGE.

DOCTOR. Sajit tells me you have a coal shed, Mrs Khan.

ELLA. Yes, I feel like locking meself in there sometimes, get away from this silly bugger. (*Nod of the head towards*

GEORGE, *then to* SAJIT.) I told you, stop playing with that, you'll break it and someone else has got to use it.

DOCTOR. It doesn't matter, Mrs Khan.

ELLA. Does to me, doctor, I'm not having my kids being accused of bad manners. People are a lot quicker to point the finger if they see they're a bit foreign. Well, not with mine. George, go order a taxi.

GEORGE *goes off.*

DOCTOR. Well, Sajit's agreed to come back and visit us, haven't you Sajit?

SAJIT. Yeah... I sunbathe on the shed as well, I don't always sit in it. I'm not mad, you know.

DOCTOR. Do you wear your coat when you sunbathe?

SAJIT. Yeah, and sunglasses.

DOCTOR. Tell me about cutting the string when you go round corners?

SAJIT. That? I don't do that any more.

GEORGE *comes back, takes* SAJIT*'s bag.*

GEORGE. Ella, taxi become downstairs.

DOCTOR. Well, that's very good, Sajit, 'cause when we get together and...

SAJIT. I use an axe now, 'cause the string's turned to rope.

End of Act One.

Interval.

ACT TWO

Scene One

MEENAH *and* TARIQ *are sat with a plate of bacon and sausages between them.* MEENAH *gets up and sprays air freshener around.* SALEEM *tries to cover the food.*

TARIQ. 'Kinell, Meenah, watch what you're doing!

MEENAH. It stinks of burnt bacon in here, me dad'll smell it a mile off.

TARIQ. Chuck some curry powder about, that'll cover it.

She goes into the kitchen and comes out sprinkling curry powder around.

How long's me mam been at the hospital?

MEENAH. 'Bout an hour, we got plenty of time. Where's Saleem, not like him to miss a fry-up?

TARIQ. Said he'd be late, something to do with his model, said to save him some though.

MEENAH. He can piss off, he should be taking the risk if he wants to eat. 'Kin college boy. Me mam's mad, she keeps buying him felt-tip pens from the market. He's got 'em all piled up upstairs. Even Auntie Annie gets them for him now, he'll be able to open a shop soon.

TARIQ. See that dressing gown me dad bought for Sajit, just because he's getting the chop?

MEENAH (*cynically*). Yeah right, it'll look great under his parka, you spoke to our Abdul yet?

TARIQ. I tried to, but he won't say owt.

We hear a knock on the door, they both freeze.

MEENAH. Who is that?

She goes into the parlour, TARIQ *picks up the plate of food ready to run.*

(*Off.*) It's alright, it's only Saleem.

She goes out of the parlour to let him in. They both come into the living room, SALEEM *carrying his portfolio.*

SALEEM. I hope you saved me some of that?

He grabs some sausage and bacon.

MEENAH. Alright Saleem, it's not leaving the frigging country, 'kinell, he's like a bleedin' gannet. (*Mimics* SALEEM *grabbing the food.*)

TARIQ *and* MEENAH *laugh.*

SALEEM. Oh cool it Meenah, you're a drag.

MEENAH *and* TARIQ *laugh at this.*

MEENAH (*taking the mickey*). Yeah, right, Saleem, I'll cool it, hey yeah. Let's go to college. Cool it! Who the fuck do you think you are?

Suddenly the door opens behind them. They all scream at the prospect of it being GEORGE, *but it is only* MANEER.

Ahhh!

SALEEM. Ahhh!

TARIQ. Ahhh!

MANEER. I can smell that from outside!

TARIQ. Where did you get a front-door key from, Gandhi?

MANEER. Off me dad.

TARIQ. Can you believe that, old enough to get married to some bird who dresses like Sinbad the sailor, with a hole through her nose, and he gives Gandhi his own key.

MEENAH. What a twat!

MANEER. Yours is called Nigget, not Sinbad.

TARIQ. Nigget! Bleeding Nigget! What sort of a come on is that? Nigget my lovely, shed those silken pantaloons and lay your head on my palliasse.

SALEEM. Thought about what you're gonna do, Tariq?

TARIQ. Not marrying Nigget, put it that way!

SALEEM. You've no choice really.

TARIQ. Oh shut up Saleem!

SALEEM. I'm only stating facts.

MANEER. What's Abdul said about it?

TARIQ. Oh he's fucking useless.

SALEEM. I still think you've no choice.

TARIQ. I have. I either stay here and have me dad tell me what to do for the rest of me life, or I do what our Nazir did and go.

MEENAH. You can't do that Tariq, what about me mam?

MANEER. She's right, me mam got a right bollocking when Nazir left.

SALEEM. You can't let her go through that again.

TARIQ. Yeah, alright, I know what happened, but I think she got bollocked 'cause he wanted to be a hairdresser, not 'cause he didn't get married.

We hear banging on the door.

MEENAH. Who the fuck's that now?

TARIQ. Go and see, Meenah.

MEENAH. No way, I went last time.

MANEER. If me dad finds me here, he'll kill me.

TARIQ. He'll do the lot of us if he sees what we're eating.

We hear GEORGE *shout through the letter box.*

GEORGE. Open door!

SALEEM. Oh shit!

GEORGE. Open bloody door!

MEENAH *grabs the air freshener and starts to spray round the room, while* SALEEM, TARIQ *and* MANEER *hide the food. They run, leaving* MANEER *alone. He goes to let*

GEORGE *in. Suddenly* SALEEM *sprints in and grabs his portfolio and sprints out again.* ELLA *enters the parlour with* SAJIT. *She lays him on on the couch, which has been made up into a bed.* GEORGE *is there as well.* MANEER *is now in the sitting room. He checks for any evidence and sees a sausage on the floor. He picks it up, doesn't know what to do with it.*

I go watch the news. You want tea?

ELLA. Yeah go on then.

GEORGE *enters the living room.*

GEORGE. What you doing?

MANEER *has now thrown the sausage under the couch.*

MANEER. Just looking for my other shoes, Dad.

GEORGE. What time Abdul get back from work?

MANEER. About half past five, Dad. How's Sajit?

GEORGE. He fine now. Put kettle on for your mam, make tea.

MANEER *goes into the kitchen.*

You go to mosque today, puther?

MANEER (*off*). Erm, no Dad, tomorrow.

GEORGE (*lights fag*). You good boy, God will help you, if you live your life believing in God. People who no follow the rules of God, he sending bloody hell. They have no chance in the world, like man we see on Sunday, he say, God say, send money, he bloody stupy, I tell you son. (*Clears his throat.*) He have nothing because he no understand God. Not educated you see. He say there is no God, we all God. This man bloody pagan... bhenchoud badahmarsh, if they no God, what we all bloody doing?

MANEER *is completely confused in the kitchen.*

MANEER. Yeah, Dad.

GEORGE. You see, puther, this country not like our peoples, I been here since 1936, I try to make good life for my family. Your mother is good woman, but she not understand, son. I love my family, but all time I have trouble with people, they not like I marry you mother. Always calling you mother bad name. That why I always try to show Pakistani way to live is good way, parent look after children, children look after parent. English people not like this. All my family love each other. Bradford, Pakistan. All same, nobody different.

MANEER. I know what you're trying to say, Dad! (*To himself.*) It's the others you've got to convince.

Fade out in the living room and kitchen and up in the parlour.

ELLA sits next to SAJIT on the couch, he's dropped off to sleep. She hums to him and strokes his hair. ANNIE pops her head round the door. ELLA beckons her in, she's got a bag of fruit and some comics for him.

ANNIE. How's he doing?

ELLA. Alright, just a bit sore.

ANNIE. Poor little bleeder, where's old bothered-balls, he happy now?

ELLA. Next door. He bought him a new dressing gown and a watch.

ANNIE. Not much of a swap, but it's better than nowt I suppose.

Pause.

ELLA. Annie… Do you think I'm a good mother?

ANNIE. What sort of bleeding question's that? Course you are. What's put that in your head?

ELLA. Well would you have put one of your lads through this?

ANNIE doesn't answer.

ANNIE. You had no choice.

ELLA. I did though, Annie, I should have put me foot down and said no.

ANNIE. And given yourself a load of bleeding grief, you know what he's like.

ELLA. I know, but now he wants to marry Abdul and Tariq off. Am I to just stand by and let him throw them out when they say no?

Pause.

ANNIE. Have they said owt to you?

ELLA. Abdul won't talk about it, I think they blame me for not sticking up for them. I only found out meself the other day.

ANNIE. They're big enough and daft enough to look after themselves, Ella, you've warned them and that's all you can do, you've four more to think about. If they want to leave it's their choice. You put your foot down when it comes to Meenah, that's where you make your stand and you know it.

ELLA. Meenah? I don't think even George would tackle her.

They laugh.

ANNIE. You're a good mother to those kids and a bloody good wife to him as well, but you're in the middle, Ella, you have to keep your head down.

Fade out.

Scene Two

Same day. MEENAH, SALEEM *and* MANEER *are sat on a canal bank.* SAJIT *charges past now and again, pushing an old pram.* TARIQ *throws stones into the canal,* SALEEM *draws* MEENAH.

SALEEM. Meenah, will you keep still.

MEENAH. 'Kinell Saleem, how long you gonna take, it only took you five minutes to draw a knob and a foreskin last week.

SALEEM. You can't rush an artist.

Enter SAJIT.

MEENAH. Will you look at that freak!

MANEER. Oi, Twitch! Get home.

TARIQ. He moves quick for someone who's just been circumcised. Me dad say owt to you yesterday, Gand?

MANEER. No, just talked about *Songs of Praise*.

MEENAH. Yeah, I bet.

MANEER. Shut it, Meenah.

TARIQ. You wouldn't tell us if that Paki said owt anyway.

MANEER. You don't have to call him that, Tariq.

TARIQ. It's what he is innit?

MANEER. What does that make you?

TARIQ (*dismissively*). Oh fuck off, Maneer.

MANEER. No, I won't. I've seen you with your friends taking the piss out of him on the road behind his back and it's not right, and it's not fair – (*Starts to get a bit upset.*) 'cause it's me dad, you bastard! They're not your friends, they're just laughing at the stupid half-caste laughing at his own dad...

TARIQ. Oh stop whinging, you soft twat.

SALEEM. I thought we were Anglo-Indian.

MEENAH. We're Eurasian.

SALEEM. Sounds more romantic than Paki, I suppose.

TARIQ (*pointedly at* MANEER). We're English!

MANEER. We're not Anglo-Indian, not Eurasian and not English.

TARIQ. Look Maneer, if you want to be Pakistani, go live in Bradford, and take me dad with you.

SALEEM *and* MEENAH *laugh*.

MANEER. No one round here thinks we're English, we're the Paki family who run the chippy, and as for our religion...

TARIQ. And you're well in with me dad on that one aren't you?

MANEER. It's my choice, I like it, I wouldn't force it on anyone, I don't think me dad should either. He's wrong to do that. But being Pakistani is more than just a religion, Tariq, you hate me dad too much to see it.

TARIQ *says nothing.* MANEER *walks off. Fade out on them; fade in on* ABDUL *and* SAJIT *as they enter stage right.* ABDUL *has his work bag slung over his shoulder.*

ABDUL. What are you doing out here on your own?

SAJIT. The others are over there. Have you got any cold coffee left in your Thermos, Abdul?

ABDUL. No, what are you doing down here on your own?

SAJIT. Hey, you're gonna get married, aren't you?

ABDUL. Who told you that?

SAJIT. I heard. So's Tariq, but he said he isn't gonna marry a Paki.

ABDUL. Did he? Well, take no notice of him, and don't call people Pakis, it's not nice.

SAJIT. Have you seen me new watch? (*Shows* ABDUL.)

ABDUL. It's a belter that, Saj.

SAJIT. It's got Arabic writing in it. You can have it if you want.

ABDUL. Me dad bought it for you, why'd you not want it?

SAJIT. I can't tell the time, and I don't understand Arabic.

ABDUL *laughs and* SAJIT *joins in.*

ABDUL. What you bleeding like, hey? I can teach you to do both if you like.

SAJIT. You teach me to tell the time, but not Arabic.

ABDUL *laughs again, grabs* SAJIT *and picks him up.*

Ahh, get off, Abdul.

ABDUL (*smells his hands*). Hey Saj, innit about time you got that parka washed?

SAJIT. Me mam keeps on shouting at me 'cause of it.

ABDUL. Why'd you keep it on?

SAJIT. I like it.

ABDUL. I like chappatis, but I don't eat them twenty-four hours a day.

SAJIT. This is different.

ABDUL. Why?

SAJIT (*his mood changing*). It doesn't matter.

ABDUL. Go on Saj, tell us.

SAJIT. 'Cause… when it's all done up… I'm not there…
I don't have to listen to anyone arguing and shouting at me…
Is that mad, Abdul?

Beat.

ABDUL. Naa, Saj, it's not mad.

Fade out, and fade up on TARIQ, *who comes over to meet them.*

TARIQ. Get lost, Twitch!

SAJIT. Get stuffed!

ABDUL. Go on up to the others Saj, I'll see you in a minute…
go on.

SAJIT *runs off.*

TARIQ. I spoke to our Nazir on the phone, he said if me dad
chucked us out we could stay with him.

ABDUL. I don't want to live anywhere else.

TARIQ. Alright, so we both stay here and say no. If we stick
together he can't do anything.

ABDUL. There's no point, Tariq, he can do anything he wants.

TARIQ. What do you mean no point, you can't just sit back and
let this happen!

ABDUL. I'm not like you, Tariq, I've never gone against him.

TARIQ. You mean you've let him walk all over you.

ABDUL. No, I haven't.

TARIQ. Oh come on, Abdul, I've been there, remember? I
swore then he'd never treat me the way he treats you.

ABDUL. There were times I could have said something, Tariq,
but I didn't.

TARIQ. Why didn't you!

ABDUL. You wouldn't understand.

TARIQ. Try me.

ABDUL. Because... I want... I want him to treat me like a proper son. I want him to talk to me, to trust me. I don't want to feel as if I'm some investment for his future.

TARIQ. Oh come on, Abdul, he's never gonna give a shit about how you feel or what you think. 'I am your father, you are my son, you do as I say, bass.' That's not fucking trust.

ABDUL. I don't know...

TARIQ. You've been told what to do all your life, all that respect crap, it's just brainwashing. Nazir got away from it, so can you.

Pause.

ABDUL. Alright, I'll see what I can do, but you'd better pack your bags 'cause as soon as we say anything we'll be out.

TARIQ. Nice one, Abdul, welcome to the West.

TARIQ *makes to go.*

ABDUL (*to himself*). I wish I had a parka.

TARIQ. You what?

ABDUL. Nothing, let's go.

Fade up on the living room. ANNIE *and* ELLA *sit listening to the radio, drinking tea and smoking.*

RADIO. 'There have been further reports of the indiscriminate destruction of buildings and summary executions by the West Pakistani army in Dacca, capital of East Pakistan. Eye-witness accounts claim the university had been attacked, and many students killed. In India a statement has been issued condemning the attacks, and has called for negotiations to take place. The Indian army has been put on full alert all along the border.'

ANNIE. Well, they're up shit creek without a paddle now.

ELLA. Try telling George that they're fighting a losing battle, and will he listen? Will he bugger. It's that army lot I blame.

Blackshirts the lot of them. Once they took over it all went up the spout.

ANNIE. We had a blackshirt, lived next-door-but-one to us during the war. Tried to get the dockers out on strike, no one listened to him mind, except Billy Thomas, and that was only 'cause his dad told him his granddad was killed by a fuzzy-wuzzy at Omdurman. Me mam used to hang a paraffin lamp on his back door in the air raids hoping the Germans would bomb him. He kept his bleeding head down on VE Day though, and he got no bunting round his door either.

ELLA. He's getting on me nerves with this war, we were in Bradford the other week, he tried to get the kids to sing the Pakistani anthem. I said they don't speak Urdu, he said tell 'em to hum.

ANNIE. You got rid of that barber's chair, I see.

ELLA. It's in the shop. Hey, you remember Sabu, don't you?

ANNIE. Which one was he?

ELLA. The one George used to call Blackie… he had a little black moustache, made him look like Fernando Rey.

ANNIE *thinks*.

ANNIE. Oh I remember, he had hazel eyes, always laughing. What about him.

ELLA. Dead. Killed with his wife on the Snake Pass coming back from Bradford. Not a mark on 'em.

Enter GEORGE.

ANNIE. Hiya George.

ELLA. Do you want some tea?

GEORGE. I have half a cup.

ELLA *pours* GEORGE *some tea*.

Any news 'bout war?

ANNIE. You just missed it George, the Indians are moving troops up to the border.

GEORGE. These baster, I tell you they want do this. No help East Pakistan, wanting bloody Azad Kashmir.

ANNIE. Do your family live near the border, George?

GEORGE. Near to, see, in't it?

ELLA. West Pakistan should pull out, George, and you know it.

GEORGE (*frustrated*). Oh stupy, listen what I tell you, India only interested in Azad Kashmir.

ELLA. What about all those people they have killed in the east? (*To* ANNIE.) They had it on telly last night, Annie, it was disgusting what they'd done to them.

ANNIE. Well, I'm off, he'll be home from work soon wanting to know where his tea is.

GEORGE. You good wife, cook dinner for husband.

ANNIE. Well he's only getting fish fingers and a tin of beans. I'll see you in the shop after. Taraa.

She exits.

GEORGE. What you talking 'bout?

ELLA. What do you mean?

GEORGE. Why you telling people, Pakistani do disgusting thing?

ELLA (*bemused*). They were last night, I don't have to tell anyone, they can see it for themselves on the news.

GEORGE. You don't know what you see, could be criminals.

ELLA. They looked like ordinary people to me, except they were chained up, holding Korans, and being hit with machetes. Now to me, I find that disgusting.

GEORGE. These bad people, want breaking country, they bloody traitors.

ELLA. I thought you were all supposed to be brothers, isn't that what Islam teaches you? And these people were murdered with Korans in their hands.

GEORGE (*getting angry*). You not wanting to understand.

ELLA. You're bloody right I don't understand, I don't want to when they behave like that.

GEORGE. I your bloody husband, you supposed to be Muslim. You should agree with me.

ELLA. Oh, yeah, right, I'm a Muslim wife when it suits you. I'll stop being a Muslim wife at half past five, when the shop wants opening, or one of your relatives wants help at the Home Office. Don't make me bleeding laugh, George.

GEORGE. I tell you missus, don't starting 'cause I fix you like I fix your baster kids, you all pucking trouble with me.

ELLA. They're only trouble 'cause you don't listen to them, you never have.

GEORGE. I no have to listen, I their father. Should be respecting a me!

ELLA. George, you've got to understand, things aren't like they were when you were young. Kids are different today, our kids are different, they're bleeding half-caste for a start. You knew it was never going to be the same with the kids growing up here.

GEORGE. This make no difference.

ELLA. Oh it does, George, 'cause you've been stricter with them than your own family have been with theirs. Stop trying to squash 'em down all the time.

GEORGE. They have to knowing who they are.

ELLA. Their lives are here, George, so's yours. It's not in some bleedin' village in Pakistan.

GEORGE (*very angry*). You never understand how I try to teach my children! Every time I tell you, you no listen, you no want a bloody listen! Only wanting you own mind. You married to me twenty-five year and know nothing. You no like my family, no respecting me, just like your baster children!

ELLA (*full stride*). I'll tell you why I don't like your frigging family, 'cause they're a bunch of money-grabbing bastards, they only come round here when they want money, or when money wants sending to Pakistan, to buy more bleeding land we're not gonna live on.

GEORGE. Bas! (*Enough!*)

ELLA. And do you think any of my kids are gonna get a look in, if owt happened to you?

GEORGE (*standing*). You don't talk to me like this!

SAJIT *watches them from the back window.*

ELLA. No, you haven't got an answer for that, have you? Yes, twenty-five years I've been married to you, George, I've sweated me guts out in your bastard shop, and given you seven kids as well, and I'll tell you this for nothing, I'm not gonna stand by and let you crush them one by one because of your pig bloody ignorance.

GEORGE *grabs* ELLA *violently by her hair and pulls her to the ground. He kicks and beats her. We see* SAJIT *crying in the yard.*

GEORGE. You baster bitch! You call me pig, you pucker, you talk to me like this again I bloody kill you bitch, and burn all your baster family when you sleep!

GEORGE *storms out leaving* ELLA *crying.* SAJIT *watches* ELLA.

Scene Three

The KHANS' *house.* TARIQ, MANEER *and* MEENAH *are sat watching the TV.* ELLA *comes in, buttoning her apron for the shop. She sits down and starts to read the paper.*

ELLA. Meenah, put the kettle on cock, I'll have a cup of tea before I go to the shop.

TARIQ. And me.

MANEER. Me too.

SAJIT. And me.

MEENAH. Don't even think about it Twitch, I'm only brewing it, Maneer can pour.

MANEER. Oh Mam, I did it last time, tell Tariq to do it.

SAJIT. Yeah, let Tariq do it.

TARIQ. Button it, spaz.

ELLA. You can all shut it, Gand – erm Maneer, you can pour, Tariq get some coal.

TARIQ. Touch wood I want me chair back.

He goes.

MEENAH. Mam do we all have to stay in on Sunday?

ELLA. Yeah you do, your dad said to wear that sari your Auntie Riffat brought you from Pakistan.

MEENAH. I look stupid in it.

ELLA. Don't be daft, you look fine.

MEENAH. Can't I just wear me jeans instead?

ELLA. No you can't.

MEENAH. Well I'm not putting that stud in me nose, it makes me go cross-eyed.

ELLA. Alright, but make sure your head stays covered, and Sajit I don't want to see you in that bleeding parka, d'y'hear me, lad. If your dad sees you in it, he'll wipe the floor with you.

SAJIT *bolts out of the room, almost knocking* TARIQ *over.*

TARIQ. What's wrong with him?

MEENAH. Nothing decapitation couldn't fix. Maneer, the kettle's boiled.

Enter SALEEM.

SALEEM. Hiya!

ELLA. Hiya cock, just finished college? Hurry up with that tea Maneer, and make Saleem one as well.

MEENAH *and* TARIQ *exchange looks at this obvious favouritism,* MEENAH *makes a wanking gesture.*

SALEEM. Mam I need another two and six for me model.

ELLA *gets her purse out and gives him the money.*

ELLA. I've got you some new felt-tips as well.

TARIQ. When are we gonna see this great work of art.

SALEEM. Sunday, when it's finished, it just needs the hair putting on it.

ELLA. Don't forget we've got visitors on Sunday, so make sure you're not late.

TARIQ. How can we forget that.

MANEER *gives* ELLA *her tea.*

ELLA. Bleeding hell, Maneer, what've you put in this, it tastes like piss.

MANEER. I'll make another one.

ELLA. Never mind I'm going t'shop.

She exits.

MEENAH. Sajit said me dad had a go at me mam the other day.

TARIQ. What do you want me to do about it?

MANEER. You can unpack that bag you've got upstairs for a start.

TARIQ. I've told you to mind your own fucking business, Gandhi!

MEENAH. What about me mam, Tariq?

TARIQ. Look, it's just in case me dad throws us out, which he will do as soon as we tell him we're not gonna get married.

MANEER. Just try to talk to him.

SALEEM. He's right, at least try.

TARIQ. What's the use, you know what he's like!

SALEEM. Let me try and talk to him.

TARIQ. Yeah sure, that'll make all the difference.

SAJIT *runs in.*

SAJIT. Me dad's coming, he said to put the news on, something's happened in Pakistan.

TARIQ. This might not be a good time.

SALEEM. There never will be, Tariq.

MEENAH. Let him try, Tariq, he'll be able to put it differently, and not just start shouting.

TARIQ. Yeah but...

MEENAH. Shut it, Tariq, and get in the kitchen, Maneer, Sajit... Kitchen now!

They all hide in the kitchen, leaving SALEEM *on his own. Enter* GEORGE.

GEORGE. News on yet?

SALEEM. Not yet. I think they're still fighting though.

GEORGE. We not win this war I think, India bloody clever, see.

SALEEM. Dad, can I talk to you?

GEORGE. All world 'gainst Pakistan see.

SALEEM. It's about Abdul and Tariq. You know, Dad, I don't think they think it's the right time to get married.

GEORGE (*irritated*). What you talking about 'no right time'.

SALEEM. I don't know about Abdul, but Tariq's not much older than me, he doesn't know what he wants to do with his life yet.

We can see the others wince in the kitchen.

GEORGE. Is not your business what I talk to Abdul and Tariq 'bout. Who bloody hell you think you are? You maybe go college, but you no bloody tell me what I doing. Understand?

SALEEM. No, Dad, I don't, I don't think you do either, it's not just them two, we're all fed up of being told what to do and where to go.

GEORGE. I warning you mister! You no talking to me like this, I your father, you treating me with respect. I not bringing you up talking me like this. Pakistani son alway show respect.

SALEEM. I'm not Pakistani, I was born here, I speak English, not Urdu.

SAJIT *bolts out of the kitchen.*

GEORGE. Son, you not understand 'cause you not listen to me. I try to show you how a good way to live. You no English, English people no accepting you. In Islam, everyone equal see, no black man, or white man. Only Muslim, it special community.

SALEEM. I'm not saying it's not, I just think I've got a right to choose for myself.

GEORGE. You want choose like Nazir, han? Lose everything, go with bloody English girl? They not good, go with other men, drink alcohol, no look after.

SALEEM. Well if Pakistani women are so great, why did you marry me mam?

SALEEM *has hit a raw nerve.* GEORGE *grabs him, and pushes him on the ground and kicks and slaps him.*

GEORGE. Oh, bhentured baster! I tell you no go too far with me, you think you bloody clever han? Pucker! You next time die baster!

He exits leaving SALEEM *crying on the floor, the others burst in.*

MEENAH. Are you alright, Saleem?

SALEEM. He beat me up! The bastard beat me up. I won't ever forgive him for that, not ever. I hope he fucking well dies.

TARIQ (*turns to* MANEER). Well, if that's got owt to do with being Pakistani, you can stick it.

Scene Four

Fade up on GEORGE *as he is finishing his prayers in the parlour, there is something poetic and gentle in the movements. He does not notice* ABDUL *who is standing by the door.* ABDUL *is visibly upset, he moves into the room, sits and watches* GEORGE. GEORGE *completes his prayers, turns and sees* ABDUL.

GEORGE. What wrong, puther?

ABDUL *sobs into his hands.*

Son what wrong with you?

He puts his hand on ABDUL*'s head,* ABDUL *falls against* GEORGE *in a kind of embrace.* GEORGE *strokes* ABDUL*'s head. Fade out and fade in on* ABDUL *sat in the same chair alone listening to some Indian music. Enter* TARIQ.

TARIQ. Where've you been? Steve said you left work hours ago.

ABDUL. Maneer came and told me about Saleem. I went to the pub.

TARIQ. You don't drink.

ABDUL. It was gonna be my first act of defiance, me dad's right, it does make you sick, but not physically.

TARIQ. Are you a bit pissed? Look, it's obvious me dad's not gonna take any notice of us. So we should just go.

ABDUL. Go, and do what, live with Nazir, what happens then? I don't want to live without my family.

TARIQ. Look, you're just feeling bad about Saleem, it wasn't our fault, even Saleem said that. That's been brewing for months.

ABDUL. How can I not feel responsible for him, or me mam for that matter. I suppose you heard about that?

TARIQ. We heard he had a go at her.

ABDUL. He gave her a fucking good hiding, Auntie Annie came into work and told me, 'cause she knew me mam wouldn't. So yes, I do feel responsible. Tariq. You know it doesn't even bother me about getting married, I just wanted to be consulted.

TARIQ. You've changed your tune, I thought you were gonna tell me dad where to get off?

ABDUL. You're not listening, are…

TARIQ. Shut up, Abdul, you're pathetic!

ABDUL. No! You shut up, Tariq! You're right, I was pathetic, tonight in the pub with the lads. We were sat drinking, telling jokes, playing music, telling more jokes. Jokes about sex, thick Irish men, wog jokes, chink jokes, Paki jokes. And the biggest joke was me, 'cause I was laughing the hardest. And they laughed at me because I was laughing. It seemed as if the whole pub was laughing at me, one giant grinning mouth. I just sat there and watched them, and I didn't belong, I was crying, crying so hard I couldn't catch my breath, so I ran and kept on running. When I got home, me dad was here praying, I watched him Tariq, and it was right, to be here, to be a part of this place, to belong to something. It's what I want. I know me dad'll always be a problem, but I can handle that now, perhaps I might make him change; but I don't want that out there, it's not who I am, it's as alien to me as me dad's world is to you.

Pause. We can just hear the music playing in the background.

TARIQ. I suppose that's it then?

ABDUL. He might be satisfied with just one of us getting married. Will you still leave?

TARIQ. I don't want anyone hurt any more… I'll think of something.

He goes, but pauses at the door.

Abdul.

ABDUL. Yeah?

TARIQ. I do understand, you know… more than you think.

Scene Five

The KHANS' *house, Sunday.* ELLA *is plaiting* MEENAH's *hair.* SAJIT *sits oblivious to all the confusion around him, reading a comic.*

MEENAH. Ouch! Mam, you're pulling me hair out.

ELLA. Keep it bloody still then. Sajit – go upstairs and ask your dad to give you the nit comb.

SAJIT. I 'aven't got nits.

ELLA. Well, stop scratching your bleeding head. (*To* MANEER.) Are you out of that bath yet, Maneer?

MANEER. I've not been in yet.

ELLA. Well, don't bother, you haven't got time. Just have a quick wash.

MANEER. Oh Mam, I want a bath.

ELLA. Alright. In and out quick. (*To* MEENAH.) Did you use the big pan for the curry like I told you?

MEENAH. Yeah, and I got some more chappati flour, Mam, as well. Will you tell Maneer to help with the chappatis, Mam?

SAJIT. I can make chappatis, Mam.

ELLA. You don't go near that flour with those hands.

SAJIT. Why can't I?

MEENAH. 'Cause we'll all end up with scabs, you mong!

Enter TARIQ *and* ABDUL.

TARIQ. Mam – I can't do this tie.

ELLA. Hang on, I haven't got two pairs of hands. Abdul! Fix Tariq's tie. (*Pause.*) Where's Saleem?

TARIQ. He said he was gonna pick his model up. Mam, this tie's not right.

ELLA. Come here. (*Does* TARIQ's *tie.*) There, that'll do. (*Strokes his hair,* MEENAH *and* ABDUL *exchange looks.*) Go on get lost.

Sajit, go upstairs and ask your dad to get me jewellery out of the safe. (*As* SAJIT *goes.*) And take that bleeding parka off! Abdul, get the posh cups out of the cabinet in the kitchen.

MEENAH. I don't know why they can't have mugs like everyone else, they only slurp it out of the saucers.

ELLA. Well if he does, don't look, I'm not having you lot laughing and showing me up. Right, Meenah, veil on! Tariq, Abdul, let's have a look at you, you'll do. Maneer!

MANEER *appears from the kitchen,* ELLA *looks at him.*

Brylcreem!

MEENAH. I feel stupid in this.

SAJIT *enters.*

SAJIT. You look it.

MEENAH. Shut your gob, or I'll shut it for you.

ELLA. If I catch you fighting in that sari, I'll wipe the floor with both of you. Now go and get me some fags from Butterworth's.

MEENAH. No way, I'm not going out dressed like this.

ELLA. Sajit go and get me twenty Park Drive. Maneer, have you emptied that bath out?

MANEER. Yeah, can you get zinc poisoning from it, Mam?

ELLA. Don't be so bleeding stupid.

MEENAH. I wish we had a proper one, that one don't half scratch your arse.

MEENAH *gets a clip round the ear from* ELLA.

ELLA. Hey, gobshite, I've told you once, keep it shut. We've got visitors.

SAJIT *bursts in.*

SAJIT. Mam, quick, the Pakis are here!

ELLA. Oh for Jesus' sake. Abdul, muzzle him, will you?

ABDUL. Sajit, get over here!

MR and MRS SHAH *enter greeted by* ELLA. ELLA *leads him into the parlour, followed by the others,* SAJIT *bringing up the rear trying to see.* ELLA *has now got her slightly posh voice on.* MR SHAH *has with him two large photographs, in ornate frames, of his daughters.*

GEORGE (*off*). Ella, this is Mr Shah and a Mrs Shah.

MR SHAH. Asalaam-a-lekum.

MRS SHAH. Asalaam-a-lekum

ELLA. Walekum-a-salaam. Would you like to come through to the parlour?

MEENAH (*to* TARIQ). What's she talking like that for?

GEORGE *introduces the boys to* MR SHAH *and* MRS SHAH.

GEORGE. This is my son Abdul.

MR SHAH. Asalaam-a-lekum.

ABDUL. Walekum-a-salaam.

GEORGE. Tariq.

MR SHAH. Asalaam-a-lekum.

TARIQ. Walekum-a-salaam.

GEORGE. Maneer.

MR SHAH. Asalaam-a-lekum.

MANEER. Walekum-a-salaam.

ELLA (*calls*). Meenah.

Enter MEENAH.

Would you bring in the tea, love?

GEORGE. This is my daughter Meenah.

MEENAH (*posh*). Righty-ho. (*Goes out to fetch the tea.*)

Pause. MRS SHAH *looks at the room uncomfortably.*

ELLA. Did you find it alright?

MR SHAH. Oh yes, no problem.

Pause.

You have a very nice family, all boys, this is very good. God has blessed you.

ELLA. Well I could have done without so much blessing.

MR SHAH. I'm sorry?

ELLA. Doesn't matter. (*Changing the subject.*) Lovely frames you've got there.

MR SHAH. Yes, let me show you, these are my daughters, Nigget and Afsal-jaan. (*Passes them over, they're quite heavy.*)

ELLA. Oh they're quite hefty... the frames I mean! Look George, aren't they lovely?

SAJIT. Which one's Tariq's?

ELLA. Sit down cock, over there by the door.

GEORGE. Very nice photo. Where you buy frame like this?

MRS SHAH. We had them especially made for our girls, gold leaf, you know.

Enter MEENAH *with the tea, she sees the photos. She can barely control her laughter, this could be dangerous. She scuttles out of the room quickly.*

MEENAH. I'll just go and get the biscuits. (*Almost snorts this.*)

TARIQ and ABDUL *hear this but* ELLA *kills another outbreak with a look.*

MRS SHAH. Do all your sons live at home?

ELLA lights a fag, MR SHAH *looks on disapprovingly.*

ELLA. All except Nazir, he's the eldest.

GEORGE. He travelling salesman.

SAJIT moves closer to the SHAHS, *he does a large twitch.*

MR SHAH. Erm. And this must be your youngest. (*To* SAJIT.) And how old are you?

SAJIT. Not old enough to get married, so don't ask me.

GEORGE (*veiled threat*). Sajit puther, go see if Saleem here yet.

MR SHAH. Ah yes, Saleem your college student, the engineer.

SAJIT. He's not, he's an artist, I've got a picture he drew of a...

> SAJIT *is about to take out the picture* SALEEM *drew of a foreskin.* MANEER *retrieves it just in time.*

MANEER. He means engineer... who erm paints engines, Mr Shah...

ELLA. Sajit. Saleem. Now.

> SAJIT *gets the message and goes.*

Sorry about that, Mr Shah, he's erm... just been circumcised...

MR SHAH. Indeed.

ELLA. Where's that Meenah with them biscuits?

TARIQ. Shall I put the pictures of your daughters on the radiogram, Mr Shah?

MR SHAH. So Tariq, do you have hobbies?

GEORGE. Only good ones. He like to work in shop most time.

> *Enter* MEENAH *with biscuits.*

MEENAH. Would you like a biscuit, Mr Shah?

MRS SHAH. Where did you get this sari?

MEENAH. Me Auntie Riffat in Pakistan.

MRS SHAH. This is not what we wear. You should wear shalwar kameez. It will look much better on you than this thing.

ELLA. Her Auntie Riffat said all women wear saris in Islamabad, and she's quite well to do, in't she George.

GEORGE. Riffat bloody stupy. (*To* MR SHAH.) Even in Pakistan women getting too bloody moderns.

MR SHAH. It's the government people I blame. They should set an example to the country.

ELLA. I think it looks lovely.

MRS SHAH. It is not traditional dress in Pakistan.

GEORGE. Tradition see, Ella.

ANNIE (*off*). Youuu! Only me!

> ANNIE *pokes her head round the door.*

> Oh, I didn't know you had visitors. I won't stay long.

GEORGE. Annie, this is my friend Mr Shah, he daughters go be marry Abdul and Tariq.

ANNIE. Congratulations Mr Shah. (*Notices the pictures.*) Are these 'em? Oh, they look bleedin' gorgeous, you're lucky you two, landing a couple of belters like that.

GEORGE (*to* MR SHAH). Annie working for me since we first getting shop.

ELLA. I suppose you'll want tea now?

ANNIE. Seeing as you've asked me so bleeding politely I will.

ELLA. Meenah go and put the kettle on.

> MEENAH *exits.*

ANNIE. Yeah they're lovely them, Mr Shah, you must be very proud of them. Beltin' frames as well.

MR SHAH. Yes, gold leaf you know.

ANNIE. I do know, I got something similar meself off the docks.

ELLA (*trying to shut her up*). Do you want a biscuit?

ANNIE. No ta. Three bob the pair they were. I've got a view of Kinder Scout in one and a three-dimensional of our lady in the other, looks beltin' don't it, Ella?

MR SHAH. Mrs Khan...

ELLA. Call me Ella.

ANNIE. Everybody does.

MR SHAH. Erm... Mrs Khan, I am very proud that your sons are joining my family.

> *This makes* ELLA *sit up and take note, even though she knows it's the girls who are joining her family.*

I can see you have brought them up to be very respectful, which is very difficult in this day and age.

ANNIE. You're right there Mr Shah, they're a credit to her, and you George.

GEORGE. Oh yes, they good boys, no bring a trouble.

ANNIE. They'll do owt for you these two, you know last Whitsun they carried the banner of the Sacred Heart at a moment's notice, all the way from Regent Road t'town hall in Albert Square and back.

MRS SHAH. What banner is this?

ANNIE. For the Whit Week Walks. Abdul and Tariq on the banner, Saleem, Maneer and our Clifford holding ribbons from the model of the holy sepulchre, with Sajit and Meenah chuckin' petals about in front.

GEORGE. Ella, what she bloody talking about?

MRS SHAH (*slightly perturbed*). Is this a religious ceremony?

ANNIE. In a way I suppose you could say it was, but hardly anyone round 'ere's religious. It's just a day out f'kids and a new set of clothes.

ABDUL. We just helped out that once, lucky we were all there really.

Lights up on living room.

MEENAH. Brew up Twitch.

SAJIT. Get stuffed you fat cow!

MEENAH. I'll stuff you, you little twat!

MEENAH *flings herself and her sari over the sofa and onto* SAJIT. *He screams.*

Up on the parlour.

ELLA. Well you've got to lend a hand haven't you, I mean that's how we brought them up.

MRS SHAH. But this was not their religion.

ANNIE (*digging herself out*). Well that's what a couple of belters you're getting, Mr Shah, they just jumped in there and gave help where help was needed, good Samaritans they were, just like in the Bible when...

We hear SAJIT *scream. This is a good time for* ELLA *to cut* ANNIE *off before she puts her foot in it again.*

ELLA. Tariq cock, will you go and see what they're up to? (*To* MR SHAH.) Kids eh? Were your two like that when they were younger?

TARIQ *exits.*

MRS SHAH. No, I was a schoolmistress before I married. I've always believed in firm discipline. Especially in a non-Pakistani environment.

ELLA. Oh I think you can be too harsh, don't you Annie?

ANNIE. Oh aye, yeah, mind you, our Peter knows how far he can go, before I knock him to kingdom come – and that's just me husband, Mr Shah!

She bursts into laughter, ELLA *also but not as much as she would like.* GEORGE *and* MR SHAH *do not find it funny.*

Do you smoke Mr Shah?

He declines, she offers one to MRS SHAH *and recieves a withering look. She gives one to* ELLA.

You could even say that in a Pakistani environment you'd still have to know where to draw the line with them, whereas with Ella and George they didn't have that environment, did they, so they had to find their own line here in Salford, in this area among non-Pakistanis, but even without other Pakistanis, they've got what you have as well, and done very well with it... like you have done. (*Got to get out of this.*) You know they look just like you Mr Shah. (*Indicates the photos.*)

MR SHAH. Oh, no, no.

ELLA. She's right Mr Shah. They've got your eyebrows.

MRS SHAH. I think there is a great preponderance placed on looks.

ANNIE. A what sorry?

GEORGE. 'Ponderance. (*To* MR SHAH.) What is latest news from East Pakistan?

Lights up on living room.

MEENAH. Have you seen them pictures though!

TARIQ. The one in the red looked like she had a hairline that started from her eyebrows.

MEENAH. At least she had a neck. Our Abdul's looked like Smiffy out of the Bash Street Kids!

Enter MANEER *with a teapot.*

MANEER. Me mam said to hurry up with that tea.

TARIQ. What's going on in there?

MANEER. Me dad's building up to the war.

Up on the parlour.

GEORGE. Is bloody Indians see!

ANNIE. I'd better be going, got to go and see the undertaker about Scots Bertha, see you later George. Nice to meet you Mr Shah.

ELLA. See you later.

ANNIE *exits.*

MR SHAH (*to* GEORGE). General Yahya Khan will hold the country together.

GEORGE. Ah yes, he's the man for that…

ELLA (*trying to make conversation*). Do your family come from Azad Kashmir, Mrs Shah?

MRS SHAH. My husband's. My family, are from Lahore, a beautiful city, the home of the arts in Pakistan. Have you been to Pakistan Mrs Khan?

ELLA. Never been asked.

MRS SHAH. But you must go on holiday some time, two months at least, see the whole country.

ELLA. Yeah, well, we can only manage two weeks in Rhyl. Even then George has to stay home and mind the shop.

MRS SHAH. Really... well Pakistan is very different to Rhyl.

ELLA. Yeah right... it's got the sun for a start... have you been in England long Mr Shah?

MR SHAH. Since 1949. My wife studied here, in London, but later returned when my daughters were young.

MRS SHAH. I don't think this is a fit society to bring up girls.

ELLA. All depends how you bring them up, I think.

MRS SHAH. But you have experienced only boys, Mrs Khan.

ELLA. I've got Meenah as well Mrs Shah.

MRS SHAH. Yes this is true Mrs Khan, but... our girls are different.

ELLA (*does not like this*). Really.

GEORGE. Han, this is true, too much tickle-tackle go on see. You go to town, and you bloody see all bloody Indian girl. All bloody up to tickle-tackle with boy.

MR SHAH. This is the problem with our community, they don't realise what a great danger it is to leave your children to grow up in this country.

GEORGE. I been in this country since 1930, an' I telling you no even bloody English same.

ELLA. What sort of work did you do when you first came Mr Shah?

MR SHAH. Very degrading work, I assure you, Mrs Khan, very degrading. I was overqualified you see. First I swept the floor in a mill, then I worked on the buses. Now I have four butchers' shops, two cars and a semi-detached house in Trafford Park.

ELLA. Really?

MR SHAH. With double extensions.

ELLA. That's nice and roomy for you. Abdul go and see where that tea is, will you.

MR SHAH. My daughters both have their own bedrooms, you know. With Axminster carpet.

ELLA. Nice.

MR SHAH. They have attached bathrooms with same carpet.

MRS SHAH. My idea.

ELLA. I've always found oilcloth better for the bathroom, stops that smell of damp.

GEORGE. We have bathroom soon I think.

MRS SHAH. How do you manage with so little room and so many children Mrs Khan? It must be a bit of a squeeze.

ELLA. I've got three double beds and one single for Meenah.

MRS SHAH. But where do you propose to put my daughters?

ELLA. One in the attic, the other on top of the chippy with Abdul.

MR SHAH (*making his move*). But we have so much room at our house, it seems such a shame to waste it. Would it not be more convenient if your sons were to move in with us?

He looks to GEORGE *for agreement.*

ELLA. Erm, I thought the daughters-in-law moved in with their husbands' family.

MR SHAH. But my daughters are used to modern conveniences. Perhaps when you get your bathroom fitted they may be able to move back.

MRS SHAH. I'd have thought you'd be grateful for the extra space, I know I would be.

ELLA. But you don't know what you'd be getting yourself into, Mrs Shah. You've never experienced boys, have you?

Up on living room.

ABDUL. Saj, go and see if Saleem's at Roy's.

SAJIT *runs out.*

Better not let him back in the parlour, Mr Shah thinks he's retarded.

MEENAH. He is.

TARIQ. Well if Sajit can't scare them off, nothing will.

SAJIT *enters with* SALEEM.

ABDUL. You'd better hurry up and get changed, Mr Shah's waiting to meet you.

TARIQ. And if you're asked what you do at college, you're an engineer who paints engines. Nowt to do with me, it was Twitch.

SALEEM (*to* SAJIT). You gobby little twat! (*Hits him.*)

TARIQ (*referring to model*). Is that it then?

MEENAH. It looks dead interesting that, doesn't it, Tariq?

TARIQ. Let's have a look at this great work of art then?

SALEEM *puts the model on the table, with its back to the audience, and lifts off the cover. The others look open-mouthed.*

SALEEM. What do you think?

ABDUL. What are you gonna do with it?

SALEEM. I'm not gonna do anything with it, Abdul. It's an example of female exploitation in art.

MANEER. It looks disgusting.

TARIQ. I wouldn't say that.

MANEER. It's perverted.

MEENAH. Not even Twitch would do something like that.

SALEEM. It's art, you pillocks.

ELLA *enters, muttering 'Axminster my arse', she does not see the model.*

ELLA (*to* MEENAH). Oi you, where's that bleeding tea, get a move on, your dad's waiting for it. Abdul, Tariq, parlour. (*To* SALEEM.) Hurry up and get ready, you should have been back half an hour ago. Sajit, where'd you put those fags?

SALEEM. I said I was going for me model.

ELLA. Show me later, I haven't time now. (*Makes to go.*)

SAJIT. He's got a woman's fanny in a box, Mam!

The model is of a vagina complete with pubic hair.

ELLA. You dirty little bastard!

SALEEM. Mam, it's art.

ELLA. I'll art you, you little sod, I'll burn the bleeding thing.

ELLA goes to grab the model, but SALEEM gets there first. She begins to chase him round the room.

Give it me!

SALEEM. Art's changed, Mam.

ELLA. Aye and I'll change it some more when I get me hands on it.

We see her chase him into the hallway, followed by the others.

Up on parlour.

We are aware of the commotion outside the parlour door.

SALEEM (*from outside*). Mam let go, you're pulling all the hair out! Maam!

SALEEM *falls through the door clutching the model. He lands in front of* MRS SHAH.

MR SHAH. Arghhh!!

SALEEM. Mr Shah, I'm Saleem, I'm an art student… erm… engineer!

GEORGE. Up baster!

MRS SHAH. What is this thing, move it, take it away from me!

ELLA comes through the door, followed by the others.

ELLA. I'm very sorry Mrs Shah, it was an accident, the hair came off in me hands.

MR SHAH. This is an insult to me, and to my family! How can you allow your son to behave like this?

MRS SHAH. I will never let my daughters marry into this jungly family of half-breeds!

ELLA. They may be half-bred, but at least they're not bleeding in-bred like those two monstrosities. (*Indicating the pictures*.)

GEORGE. Ella!

ELLA. Never mind 'Ella'. (*Back to* SHAH.) Who the frig do you think you are, coming in here telling me my house isn't good enough for your daughters? Well your daughters aren't good enough for my sons or my house. And if I hear you say another word about my family, I'll put that fanny over your bastard head.

MR SHAH. How dare you speak to me like this!

GEORGE. Ella you stop now or I bloody killing you!

MR SHAH. I won't stay here another minute, your wife is a disgrace!

ELLA. Sling your bleeding hook, go on, piss off! (*Points to the pictures.*) And take Laurel and frigging Hardy with you.

MR SHAH *takes the photos and ushers his wife out of the room.*

GEORGE. You baster bitch, you insulting guest, bring bloody shame on family!

ELLA. You ought to be ashamed George, you're not getting these lads married, you're selling them off to the highest bidder. Who's gonna get Meenah? Someone with double glazing and a detached house!

GERORGE. Why you never baster listen!

GEORGE *grabs* ELLA, *and pushes her to the floor, he starts to hit her.*

MEENAH. Maam! Maam! Abdul stop him!

SALEEM *and* TARIQ *run over to try and stop him,* MANEER *grabs* ELLA *and tries to pull her away.* SAJIT *takes off his coat, runs over, and starts to hit* GEORGE *with it.*

ABDUL. Dad! (*Grabs* GEORGE *and pushes him against the wall.*) Get off her, stop it.

SALEEM. Smack him one Abdul!

ABDUL. Dad, if you touch her again I swear I'll kill you!

GEORGE. You don't talk…

ABDUL. No Dad, it's over, alright, it's finished!

SAJIT *is still hitting him with his parka.*

Sajit stop it!

SAJIT *carries on hitting* GEORGE.

I said stop it!

SAJIT *stops and runs off to the shed crying. Pause. There's just the sound of* ELLA *crying. The others help her into a chair.*

Just calm down Dad, alright?

GEORGE *starts to cry.*

GEORGE. I only try to help you son, I no want to bloody hurt you, I love my family. I have to bloody stick up for family when people calling.

ABDUL. Go on over to the shop, go on, I'll come over in a bit.

GEORGE *looks at* ELLA *and the others, he looks at* ABDUL. *Ashamed and upset, he walks slowly out of the room.*

MEENAH. Don't cry Mam, it wasn't your fault. Maneer, go and make some tea.

SALEEM. You should have stopped him from hitting her, Abdul.

TARIQ. Leave him out of it, Saleem.

ABDUL. I couldn't hit me dad.

SALEEM. Dad, that bastard's not a father, I don't know 'bout holding him back, you should've broken his neck.

ABDUL. What I did or didn't do has got fuck-all to do with you Saleem.

SALEEM. Feeling guilty now, are you?

ELLA. Just pack it in the lot of you, you get on me nerves. I can't do anything to please you, if it's not you it's your dad, if it's not your dad it's you. You're nothing but bleeding trouble. And – (*To* SALEEM.) Pablo bleeding Picasso, that 'bastard' you've just been talking about is my husband, and

whatever you may think of him he's still your father. So if I
hear another foul-mouth word from anyone I'll have you.
Now where's Sajit?

Enter MANEER *with the tea.*

MANEER. He's in the shed.

ABDUL. He took his parka off though, he hit me dad with it,
when he slapped you.

ELLA. I don't believe it, I spend a year trying to get him out of
that bloody coat, your dad hits me, and he whips it off and
tries to kill him with it. I'll go have a word with him.

ELLA *goes to the shed.*

SALEEM. She's just gonna leave it, isn't she?

TARIQ. What else do you expect her to do?

SALEEM. She'll just let him walk back in here after what he's
done?

MEENAH. He did after Nazir left, didn't he.

SALEEM. So you're just gonna sit there, with your heads in the
sand, until it happens again?

ABDUL. No one's hiding. Me mam's just trying to hold her
family together.

SALEEM. Family! This isn't a family! Normal families sit
down and talk. We say something out of line, me dad hits us
and that's it.

ABDUL. It's not as simple as that, and you know it.

SALEEM. She should divorce him.

ABDUL. You're all missing the point, have you not thought that
she might love him?

MEENAH. Me dad?

ABDUL. What else do you think has kept them together for so
long? We're the cause of most of the arguments between
them, 'cause she always takes our side.

TARIQ. So what do we do now, Abdul?

ABDUL. Try and make things easier for her, don't make her job any harder than it is. It's me dad that's gonna have to change.

MANEER. He was only trying to show us our culture.

ABDUL. He's got no right to tell us what our culture should be, he lost that when he settled here and married me mam.

MEENAH. God Abdul, you sound dead different.

SALEEM. Say that when you get married off.

ABDUL. That's not gonna happen to her, it's not gonna happen to anyone who doesn't want it. I'm telling you, things are gonna be different round here.

He picks up SAJIT's *coat from the floor and goes to the yard.*

MEENAH. 'Kinell.

ABDUL *meets* ELLA *in the sitting room.*

ELLA. He's all yours. I want to go over and see your dad in a bit, we've got to talk, will you come with me?

ABDUL. Course I will.

ELLA *gives* ABDUL *a hug. This is quite awkward as they're not a physical family.*

Thanks for sticking up for us, Mam.

ELLA (*pulling away*). Go on you big daft get, go give him his coat.

ABDUL *goes into the yard.*

ABDUL. Sajit, are you still in there?

SAJIT. Get stuffed you!

ABDUL. What have I done?

SAJIT. You shouted at me for hitting me dad.

ABDUL. I know, I'm sorry, come out I want to talk to you.

SAJIT *emerges slowly.*

SAJIT. I was only hitting him 'cause he hit me mam. He always does it. He said he was gonna burn the house down.

ABDUL. You don't have to worry about that, I won't let him. Here I've brought your parka.

SAJIT. I didn't half give him a belt, didn't I?

ABDUL (*smiling*). Yeah, do you want it or what?

SAJIT. No.

ABDUL. Stick it in the bin then.

SAJIT *takes the coat, goes over to the bin, lifts up the lid, takes one last look at his coat, and throws it in.*

SAJIT. Abdul.

ABDUL. Yeah?

SAJIT. Can I have another look at our Saleem's model?

ABDUL (*laughing*). No!

The End.

NOTES ON FALLING LEAVES

for
Zaffa

'ere y'are now

Notes on Falling Leaves was first performed at the Royal Court Theatre Downstairs, London, on 11 February 2004. The cast was as follows:

WOMAN   Pam Ferris
MAN   Ralf Little

Director   Marianne Elliott
Lighting Designer Trevor Wallace
Sound Designer   Ian Dickinson

Characters

MAN, *twenty-six*

WOMAN, *early fifties*

Leaves completely cover the stage and wings. A rusty iron bench is centre stage. A WOMAN *in her early fifties stands upstage centre in the semi-darkness.*

The WOMAN *has short grey hair. She wears a large maternity-type dress with a Peter Pan collar. She plucks at the waist of the dress all the time, as if irritated in some way. On her arm she carries a handbag. When she moves, it is in a stooped shuffle. She slowly bends and picks up a leaf and whispers to it and then drops it again. She shuffles towards the bench and contemplates it. She knows there is something she has to do with it, but it doesn't come to her.*

Beat.

She looks about her, a pained expression on her face.
She moans little moans. She comes to the front of the bench and lowers herself down towards the seat, but misses it completely. Slowly she squats down in front of it, whispering to the leaves as she picks them up. Upstage, a MAN, *twenty-six, slowly follows her forward. He lights a cigarette. He clears his throat. He does this throughout his speech. He stands and stares at her. In his hand, he holds a bright-pink child's drinking beaker with a lid and two handles.*

MAN. I stayed at the house last night. Your house... Last night...

He clears his throat again. The WOMAN *does not acknowledge him but carries on handling the leaves.*

I stayed in your house last night... Our house. The house we all lived in.

The WOMAN *pays no attention to anything the* MAN *says. Her focus is never on him.*

WOMAN. Hanawahd. I couldevin...

She moans. He clears his throat again.

MAN. It was there... but it wasn't... bit like you really.
Shadowed. Dirt on the handle of the fridge. Fingerprints that
belong to fingers that don't feel any more. I touched them.
Ran my fingers over them. You. Everything I touched had
you on them. Every room had conversations in them.

It was all there exactly as I remembered it, nothing changed.
But it's a dead house. If houses can die, then your house is
dead. The girl I'd brought with me thought it was spooky.
She sat in a chair afraid and wouldn't move. Followed me
about like you did... Could hardly tell her to 'Fuck off and
sit down,' could I? It was cold. Soulless. There was still a
distinctive odour of stale piss around the place... not your
fault, I know. She smelt it. The girl. The moment we walked
in. She didn't let on but I know she smelt it. I knew it was
coming at the top of road. Even before I put the key in the
back door. You'll be pleased to know I used the back door.
Even though I'd brought a visitor. It made me laugh...
Shocking, to come to your boyfriend's parents' house
permeated with the smell of age-old piss.

I didn't care. 'What d'you think?' I said in a very 'I've just
had the whole place redesigned' kind of voice. 'Oh it's very
nice,' she said. 'It's council,' I said. 'Oh right... I've never
been in one before.' She sat down in your chair. She probably
thinks all council houses smell of piss. She lives with her
parents in a house in Mayfair... It's very nice. You would have
liked it. Not a whiff of piss in that place. I watched her. I think
I was enjoying her discomfort. She didn't know what to say or
do. She didn't seem to want to touch anything...

She'd have freaked if I'd told her she was sat in your chair.
Your pissy old chair... I could still make out the ash in the
carpet from your fags missing the ashtray.

I began to resent her being there. She looked clean and fresh.
So was I, but I was part of it... I still belonged there. Even
now, after all this time. It all looked the same. But dead. There
was a Christmas tree bulb on the floor behind the telly...
Papers still in the two pouffes by the electric fire. Bills behind
that awful glass swan. Are they called pouffes? You used to
call them pouffes. I've heard them called Ottomans...
Ottoman pouffes? Probably a grain of truth in that. They were

partial to taking it up the shitter I believe... I fucked her in our
kid's old bedroom. She wouldn't use yours or mine. The only
two with beds still in them. The others took theirs with them
when they left. Four gone, two to go. Mine and yours. Not that
I'm gonna take mine... I stuck my mattress on the floor in our
kid's room. Hope you don't mind...

It was dead... the sex. Dead sex in a dead house. Cold,
clammy, shadowed, dead sex.

*Offstage we hear the faint sound of a vacuum cleaner moved
across a floor.*

Sex with the smell of piss and decay. It was hard getting into
her, entering her... I hope you don't mind me mentioning
this to you... it's not therapy or owt... I'm not looking for a
reaction from you. We're well beyond that now... I just feel I
can. 'Cause you don't hear or understand and it helps me in
some odd... fucked-up kind of way. Where was I? It was
hard... I think she was a virgin. I don't know... I've never
consciously had a virgin, Mother, though it's not through
lack of trying. It's not something you ask, is it? We haven't
been seeing each other long. A couple of weeks. I don't
know why I asked her to come.

There was blood... lots of it... even in the dark I could see it
dark on the sheets. I understand blood... I know there's
something wrong when I see blood. There's something you
can do. She didn't scream out like I've heard virgins are
supposed to do their first time. I'm not saying I was
disappointed or anything... A scream I understand... pain I
understand. She's worried about the bloodstains on the
sheets. She wants to wash them. Your sheets. Your
best sheets. The ones you won at Bingo. Your big win.
Remember how happy you were when you won all those
prizes and they sent you home in a black taxi? Sheets, a glass
swan that you could put flowers in, a photo album for all
your happy memories, a thatched-cottage tea set...

I told her not to worry about the sheets as everything's being
dumped by the council next week. Your house and its
contents. All our lives. Going to the dump. It freaked her out
even more. She cried. I was worried, in an oddly detached
way, that she might become hysterical. I ran her a bath, I

thought it might help... I sat outside the door listening to the water splash about. I took a towel in for her... she stood up in the bath, smiling, waiting for me to wrap her up in the towel and lift her out, the way you used to do to us when we were kids... She looked fuckin' horny standing there... drips of water running down her body... I started to get a hard-on again. But then you were standing next to her... wet and scared with your saggy old tits dangling down and your sad old bush... Sons shouldn't see their mothers' bush... They shouldn't give directions on how to wash from outside the bathroom... She looked at me strangely and took the towel.

Sitting in her water, I washed the blood off my cock... all looked a bit like fuckin' *Psycho*. By the time I'd finished she was asleep. I lay awake and listened for your snores.

Nothing... you're not there. I sit on the stairs and listen to the house. It's breathing low and shallow... it must be getting harder now... can't be long. I wandered round the rooms in the blackness... Just like you used to do. What were you looking for... Who were you whispering to in the dark? Would I bump into your ghost... but you're not dead... you're as good as, if you don't mind me saying... you may as well be... everything's basically working but... I can't speak to your spirit if you're not dead... bit of a disappointment in the dead-parent-conversation department. I've a friend who speaks to his dead mother all the time in his head. He finds this very comforting... I can't. You're not dead... Which is inconvenient sometimes. It feels like you're dead... I try to pretend that you're dead, but you won't die. You blink. It's amazing how much life there is in a blink. I think sometimes, you're about to say something... but then you don't. You blink.

I'm here for the others. I'm here 'cause it's expected. When I'm in London I don't even think about you. You rarely cross my mind. 'I won't take my coat off, I'm not stopping,' so to speak.

He clears his throat again. He hums to himself. He lights a cigarette.

Last night. In the middle of the night. I walked our walk again. That walk. The walk we took that day. The girl would've freaked if she'd woken and I wasn't there. But I thought... Fuck it! I'm going! Fuck it! This'll be the last time I'm here. The last time the house is here.

I leave. It's three o'clock in the morning and I'm running through the estate to the medical centre. Past St Joey's, past what's-his-name's house who was in my class at school and got his eye poked out in a fight at the fifth-year disco... Not so fucking hard now, are you, you one-eyed bastard! Through the shitty precinct, six derelict shops, a chippy and a fuckin' Spar.

I'm outside the medical centre. It's a burnt-out shell. I wander through what's left. I'm in the room. That room. It smells of piss as well. Used needles on the floor... It's dark in here... empty. No sun. When we were here, there was bright, bright sunshine, streaming through the windows. A doctor and six fuckin' medical students!

Six fuckin' students and...

'I'm afraid she'll have to have more tests.'

Six fuckin' students and...

'It won't get any better.'

Six fuckin' students and everything that was, before we came into this room, has gone! You're brought back in and you sit next to me. You smile politely. That working-class deference to authority... I can't hear anything. I can't see anything. I'm not sure if I'm still breathing. There's something in my stomach. It's starting to rise into my chest. It's in my throat.

I'm out the door. We're walking back together. You and me. Mother and son... I want to... I want... There's something in my throat. I force it down. You're by my side. You look worried. I've never seen that look before. You look scared. I shouldn't be seeing this. Children don't see these things. They can't. They just can't. I walk faster. You're trying to keep up. Pathetic little steps... Looking up at me...

'What did he say?'

I force it down.

'Must be the change.'

I force it down.

Not here. I've got to get home. I walk faster and faster. The sun's shining, it's a beautiful day. People sit on their steps talking, drinking tea. Through the precinct, busy shops, people queue in the chippy. 'Do we need owt from t'Spar?' I force it down. It aches... I'm beginning to ache... Oh, Mam, it hurts... it hurts so bad... I want to scream. I'm screaming inside! And you run to keep up. Cubs and Brownies playing games outside St Joey's. We're home.

Upstairs in the bathroom. I lock the door.

Pause.

Nothing. Nothing comes. I look in the mirror and nothing comes. I hear you call up the stairs, asking if I want tea and nothing comes.

The WOMAN *moans and attempts to rise, but slumps back down. The* MAN *clears his throat and lights another cigarette.*

I checked on the girl. She was still asleep. I wander back downstairs. I find myself by the coat cupboard. I open it and shit myself. I thought it was your ghost, but it's only your long white lollipop-lady's overcoat hanging there. Your lollipop stick stands there as well – 'Stop!' illuminated briefly as I walk inside and close the door. 'Stop!' Is it some kind of message from beyond your brain I think to myself.

It's dark in here... darker than the dark outside. Darker than the shadows. I'm next to one of your old coats. Not a poorly coat. An old one, from before.

The MAN *lifts his hands to his face and smells them. He takes deep breaths.*

I'm next to you again. The old you. The you I know. That makes me laugh. I put my head under your coat and breathe you in. All of you. All over. I can almost feel you warm by my side. You're with me, you're with me, you're with me, you're with me! I can smell you. I can smell you. I remember! I remember when our kid took you out... I got you ready. Helped you to put your tights on... you kept trying to put both legs in the same hole, we shouted at each

other, we fell on the floor and we laughed. We laughed
like we'd laughed before. Before the lump. Before the dark.
You put your arms around me and you kissed me. You
looked at me and saw me. The last time, the very last time
you were you and I was me. I remember...

I cry... my eyes pour... but I make no sound. The lump is in
my throat again. The lump from the room. The lump you
gave me. The lump that I forced down as we walked home.
The lump I tried to save till we got back. The lump I didn't
want you to see.

Beat.

Your lollipop stick falls and hits me on the head. I'm under
your coat. I'm a twenty-six-year-old man crying in the
darkness and your lollipop stick has just hit me on the
head... It fuckin' hurt as well... Maybe it is a message I
think or maybe it's just a falling lollipop stick. Everything's
gone... you're just a lovely smell on an old coat. No
memories, memories have decayed, decomposed in your
head. Black, rotten, putrid sludge. Time stopped. All life
stopped in this house when thoughts stopped. When your
thoughts stopped feeding the walls.

I look at you, but I don't see you any more. If you could talk
what would you say? Mmmm?...

MAN/WOMAN (*simultaneously*). If you/I could talk what
would you/I say.

The MAN *turns away and lights a cigarette. He wanders
slowly towards the shadows, where he stands, smoking.*

WOMAN. I'd say I hate... this dress. Hate the colour. It looks
like sack. Trim on the collar. Peter Pan collar... Gyave...
Iyave... seven and counting. Seven for the seven days. Yes.
Seven and counting seven. For senniven... finseev...
sauurrvev... fannar... fanssrarven. What days? What they
called days? When do they come? How do come? Howmen-
in... Come light and dark. Mmmm. Always light an a dark.
Every dressincome round light an a dark. Blue one. Green
one. Red one. Blue... Red. All with the collar. Flowers. All
flowers. Bright flowers and swan. Nice flower an a white
swan. They flower me with flowers. Flowers that can't smell.

Flowers that don't… pick. Flowers that don't… flowners that
don't… stand in the… things. The bird… things… the swan
things… Floweres… Flowers I piss on. Flowers I shit on.
Flat flowers. Flowers that getting wash and fade. I've got
them in bunches. All over me bunches. Every dark and light.
Bunches. I know them… I know they are them… I know
they are all. I cannnnn… know.

She looks at the audience and smiles at no one in particular.
She focuses on nothing. Her face is blank. She looks at the
bench, makes to sit on it. An anxious look crosses her face.
She is incapable of following through the movement. She
stands. She has already forgotten what she was going to do.
She sighs and smiles.

It's all of an all. All of all, of all of it. I am. I alwayam. It.
Iyam here. I be am. Me. Me am. Is where it is for me. This…
all it am. Is all it is. All it is all…

She closes her eyes and quickly says…

Dark and a light… dark an a light. An in all flowers.
(*Slower.*) Them flowers that don't feel like them. Floweds
that don't smell like them. The space of it. All in me and a
out of me, the space of it. Quietlyness space of it. Inside…
me… inside me the space of it. Of it all…

Pause.

I see an not see. I hear and not hear. To think the think of
things and not do. Not feel their… vermmm… feelness.
Not… mmmoove wivth the feelingness of it. Not feel.

She starts to become very agitated.

Making a mess… offff me. A mess of myself. Oh is terrible.
Terrible, terrible, terrible, terrible, terrible. Stop it! Stop it!
Now! Don't want it… don't wantdo… Think of yourself…
Think of the others. What musthey think… Whaaaam…
whahaamaduy… whamidey… whamuusey.

She moans little animal moans.

Thoughts. The thought of it, the thinking of it. I see them, the
thoughts. I sit and see them all. I see the people round me. Me.
My mess. The scurrying. The worry. The rush. The smiles.

The concern. The loathing. The disgust. The bile. The heaving. The bile. The smell. The wetness. The bile. The warmth.

She raises her face to an imaginary sun.

(*Whispered.*) The warmth. The warmth. The warmth. The sun on my face. Washing me, across me, in me, through me. It's me! I'm here. I'm here again and it's me. I'm here again and the flowers! I'm here again and the smell! I'm here again and the all of it! The completeness of it. Of me. I'm here in the hereness of it and I am. Knowing one will come… It'll come and I'll catch it. Grab it. Don't know what it's going to be. Don't care. Anything. Anything that takes me…

This wrongness. On my back. The mess between my legs. Between my legs. Oh God. The mess. The smell. Wiped. Powdered. Plastic pants.

My baby.

He stands. Watching me. Silently. Silently me. He doesn't speak. Don't hear his voice. No soft voice. No comfort. He doesn't touch. Stands away. I can feel the space. The distance of him. The loss of him. Oh, the loss. The things felt. Everything inside of him. All away. In the blackness of it he is. In the farness that it is. Out… in a goneness.

I. Can't. Smell. His. Him.

I can't smell that which is him. His him, see. His him that is part of me. The him, that makes him, him. That I no longer have. That he no longer sees. Or looks to see. Or expects to see. He doesn't know I'm here and that I still am. Am the one, the person in the flowers, the one he knows. I'm flowered, I'm flowered, my baby, I'm flowered. Standing watching. Watching, watching. Clearing his throat. All the time clearing his throat. He never got rid of the knot. Big… rises up… all the time rises up. Big grey wave thing. Not skin. Not muscle. Energy. A bile. A lump… all the time it is.

She becomes agitated, pulling at her dress. She speaks faster.

I know how he got it. I was there. In the place. In a that room. I felt it. Felt it there. I became part of him. Into his body. Into him. A part of me in him. Me in him. A bad part of

me in him. It wanaaammin... wusss in... It was in the room
with us. In the room with the smiling people. In the room.
Inre thre room. Inaeroom, neroomah. (*Whispering*.) The knot
was there, the knot was there, the knot was there and it
was mine. It was mine and I gave it to him. I gave it to him, I
gave it to my son. I gave it to my son, I gave it to my baby.
In a room full of strangers asking strange questions. I gave
my son a knot. I gave him me. A piece of me. Of me. Of me.
Of me.

Elizabeth the Queen. The Thatcher... Is not Christmas?...
Don't know, love... Bull, car, man. Could you repeat please?
Bullmaaah... car, sorry... Try again... Bbbbul, car... man.
No? Backwards. Reverse them please... No if's and annnns,
no if andnns but's. Where are you? What country are you in?
What day is it? Don't know... don't ask sstu milly mally
thingys. I look at the strangers, the young people. My son's
people.

Smiling smiles of smiles and smiles and smiles and smiles
and smiling smiles of smiling smiles. Malinga malyle,
maliyle, malyle, malyle, smiles. Standing there and standing
there. Stands my baby standing. Not smiling malinga malyle
smiles. But standing. His face is stiff. His face is angry. His
face is hard. A rock.

His face is wet.

His face is wet.

My baby's face is wet.

A fly is buzzing around the room. A fly is buzzing around the
room.

My baby's face is wet. My life has gone and a fly buzzes
about the room.

My brightness has gone and a fly buzzes about the room.

My motherness that mothered him gone... zzzzz...

My fingertips that touched his face have gone... zzzzz...

The way I looked my looks, that made me, me, have gone...

My me has gone.

All that is me has gone...

All that I was has gone in the buzzing of a buzz.

Pause.

Oh the sadness of it. Oh how sad, how sad, how sad, how sad it all is. The terrible, terrible sadness.

I just want me again for a momentness.

That that I was. That that I was to be. To smell my baby. To use my fingertips. To wipe the wetness of it from his face. For a momentness of time. Is all, that is all, that is all.

Pause.

The sun is warm on my face. I sit in the centre of the room. It pours through the window in front of me. Behind the smiling people. Smiling their smiles of smiles and smiles and smiles and smiles. They have no eyes. They are dark and the sun is bright. But they smile. Strangers' smiles. They've ended it. My world. My me. They've questioned my world and they've ended it. My baby and my's world. The world we lived in, brought into this room, is gone. Stripped clean. Stripped by questions. Nothing remains standing. Not even you my baby, my baby with the wet face.

The MAN *walks over to her, and tenderly helps her to her feet and gently sits her down on the bench. He sits down beside her.*

MAN. I was eight, the needle nurse came to school. I was so scared I couldn't catch my breath... screamed the place down. The door opened and you were there with the other mums. I ran to you. You held me. You dressed me. You said I could come home. You bought me an ice lolly. I held your hand and ran to keep up with you as we walked. Walked home through the streets with the sun on our faces...

The sound of the projector gets louder, until we are left with just the sound of the loose end as it slaps around the spool. The lights slowly fade.

Blackout.

ALL THE WAY HOME

All the Way Home was first performed by The Library Theatre Company at The Lowry, Salford, on 29 September 2011. The cast was as follows:

JANET	Susan Cookson
CAROL	Kate Anthony
SONIA	Julie Riley
PHILLIP	Paul Simpson
AUNTIE SHEILA	Judith Barker
SAMANTHA	Naomi Radcliffe
BRIAN	Sean Gallagher
MICKEY	James Foster

Director	Mark Babych
Designer	Hayley Grindle
Lighting Designer	Ciaran Bagnall
Sound Designer	Paul Gregory

Characters

JANET, *forty-five*

CAROL, *forty-nine*

SONIA, *thirty-nine*

PHILLIP, *thirty-seven*

AUNTIE SHEILA, *seventies*

SAMANTHA, *thirty-nine*

BRIAN

MICKEY

ACT ONE

Scene One

Salford, Bonfire Night, present day.

The back kitchen of a terraced house. The set is a skeleton of a kitchen. We can see through it. Pipes, taps and wires should all be free-standing, with just the bare carcasses and shelves of cupboards. The only furniture, a mismatched fake Chippendale table, with six chairs, and a battered armchair. The armchair should bear the greasy stains from the head and hands of someone that has sat there regularly. This chair is never used by any of the characters.

There are bars on the outside of the windows. A door leads out to a backyard, another to the rest of the house. Various types of fireworks should go off intermittently throughout the play. From the back entry we hear kids singing.

KIDS (*voice-over*).
>This way my lady oh!
>That way my lady oh!
>This way my lady oh!
>All the way home.

>JANET, *forty-five, stands ironing clothes from a large basket of washing. A man's shirts hang, ironed, on the cupboards behind her. She's always on the go. Cleaning and tidying up.* CAROL, *forty-nine, sits at the table flicking through a newspaper. Both women smoke and drink tea.*

>*On the table is a baby monitor. It has a big smiley clown's face. The sound is turned down, but we can see lights moving in an arc across the face, lighting up the smile and indicating someone breathing. JANET and CAROL are both aware of this. A kettle is boiling on the stove.*

>Here comes a sailor!
>And here comes another one.

> Sexy as the other one,
> All the way home.

CAROL *walks over to the back door and opens it.*

> This way my lady oh!
> That way my lady oh!

CAROL. Michaela, can you keep it down please?

KIDS (*voice-over*).
> This way my lady oh!
> All the way home.

CAROL. Michaela!... Could you keep it down, you know your Uncle Frankie's not well.

MICHAELA (*voice-over*). Fuck off, you're not me mam!

KIDS (*voice-over*).
> Here comes a soldier!
> And here comes another one!
> Buggers all the other ones!
> All the way home!

We hear the sound of breaking glass. Michaela screams, the others join in and we hear them run off. CAROL comes back, she and JANET shake their heads. JANET puts more water into the iron and lights a cigarette.

CAROL. Mouthy little cow.

JANET. I'll do this lot and I'll swing an 'oover round the front room...

CAROL. Yeah?

JANET. Yeah... Perhaps I should do the bathroom first... I meant to do it last night before I went to bed...

CAROL. I'll do it later.

JANET. I don't mind, I've gotta put some clean sheets on our Phillip's bed, anyway.

Beat.

I don't know how me mam managed with us lot.

CAROL. Me and Frankie used to look after you, Brian and Phillip. Sonia were still in a pram.

JANET. Still a lot though, eh?

CAROL. I said I don't mind doing the bathroom.

JANET. No, leave it to me. I know what needs to be done, regarding Frankie's sheets and that… He's a bit funny about things like that now… You know… about 'em being handled by anyone else.

Pause.

I'll stick some tea on first though, eh?… Yeah, that's what I'll do next. Are you stopping for your tea?

CAROL. Might do. What're you doing?

JANET. Tater hash, I think… Our Phillip likes it.

CAROL. He likes it the way me mam cooked it.

JANET. I don't use corned beef. I use mince.

CAROL. That'll be it then… I always find it leaves a greasy aftertaste at the back of me tongue – mince.

JANET. It's a different butcher you need. I get mine minced in front of me. I can see what I'm getting then.

CAROL. I won't stop. I never liked tater hash.

JANET. Maybe I'll ask Frankie what he fancies…

CAROL. Yeah?

JANET. I'll ask him. He likes to be kept in the loop.

CAROL. He were asleep when I looked in before.

JANET. I'll ask him later then. Give us a chance to tidy up his room. Give it a bit of an airing.

JANET gives the steamer button a press and it sends out a couple of jets of steam. CAROL goes back to reading the paper. She hums the tune sung by the kids.

CAROL. They found the head of that headless corpse.

JANET. I heard.

CAROL. Salford Precinct.

Pause.

JANET. Wonder what were it doing there?

CAROL *looks at her incredulously.*

CAROL. Shoppin' at Tescos... How should I know?

Pause.

JANET. He were in our Sonia's music class at school.

CAROL. Who?

JANET. That... headless-corpse bloke.

CAROL. She said that?

JANET. Yeah. 'That head did music with me at school' she said.

CAROL. Did he have a body then?

She laughs.

JANET (*shocked*). Orr, Carol, that's terrible! That's someone's son you're takin' piss out of.

CAROL. So.

JANET. You shouldn't mock the afflicted.

CAROL. I didn't chop his head off, did I?

JANET. You can bring it back on yourself saying things like that. Think of your Reece.

CAROL. I'll take an axe to his head myself one of these days.

JANET. Up to no good?

CAROL. You'd never think we live in Didsbury Village, the way he behaves. Might as well be back round here.

JANET. Thanks.

CAROL. You know what I mean.

JANET. Yeah... knocking about with a better class of scum there, is he?

CAROL. I didn't mean it like that… It's just that he's…

JANET. What?

CAROL *looks at* JANET.

CAROL. Nowt.

JANET. Did you hear that?

JANET *stops ironing. She goes over to the door.*

Was that Frankie?

CAROL *turns up the monitor. We can hear a man breathing with difficulty.*

CAROL. Fast asleep.

JANET. I'll go and check.

CAROL. Leave him, he'll be fine.

CAROL *turns the monitor down again.* JANET *is unsure, but decides against going to look.*

JANET. Brew?

CAROL *nods and* JANET *collects up her cup and walks over to the sink.*

CAROL. Our Sonia played the cornet?

JANET. Me dad made her. Made our Phillip learn the recorder as well.

CAROL. I didn't know me dad liked music.

JANET. He didn't – it were some documentary he'd seen on telly about the rise of Acker Bilk.

Pause.

CAROL. Who did music with you at school?

JANET. Bummer Walsh.

CAROL. Was it Bummer Walsh? I thought he'd left by the time you got there. There was another Mr Walsh, I remember –

JANET. Yeah, he did English. He was English Walsh. Bummer Walsh did music…

She puts her cigarette on the side and washes the cups in the sink.

He let us bring our own records in once. You know – stuff we liked.

She dries her hands, picks up her cigarette and thinks for a minute as she looks out of the window. She takes a drag on her cigarette.

I didn't take owt. I wanted to… I just didn't.

CAROL *looks at the five small, brown pill bottles. She picks them up and squints as she tries to read the labels.*

Eddie Watts took some David Bowie song about having a wank on the floor.

CAROL. You what?…

The kettle starts to whistle. She turns it off. She wraps a tea towel round the handle.

JANET. He had the lyrics an' everything! 'And I had a wank on the floor', I'll never forget it – or was it 'I fell wanking to the floor'. Might not of been the floor, but he was definitely having a wank.

She pours a hot kettle into the teapot.

CAROL. And Bummer Walsh played it?

JANET. Yeah. The whole LP. We were all pissing ourselves. Bummer Walsh just sat and listened to it. Read the lyrics and everything.

CAROL. He were always dead quiet, weren't he?

JANET. We ran riot with him… He just sat there and played classical music.

She takes the tea over to CAROL *and returns to her ironing.*

CAROL. Same with us. He just played the piano and stared at the wall. I always felt dead sorry for him.

JANET. So did I – Well, not at the time like. At the time he were just –

CAROL. Bummer Walsh.

Pause.

JANET. He had shell shock from the war, didn't he?

CAROL. I thought it was a limp.

JANET pours the tea and milk into the cups.

JANET. Anyway, he taught that headless lad the cornet with our Sonia...

Beat.

Eddie Watts... He were Bowie mad... Wore all the gear an' everythin'. We all thought he was dead cool... till he was caught with his finger up his arse in the boys' bogs.

The door bangs open and SONIA, thirty-nine, comes in with a pile of shopping bags. Her fingers are covered in home-made tattoos and sovereign rings.

She wears a couple of gold chains round her neck. She wears a baseball cap and a tracksuit. She's an ex-crack addict.

SONIA. Make us a brew, Jan, I'm as dry as me nan's twat. Has our Michaela been round?

CAROL. Out the back...

SONIA does not even acknowledge CAROL. She dumps all the bags, except one.

SONIA. Michaela!

JANET. Shhh!

JANET exchanges a look with CAROL and goes to pour another cup of tea.

SONIA. Michaela!

JANET. Keep your voice down.

SONIA ignores CAROL and heads out the back door.

SONIA (*voice-over*). Michaela! Get off that bleedin' shed now!... Are you deaf or what? I said...

MICHAELA (*voice-over*). I'm off it!

SONIA. Do I look fuckin' stupid! I said off the shed and that means the wall as well! And if you're not down in five seconds I'm gonna leather you! One! Two! Three!... Now get home. Tell your dad I'll be back later, there's baked beans in't cupboard.

SONIA *is at the kitchen door. She shouts back.*

And stay out of them bastard houses.

CAROL *looks up from the paper as* SONIA *comes back into the room.*

JANET. You'd think the council'd board them houses up by now...

CAROL. Kids only smash them in again. They don't give a toss, ought to ASBO the bleeding lot of them.

JANET. They have.

JANET *hands* SONIA *a cup of tea.* SONIA *tastes it and pulls a face.*

SONIA. Sugar on ration?

She wanders over to the counter and adds two more large sugars. On her way back, she picks up a packet of cigarettes from the table.

Few weeks ago, right... These yours, Jan?

JANET *nods and* SONIA *takes one.*

We knew them people living in 'em, neighbours and that, right?

She heads over to the kitchen door, breaks off the cigarette filter, chucks it out into the yard, and lights up. She always snaps off the filters.

Now, they're covered in shit.

JANET. You what?

SONIA. Someone's going round and shittin' in the rooms!

CAROL. That's disgusting...

JANET. What's the point in that?

SONIA. Toilets are still flushing in some of 'em. So there's no call for it. But no – covered in shit!

JANET. You haven't been in?

SONIA. Gotta have a fuckin' gander, haven't you? See if anyone left owt useful.

JANET. Sonia! I couldn't do that, me. Not in a neighbour's house. Even if they have moved.

SONIA. Don't bother me… Look what I found in Elsie Taylor's.

She pulls a couple of small ivory crosses from her purse and hands them to JANET. JANET takes one and passes the other to CAROL.

JANET. Oh, aren't they lovely. She left these? Fancy leaving these behind.

SONIA. You can have one if you like –

CAROL looks up. SONIA looks at her.

(*Pointedly.*) Jan.

JANET. Taa…

SONIA. Hold it up to the light and look through that hole in the middle.

JANET. Ohh, yeah. '1914–1918' – God, that's dead old that, isn't it. What's that say?…

CAROL. Thiepval.

JANET. Where's that?

CAROL. Belgium.

SONIA looks scathingly at CAROL.

SONIA. I forgot you go caravanning.

CAROL.…Salford Pals fought there. These are keepsakes for people who'd lost loved ones.

JANET puts the cross down quickly.

JANET. Good Jesus tonight, Sonia. What d'you bring them in here for? It's bad luck that. You'll bring it back on yourself doing things like that. Put 'em back!

SONIA. Fuck off – she left 'em.

CAROL pushes it back across the table.

CAROL. Maybe you should find out where Elsie moved to and take 'em back.

SONIA. Maybe you should mind your own friggin' business.

She sweeps up the crosses.

Sod youse then. I'm having one mounted on a ring. Might be worth something.

She holds a cross up to the light and looks through it.

Pause.

JANET. Precinct busy?

SONIA. Packed. Coppers still had it cordoned off with tape 'cause of that head.

CAROL. You went to school with him, didn't you?

SONIA ignores CAROL. She carries on looking through the cross.

JANET. What was he like?

SONIA. Pain in the arse then as well. Fancy gettin' your fuckin' head cut off. Twat!

JANET. Do they know who did it?

SONIA. Like I'm gonna tell you?

JANET. Orr, go on, Sonia.

SONIA. Forget it, motormouth… serious business this. Whole fuckin' estate's talkin' about it.

JANET. Bet it were drugs.

SONIA. Hardly a fuckin' newsflash round here, Mrs Marple!

We hear a thump on the ceiling. All focus is suddenly on the monitor. CAROL turns the sound up. We hear a man coughing heavily and moving about in bed.

JANET. I'll just go up....

CAROL. He'll be alright...

JANET. Better had, eh? Just to be on the safe side.

SONIA. Go on, Jan...

> JANET *exits. We hear her run up the stairs.*

> SONIA *and* CAROL *avoid eye contact. They sip their tea and ignore each other. The wait should feel long and awkward. We hear* JANET *come back down the stairs. She comes back into the kitchen.*

JANET. He's awake... I gave him some Lucozade.

SONIA. How were he this morning?

> JANET *looks to* CAROL.

JANET. Quiet.

CAROL. Yeah, quiet.

SONIA. Doctor been round?

JANET. Yeah... gave us the number to call for the Macmillan nurse... you know the erm...

SONIA. Yeah.

CAROL. They do a great job them nurses. Hard job and all.

SONIA. Yeah, alright, I know what a nurse does. We've got 'em in Salford as well you know.

JANET. They're different to normal nurses these, Sonia.

> *Pause.*

> SONIA *sees the tablet bottles.*

SONIA. What are they?

JANET. For the pain... different types...

SONIA. Don't tell him you've got 'em 'cause I'm telling you now, he'll go fuckin' spare.

CAROL. He'll need something sooner or later...

JANET. It's bad enough now. He can't just pretend it's not there.

SONIA. I'm not saying owt… Not up to me. I just know what he'll do.

JANET. The hospital said – and the doctor –

CAROL. He'll have to take something –

SONIA. Don't tell me… I don't want to know. I've said all I'm going to say. You know what he thinks about 'em.

JANET. There's no point having a go at us, Sonia…

SONIA. Did I say owt? Did I?

JANET. No.

SONIA. Then I'm not having a go at you, am I? He's my brother as well you know, not just yours.

JANET. I know.

SONIA. Do you not think I don't care about what he needs? I can see he's in pain as well, I'm not bastard blind.

She lights another cigarette.

So I'm telling you now, don't you two think you can start making all the fuckin' decisions all of a sudden.

CAROL. No one's doing that.

SONIA. I didn't ask you!

JANET. We're all involved in this.

SONIA. Could've fooled me.

JANET. He'll need 'em eventually and when he does, I want us all to say so.

SONIA *doesn't say anything.*

I said…

SONIA. Yeah – alright, you made your point, don't label it!

Pause.

JANET. I'll get this lot put away.

JANET *picks up the shopping bags and starts to put the shopping away.*

SONIA. Amhurst's has closed down.

JANET. They'll be no shops left round here soon.

SONIA. Only the Paki's and he'll stay and squeeze the last fuckin' penny out of us.

JANET *gives* SONIA *a look.*

JANET. Riaz has had to put serving grills up.

CAROL. That's terrible…

SONIA *looks directly at* JANET.

SONIA. Bang out of fuckin' order, that!

The other two don't say anything.

It's not right though, is it? Fuckin' Paki putting grills up against us.

CAROL. Can you blame him with the amount of robbin' that goes on round here?

SONIA. What's that supposed to mean?

CAROL. Nowt… Just saying…

SONIA. Don't look at me, Carol…

CAROL. I wasn't.

SONIA. You fuckin' were and don't deny it.

CAROL. I didn't say a thing.

SONIA. You don't have to you, with your snotty-nosed fuckin' looks.

JANET. She didn't, Sonia.

SONIA. Taking her side, again?

CAROL. Sonia, I wasn't looking at anyone, alright. If you thought I was looking at you, I wasn't.

SONIA. That an apology then.

CAROL.…If you want.

SONIA. If I want?… Not for me to say though, is it, eh? It's you that's saying you're sorry, so you're the one to say if it's true whether you're actually sorry or not, aren't you… at the end of the day… Not me…

She looks triumphantly at CAROL.

CAROL. I'm sorry… okay?

SONIA. Yeah, right – whatever.

Pause.

CAROL does not want to get into this any further.

CAROL. I'll go up and see if Frankie wants anything.

CAROL gets up and heads out of the room. JANET *gives* SONIA *a censorious look.*

SONIA. She does me fuckin' head in every time I see her.

JANET. She's your sister.

SONIA. Fuck her.

JANET. That's not nice, Son.

SONIA. I don't fuckin' care! She's a snobby bitch, so don't expect me to change 'cause she decides to show her face round here again…

JANET. He's her brother as well… At least she's making the effort.

SONIA. Yeah, well, too fuckin' late in my book.

SONIA heads over to the fridge, opens it and pulls out a can of Tennent's lager.

JANET. Frankie's pleased she's here.

SONIA. He's ill.

JANET. He's happy and that's what's important. Family's family.

SONIA. You talk some bollocks sometimes, you. Where was the family when she pissed off and moved to Didsbury? How interested in Frankie was she then, eh? I didn't see many invites coming our way.

JANET. That's not the point any more. Things are different now.

SONIA. He's been ill for months… Where's she been?

JANET. For your information, it was Frankie who called her! He wanted to see her.

SONIA. Bang out of fuckin' order she is.

JANET. I don't care any more. She's made her peace with him and she's here, that's all that matters.

SONIA (*dismissively*). Oohh… fuck off!

> PHILLIP *comes in. Thirty-seven, he's wearing a tracksuit with a hoody. He stirs a stick in an old paint pot.*

PHILLIP. That my lager?

SONIA. You can fuck off an' all, Snoop Doggy Shit Breath!

PHILLIP. What d'you want written on the wall?

JANET. Have you not done it yet?

PHILLIP. Don't say it like that, I've been at it all morning!

SONIA. You weren't there when I come in.

PHILLIP. I went and had a look to see what other people had written.

JANET. And?

PHILLIP. What?

JANET. What had they written?

SONIA. How does he know, he can't fuckin' read.

PHILLIP. I can.

SONIA. You can't.

PHILLIP. I had special classes.

SONIA. Then just write 'Janet, John and Spot the fuckin' Dog still live here'.

JANET. What's Riaz got on't shop?

SONIA. 'Still here you Paki bastard?' (*Laughs*.)

JANET. We'll have enough of that now, thank you very much. He's been very good to our Frankie since he's been ill.

SONIA. 'Cause he wants to get into your knickers…

PHILLIP. Shut it, Sonia, he's alright Riaz.

JANET *ignores her. She turns back to* PHILLIP.

JANET. Just write 'This house is still occupied' across the front door.

SONIA. You're better off askin' that fuckin' head on't Precinct to do it.

JANET. Ignore her – Come here.

JANET *takes a notepad and pen from a shelf and starts to write the sign on the pad.* PHILLIP *lights a cigarette and watches.*

PHILLIP. Can you do bigger letters than that, Jan?

SONIA. It's not Sesame Street.

SONIA *takes another cigarette and sits at the table.*

PHILLIP. I heard they've found what's-his-name's head.

SONIA (*quickly and dismissively*). Yeah-on-the-Precinct-we-know. Not news!

JANET. Did you know him?

PHILLIP. Were in't Boys' Brigade with me. Played bugle.

SONIA. Cornet.

JANET. What happened?

PHILLIP. Mixed with the wrong people in't hood.

SONIA *laughs.*

SONIA. 'Hood'? Fuckin'ell… MC Thick Twat in the house! Yo, y'alright, our kid!

PHILLIP. Spanner did it.

JANET *and* SONIA *laugh.*

JANET. Neville Taylor?

SONIA. Did he fuckin' eckkers like.

PHILLIP. He did... He's been arrested. Five-O found blood all over his walls an' that. His mam went mad.

JANET. She only moved in there a fortnight ago.

PHILLIP. Fuckin' knob were going round an' tellin' everyone he done it.

JANET. Not very clever, is it?

PHILLIP. Crackhead... They both were. Had an argument over some rock and Neville wasted him. Said he put up a right struggle...

SONIA. Not much of one if he ended up without a fuckin' head.

JANET. Ah, it's terrible though, isn't it.

PHILLIP. He were gonna chop him all up but he could only manage the head.

JANET. Can't be easy, can it?

PHILLIP. Dead sorry about it now, they say. Gutted. He were crying and everything.

SONIA. Mard-arse!

We hear coughing coming over the monitor. They listen.

CAROL (*voice-over*). Are you alright, Frankie?...

More coughing.

Come on... Drink this...

We hear the man moan, his breathing laboured, he coughs some more. SONIA turns the sound down. PHILLIP looks worried, he sits down at the table.

PHILLIP. Is he alright, Jan?

JANET. Yeah... that's just 'cause he fell asleep on his back... Carol'll sort him out...

PHILLIP. He sleeps a lot now though, don't he?... When did our Carol come?

JANET. Couple of hours ago.

PHILLIP. Has our Brian phoned yet?

JANET. No… I can't get hold of him.

PHILLIP. He'll come though, won't he?

JANET. Course he will…

PHILLIP *looks at the medicine on the table. He touches the bottles.*

PHILLIP. These for Frankie?

JANET. Yeah. Doctor left 'em… He'll need 'em soon.

Pause.

PHILLIP *starts to cry.* JANET *looks away.* SONIA *goes and stands by the door. She lights a cigarette. Outside it starts to rain.*

Beat. Time passes. Clouds pass quickly across the sky.

We hear 'La Rapture' from the album Tout Est Calme, *by Yann Tiersen, during which these things should happen:*

PHILLIP *exits.*

JANET *walks over to the kitchen area. Picking up the kettle, she takes it over to the sink and holds it under the tap. It fills quickly and is soon overflowing. She does nothing. She stands and watches it.*

The tap should emit a powerful jet of water, so that it splashes back up.

The washing machine starts to spin, juddering loudly.

Outside it begins to rain heavily.

The lights slowly fade, leaving only the yard area lit, where we can see the heavy rain falling.

SONIA *steps into the yard. She looks up into it, letting it play on her face.*

Scene Two

Lights up, as JANET *turns and puts the kettle on the stove. She strikes a match and puts a light under it. She starts to fold up some sheets.*

AUNTIE SHEILA (*voice-over*). Only me!

The door opens and AUNTIE SHEILA *comes in. She's in her seventies but still quite spry. She's followed by* SAMANTHA, *thirty-nine.* SAMANTHA *carries a baby in a papoose-type baby carrier round her middle. She is definitely on the lower end of the spectrum, gullible, but not stupid. She's more than capable of looking after herself, although she has managed to end up with a baby. Both she and* AUNTIE SHEILA *are inseparable. Her mother still buys her clothes, which are plain and not terribly fashionable.*

JANET. Hiya, Auntie Sheila. Hiya, Samantha.

AUNTIE SHEILA. Alright, kidda…

AUNTIE SHEILA shakes her umbrella, SAMANTHA *tries to protect the baby.*

SAMANTHA. Mam, the baby!

AUNTIE SHEILA. Bit of water won't do her any harm.

JANET. Give us that, I'll put it in the sink.

JANET takes the umbrella from AUNTIE SHEILA. JANET *takes a look at the baby.*

Ahhh, bless…

AUNTIE SHEILA. Go and put her down in the front room.

SAMANTHA. That alright, Jan?

JANET. Course…

SAMANTHA exits. AUNTIE SHEILA *sees* SONIA *in the yard.*

AUNTIE SHEILA. What you doing out there, you barmy bleeder?

JANET turns to see SONIA *out in the rain.*

JANET. Sonia, get in out of the rain, will you.

AUNTIE SHEILA. She boozed up or drugged up?

JANET. Neither.

AUNTIE SHEILA. We don't want any of that round here now. Not with that lad up there the way he is.

JANET. She's fine.

AUNTIE SHEILA *takes another look at* SONIA. *She starts to take off her coat and rain hat, helped by* JANET.

AUNTIE SHEILA. Doo-bleeding-lally that girl. Kettle on?

SONIA (*shouts*). You talkin' about me, Sheila?

AUNTIE SHEILA. Auntie Sheila, to you!

JANET *gives the coat and hat a shake and hangs them up on the back of the door.*

Will you come in out of that rain. The floor's soaking in here!

SONIA *rushes back in. She shakes her wet hair, to the annoyance of* AUNTIE SHEILA *and* JANET.

Give over!

SONIA. Fuckin' needed that!

AUNTIE SHEILA *gives her a disapproving look.*

JANET. Here…

JANET *throws* SONIA *a towel and uses a mop by the door to soak up the water.* SONIA *starts to dry off her hair.*

AUNTIE SHEILA. Saw your Michaela on't croft… She's gotta a gob on her an' all…

JANET. Wonder where she gets that…

AUNTIE SHEILA. Shouldn't she be in school?

SONIA. She's got verrucas…

JANET. We've got ointment for them, upstairs.

JANET *takes a T-shirt from a pile of washing and throws it to* SONIA, *who proceeds to change.*

AUNTIE SHEILA. You used to have to have 'em burnt out.

SONIA. Kids today, eh?... They don't know they're born, do they?

AUNTIE SHEILA. No need for the lip... I was just saying.

SAMANTHA *comes back in.*

SAMANTHA. Hiya, Sonia...

SONIA. You here an' all...

SAMANTHA. Nice to see you as well.

AUNTIE SHEILA. Brought some fruit for Frankie.

She takes some oranges, grapes and bananas out of her bag, and a Tupperware bowl. She gives them to JANET.

JANET. Ta, Auntie Sheila.

AUNTIE SHEILA. I made him a rice pudding and all...

SONIA. He doesn't like rice pudding.

AUNTIE SHEILA. It's easy to digest.

SONIA. Doesn't mean he likes it though.

AUNTIE SHEILA. He's always liked my rice pudding. Ever since he were little. Did he eat my shepherd's pie, Janet?

JANET. Yeah...

AUNTIE SHEILA. There you go, know-it-all, he had that as well. I'll do him a steak and kidney for the weekend.

SONIA. He can't eat that either.

AUNTIE SHEILA. Since when did you become a food expert?

SONIA. Since I bothered to read the diet chart from the hospital.

JANET. He's not that fussed any more, Auntie Sheila... just plain and simple... nothing too rich.

SONIA. He can't keep anything down.

Pause.

AUNTIE SHEILA. How's he been doing?

JANET (*non-committal*). Alright…

   JANET *looks at* SONIA. SONIA *gives a shrug*.

   Yeah, fine…

SAMANTHA. 'Cause he looked awful when he came back from hospital, didn't he, Mam?

AUNTIE SHEILA. He didn't look right.

SAMANTHA. I weren't gonna say but –

SONIA. Then don't.

JANET. He slept a bit better last night.

   AUNTIE SHEILA *sits at the table and lights up*.

AUNTIE SHEILA. That's good.

JANET. That's what I thought.

AUNTIE SHEILA. Good night's rest and that…

   She nods to SAMANTHA *and they both head for the door*.

   Come on then, we'll go up and see him.

JANET. Best pop up later.

   AUNTIE SHEILA *is taken aback by this*.

AUNTIE SHEILA. Right… If you think it's too much, Janet, say now and we'll go if you want? We don't want to get in't way…

JANET. Don't be daft, he's always happy to see you.

   AUNTIE SHEILA *and* SAMANTHA *sit*. SAMANTHA *lights up a cigarette*.

   Pause.

SAMANTHA. I didn't think he'd see this place again, me. Not the way he looked. I said, didn't I, Mam? When we got in – I said, he's not looking good – death warmed up, I said…

AUNTIE SHEILA. She did.

   SAMANTHA *catches* SONIA *giving her a withering look*.

SAMANTHA. Well... he's home now and that's the main thing, in't it.

SONIA. It's what he wanted.

JANET *goes to the sink and empties the fruit into a colander. She runs water over them.*

AUNTIE SHEILA. Make sure you give 'em a good rinse, Janet. There's that many foreigners coughing and spluttering over 'em in that market... You can't move for 'em fingering everythin' in sight.

JANET. Our Carol's here.

AUNTIE SHEILA. I'd heard she were back in't picture.

SMANATHA Is she upstairs with him?

JANET. She were just... checking on him.

JANET *pours tea into a cup and takes it over to* AUNTIE SHEILA. SAMANTHA *takes out a yogurt drink from her bag and opens it.*

AUNTIE SHEILA. What she after?

JANET. Nothing.

SONIA. Stickin' her oar in as per.

AUNTIE SHEILA. Figures.

JANET. They've made up and that's the main thing, in't it... our Frankie's happy.

SONIA. Is he?

JANET. He needs all his brothers and sisters around him now.

AUNTIE SHEILA. If that's what he wants, that's what he wants, innit... Very forgiving that... Very wise.

SAMANTHA. They make you wise though, these situations, don't they, Mam?... When you're... you know... Thingamabob.

SONIA. 'Have you done this?' – 'Did you ask the doctor that?' –

JANET. She's just making sure we've got all the information.

SONIA. Thinks we're too fuckin' stupid to ask!

AUNTIE SHEILA. What else is there to know?

JANET. That we're doing everything we're supposed to do...
Whatever's necessary for now...

SONIA. They're trained, aren't they?

JANET. I know, but Carol says...

AUNTIE SHEILA. What the heck does our Carol know about it?

SONIA. She's a fuckin' expert 'cause she's got Bupa.

SAMANTHA. They don't do death though, do they?

JANET. Samantha!

SONIA. Shits on her own doorstep. Always has and always
will.

SAMANTHA. Me mam said that, didn't you, Mam?

JANET. Will you give her a break! She's trying to help. She
doesn't need you lot on her case all the time!

AUNTIE SHEILA. Has he had his blanket bath today?

JANET. Carol's... doing it.

AUNTIE SHEILA. Says who? I give him his blanket bath. It's
me that does that. He expects it.

JANET. Well, you weren't here and... she just thought...

AUNTIE SHEILA. Aye, I know what our Carol thinks.

SAMANTHA. That's not right that. Not right. Me mam does
his blanket bath. She looks forward to that, don't you, Mam?

AUNTIE SHEILA (*magnanimously*). I'll let it slide this time.
But you'd better put her in the know regarding what's what
in these matters. She'll need time to readjust to us round here
I expect.

Pause.

Stick a bit more water in this, Jan...

JANET *takes the cup, adds a little water to it, and hands it back to* AUNTIE SHEILA. AUNTIE SHEILA *looks about the kitchen.*

You've done a great job on the house, Janet. Looks spotless, doesn't it, Samantha?

SAMANTHA. Yeah... you could eat your food off the floor... Could eat it off the table and all, now! (*Laughs.*)

SONIA. Frankie had a bit more on his mind than housework.

SAMANTHA. Just a joke, Sonia. Tut! God, Frankie'd get it...

AUNTIE SHEILA. Course he would.

SAMANTHA. 'Kin'ell! Keep me gob in future.

AUNTIE SHEILA. Still got his sense of humour, that lad.

SAMANTHA. Never lost it, has he, Mam.

JANET. Sonia and Carol helped too...

AUNTIE SHEILA. If you need owt picking up from your flat, Janet, just let us know.

JANET. I'm alright... I've got what I need.

SAMANTHA. Must be funny being back in your old room?

JANET. Least I'm not sharing a bed with Sonia and Carol this time.

AUNTIE SHEILA. And your dad's not bouncing your mam off the walls...

Pause.

I think Frankie's pleased... You being back here an' all. It's a comfort for him and God knows that lad needs that now.

SAMANTHA. Yeah.

JANET (*pointedly*). We're all here for him, Auntie Sheila...

AUNTIE SHEILA *glances at* SONIA.

AUNTIE SHEILA. Oh, I know you are but... you know what I mean.

SONIA *gives* AUNTIE SHEILA *a dirty look. She knows exactly what she means.*

SONIA. Yeah.

JANET *sees the tension and tries to defuse it.*

JANET. And our Phillip's moved back in for... for a while at least.

AUNTIE SHEILA. Yeah, but he's as thick as a piss-stone him, in't he? Not good in an emergency situation...

Pause.

SONIA *gets a can of lager from the fridge.*

Our Brian coming up today?

JANET. He left a message... Said he's gonna try... you know what he's like...

AUNTIE SHEILA. Should be here now. This is his place.

SONIA. He'll be here...

AUNTIE SHEILA. I wouldn't be so sure. Very busy these days, isn't he.

JANET. He's got a showing on or something... I think.

AUNTIE SHEILA. Yeah – last weekend it was... Important one as well by all accounts...

JANET. How do you know?

AUNTIE SHEILA. It was on the computer, weren't it, Samantha?

SAMANTHA. I internetted it – he's had a big exhibition and everyone's been dead impressed apparently. They had a big party afterwards. Elton John were there.

JANET. He didn't say... Did he say anything to you, Sonia?

SONIA. No.

AUNTIE SHEILA. That's London for you.

JANET. Don't mention Elton John to our Frankie, 'cause he'll go bang on't turn.

AUNTIE SHEILA. Hailed him as one of 'Salford's Famous Sons' it did.

SONIA. One that in't in prison.

AUNTIE SHEILA. Don't scoff, it isn't clever. Were a right big list an' all, weren't it, Samatha?

SAMANTHA. Massive.

AUNTIE SHEILA *lights a cigarette.*

AUNTIE SHEILA. There was erm... what's-his-face... Jasper Carrott's friend – oh, what's his name – Jesus of Nazareth.

SAMANTHA. Robert Powell.

AUNTIE SHEILA. Him. Erm, that little Pakistani bloke who won an Oscar, played Gandhi. Who else was there? Oh, yes, Freddie 'Parrot-face' Davis!

JANET. Good that, in't it?

AUNTIE SHEILA. Your mam'd be dead proud you know...

JANET. Yeah... Yeah, she would, wouldn't she...

Pause.

AUNTIE SHEILA *takes a long drag on her cigarette.*

AUNTIE SHEILA. I've felt her presence a lot lately...

JANET. Have you?

SONIA *rolls her eyes.*

SONIA. Here we go.

JANET. Shut up, Son.

SAMANTHA. Had full communication in church on Sunday, didn't you, Mam.

SONIA. D'you have to?

JANET. I knew I should have gone with you.

AUNTIE SHEILA. We had Mr Brewer in, from Cheadle Hulme.

SAMANTHA. They say he's the new Doris Stokes.

AUNTIE SHEILA. I knew straight off it were me he were after. He kept glancing over in my direction… he said 'I'm being drawn over here'.

She makes a reaching gesture.

JANET. He got you straight away, didn't he?

AUNTIE SHEILA. Hold your horses…

She takes another long drag on her cigarette.

He said 'I've a lady in spirit. She's got on an emerald-green cardi with brass buttons.' Well, about five on my pew shot their hands up, but he weren't having any of it. And I didn't say owt.

SAMANTHA. It were hardly evidence, were it, Mam?

AUNTIE SHEILA. But then he said 'I'd like to come to you, madame, if I may,' and he looked me straight in the eyes and said 'The buttons have got reef knots on, can I give you that, dear.' I said 'Yes.' You see, I'd bought your mam the very same cardigan from Debenhams the year before she passed over. Remember?

JANET*'s hand goes up to her mouth, she looks pensive.*

JANET. Yeah…

SONIA. So had the rest of your pew by the sound of it.

AUNTIE SHEILA *ignores her.*

AUNTIE SHEILA. He said 'She's telling me to tell you, that…'

She takes a moment to compose herself. SAMANTHA *gives her mother a rub on the back.*

'She's with you all constantly and she'll be there to take him over.'

JANET *starts to cry.* AUNTIE SHEILA *gets up, goes over to* JANET *and awkwardly tries to comfort her.*

SONIA. Now look what you've done! Are you happy now?

SAMANTHA. She's only bearing witness!

SONIA. You're sick, the pair of you!

JANET (*sobbing*). Did he say owt else?

SONIA. Haven't you heard enough of this bollocks?

AUNTIE SHEILA (*knowingly*). He asked if anyone were moving house.

SONIA. Do us a fuckin' favour! Anyone who reads the *Manchester Evening News* can tell you half of Salford's being pulled down.

AUNTIE SHEILA. No one's talking to you.

SONIA. Not dead'uns anyway.

AUNTIE SHEILA. Some people find it a comfort to know the people we loved are still about.

SAMANTHA. Giving us proof of life after...

SONIA. No one's dead yet, bog-eyes!

Beat.

AUNTIE SHEILA. There's no talking to her sometimes.

We hear the baby start to cry.

SONIA. Good. 'Cause you're about that fuckin' interestin'.

She holds out her index finger and thumb, indicating an inch. She gets up and heads to the fridge and takes a can of lager.

You spend more time talking to me mam dead, than you did when she was alive!

SAMANTHA. Ignore her, Mam.

AUNTIE SHEILA. Come on, let's go see to Whitney.

SONIA. Don't mention any of that shite to Frankie, either, when you see him!

AUNTIE SHEILA leaves the room with SAMANTHA. JANET looks at SONIA and returns to folding up the washing.

SONIA. Don't look at me like that... I'm not having her up there rattling on about the fuckin' afterlife... He's got enough on his plate.

JANET. Give her a bit of credit, Son.

SONIA. D'you think he wants to hear any of that, do you? It's bad enough you're at it. God you're fuckin' gullible you.

JANET. It's what you believe innit. It's what I believe in.

SONIA. Ghosts?

JANET. Can we just forget it.

SONIA (*mimicking*). 'You're going to meet a tall dark stranger.' Hardly fuckin' surprising with the amount of Pakis that live round here, is it? She loves all this, you know – death. She were like this when me mam were ill.

JANET. Now you're just being stupid.

SONIA. Hovering round the house like a fuckin' vulture... Me mam didn't want her here...

JANET *just looks at* SONIA.

What?

JANET. Me mam couldn't care less... She didn't want anyone around.

SONIA. Meaning?

Beat.

JANET. Nothing.

SONIA. If you've got something to say, Janet, just fuckin' say it!... Don't hide it behind Auntie Sheila...

JANET. I haven't.

SONIA. You saying she didn't want me about, is that it?

JANET. All I'm saying is me mam had her fair share of arguments with everyone, me included. I just don't think it fair to single out Auntie Sheila, alright? They were sisters. Sisters fall out. I think even you can appreciate that.

SAMANTHA *comes in.*

SAMANTHA. Sorry… Just getting me baby bag…

She picks up the bag and leaves.

SONIA. I don't expect that kind of shit off you, Janet… I thought you understood.

JANET. I never said anything.

SONIA. I was fucked up! You know I was… So why d'you always have to throw it back in me face all the time!

JANET. I'm not…

SONIA. You lot won't ever let me fuckin' forget it, will you!

JANET. I'm not getting into all this now. Not now… It's in the past.

SONIA. It obviously fuckin' in't if I have to go through this all the time.

JANET. Oh stop it, Sonia. None of this is about you, alright.

SONIA. It is about me though, in't it, eh?

Pause.

I wanted to be there!

JANET. Sonia… How could you in the state you were in? It was bad enough as it was…

SONIA starts to get upset but forces herself to hold it right back. We should see clearly how painful this is for her to do. There is a real wound here.

Oh… Sonia…

SONIA. Don't… I don't want your fuckin' pity now! I know what you lot were saying behind me back! Fucking Carol and that old cow out there!

JANET. I never…

SONIA. Liar!

JANET. I never said anything I haven't said to your face and you know that!

SONIA. I know I always give me mam fuckin' grief and that... made her cry an' everythin'. It weren't my fault... she knew that, Janet, she knew it... She knew I was out of it – that I didn't mean anythin' I said... I know she did... I didn't know half the things I were doing at the time... She didn't care though. She didn't... 'cause she loved me – she still fuckin' loved me – and she wanted me there... I know she did... She loved me, me mam... She'd never give up on me – never...

JANET doesn't know what to do. She just stares at her.

JANET. Son...

SONIA. Why didn't you let me be there?

JANET. We just thought –

SONIA. It was me mam, Janet – me mam!

JANET. Things were –

SONIA. That's all I wanted... for a few... fuckin' minutes... a bit of fuckin' time... I was worth that much at least... I never saw her again... I never fuckin' saw her...

Pause.

She wanted me there, didn't she?

JANET. Yeah... yeah she did – course she did.

SONIA takes a cigarette, breaking off the filter. She lights it and stands in the open doorway to the yard.

We hear the letter box being knocked. The front door open. We hear the voices of AUNTIE SHEILA, PHILLIP *and* BRIAN. *The baby starts to cry loudly.*

PHILLIP (*voice-over*). Look what I found wandering the streets.

AUNTIE SHEILA (*voice-over*). Hiya cock, are you alright? Give us a kiss.

BRIAN (*voice-over*). Alright, Auntie Sheila?

SONIA flicks the rest of her cigarette off into the yard.

JANET. He came then... I'd better put the kettle on.

> SONIA *goes over to the fridge and pulls out a can of lager.*
> *She lights another cigarette and stands by the door. Outside*
> *the rain gets heavier, the sound louder. The lights slowly*
> *fade.*

Scene Three

JANET *peels potatoes at the sink.* PHILLIP *leans against one*
of the kitchen cupboards drinking lager and fiddling with an
expensive-looking camera. CAROL, BRIAN *and* AUNTIE
SHEILA *are sat round the table.* SONIA *stands in the doorway*
leading to the yard drinking lager.

JANET. What time did your train get in?

BRIAN. Couple of hours ago.

JANET. You should have called... I'd have cooked something
proper. I'm only doing tater hash.

BRIAN. Weren't sure I was coming up myself till this
afternoon.

CAROL. Your exhibition.

JANET. We heard. Thanks for the invite.

BRIAN. It wasn't that kind of...

SONIA. Yeah it was. Samantha got it off the internet. You're
bum-chums with Elton John.

AUNTIE SHEILA. Ignore her, Brian. It's dead good that, cock.

> SONIA *scrunches up a can and tosses it into the night.*

JANET. Do you have to do that?

SONIA. There's no one living there...

> SONIA *heads over to the fridge and takes out another lager.*

BRIAN. I noticed most of the streets are boarded up.

AUNTIE SHEILA. They'll all be coming down soon.

PHILLIP. They're doing an urban regeneration. Not that anyone round here's gonna be able to afford to buy back.

SONIA. Sell enough drugs they can.

AUNTIE SHEILA. End of an era. Still, we'll get a bit of garden in the new place, eh.

CAROL. It's terrible, here now, Brian. Soon as people move out, kids set the houses on fire.

SONIA. Lucky you don't live round here then.

CAROL. It is, isn't it. 'Cause I'd brain the useless little bastards if I got hold of 'em!

AUNTIE SHEILA. Braining's too good for 'em! They want their skennin' fingers chopping off! Nowt but the bleedin' scruffs left round here, now, Brian…

Pause.

BRIAN. How's Frankie doing?

CAROL. No change…

JANET. Haven't seen him for a while, have you?

AUNTIE SHEILA. You'll be shocked when you do.

JANET. He has a nurse sits through the night with him now.

BRIAN. Yeah?

JANET. We were expecting you down last week, when he got back from the hospital.

BRIAN. I couldn't… I had a word with him on the phone…

JANET. He said… Weren't on long though, were you?

BRIAN. Wasn't I?

AUNTIE SHEILA. I'd come in to check on him. He said you'd just rung off. Hadn't said much.

BRIAN. Well he… He sounded a bit drowsy…

CAROL. He were very tired.

JANET. Loads of people here to see him home, weren't there, Carol. Rammed it were, here.

AUNTIE SHEILA. Couldn't move for well-wishers.

CAROL. Yeah. Took it out of him a bit.

AUNTIE SHEILA. And he weren't looking good any which way.

JANET. Everyone were asking where you were.

BRIAN. Yeah?

JANET. I told 'em you were busy.

Pause.

BRIAN. Is he… comfortable?

JANET. As much as he can be for now.

BRIAN.…In any pain or anything?

JANET. He weren't letting on for ages, were he, Carol?

CAROL. Didn't say owt…

JANET. Not to us anyway.

SONIA. Why should he.

CAROL. Was a nurse on the ward he were on…

JANET. She said, 'On a scale of one to ten, how bad's the pain?' He said eight. Eight and not a bleeding dicky bird to us.

CAROL. You know our Frankie.

SONIA. You don't.

CAROL *ignores* SONIA.

Pause.

JANET. Since then they've just been watching…

CAROL. Monitoring, you know… They're going to fit a pump…

JANET. Everything'll be automatic then. The drugs and that.

BRIAN. Can he talk?

JANET. Oh yeah, he's all there... he's not gone gaga... He's still got plenty to say...

BRIAN. Still chucking his weight about, is he?

JANET. Not quite, but you know Frankie.

BRIAN. That's good then, isn't it?

SONIA. He hasn't been down from his room since he got back from the hospital.

Pause.

JANET. Go on up and see him.

AUNTIE SHEILA. Come up with me in a bit.

BRIAN. Yeah... I will.

JANET. He wants a word with you. Talk to you and that.

Everyone looks at BRIAN.

Pause.

PHILLIP *sets the camera, the flash goes off.*

PHILLIP. Sorry, our kid.

AUNTIE SHEILA. Are you stoppin' here, Brian?

JANET. I've made your room up for you...

BRIAN (*embarrassed*). Well, I hadn't... I... I booked into The Midland Hotel...

JANET. Oh... I thought you might stop here...

BRIAN. I've brought some work and that...

JANET. You could have done that here...

BRIAN. You know what I'm like...

PHILLIP. I'll kip on't couch, if you want more space, our kid?

AUNTIE SHEILA. Times like this you need to be with your family.

BRIAN. I know but...

AUNTIE SHEILA. You can have too much privacy sometimes. There's so much nonsense talked about it these days. Privacy... There'd be five of us queuing up for the piss-bucket when I was a kid. Never bothered us none. Sends your lot round the bend, don't it?

BRIAN. Does it?

AUNTIE SHEILA. Look at Lowry...

CAROL. He was a painter, not a photographer.

AUNTIE SHEILA. Same difference. All that squiggling.

CAROL. You could stay with us in Didsbury... We've a self-contained unit at the end of the garden.

BRIAN. Thanks but... I'm all settled in now...

JANET. Suit yourself... bed's there. But I thought you might have...

The camera flash goes off again.

SONIA. Put it down, you mong, before you break it, 'kin'ell. Take it off him, Brian.

PHILLIP *pushes it away.*

PHILLIP. Sorry!

Pause.

AUNTIE SHEILA. Can't swing a cat in our house since our Samantha had the baby.

BRIAN. I didn't know she was pregnant?

JANET. Ought to try ringing us back sometimes. Amazing what you find out.

AUNTIE SHEILA. Phillip, did you tell Samantha, our Brian's here?

PHILLIP. She's still conked out with the kid.

AUNTIE SHEILA. Got post-natal depression and everything.

BRIAN. Right... What did she have?

PHILLIP. Still trying to figure it out, aren't they, Auntie Sheila?

AUNTIE SHEILA. Belt up, you. Little girl. Whitney Louise, ten pounds. Humungous, she was. Bonny now though. Hey, you could do some proper photos for us.

BRIAN. I will. I'll come round.

Beat.

AUNTIE SHEILA. The father's a coloured. Nice lad. Baby doesn't look coloured though. Does she, Janet?

JANET *doesn't know what to say.*

JANET. More like Pervaiz, in't shop, I'd say.

PHILLIP *and* SONIA *start to laugh.*

AUNTIE SHEILA. She looks nothing like him. I said her father's a coloured, not a Pakistani.

JANET. I didn't say she looked like him.

AUNTIE SHEILA. Her lips are thicker for starters.

CAROL. Does it matter? She's lovely.

BRIAN. I'll look forward to it, Auntie Sheila. Does she need any baby stuff?

AUNTIE SHEILA. Anything for a one-year-old with a bit of give. Hang on, I'll go and shift that big daft lump.

AUNTIE SHEILA *heads off out to the parlour.*

BRIAN. Fancy little Samantha with a baby, eh?

SONIA. Dead ugly it is.

JANET. Sonia!

SONIA. It is.

PHILLIP. I can't look at it, me.

SONIA. It looks like Sheila with a fake tan.

JANET. She just needs to grow into her skin a bit more. Lots of babies do.

Pause.

CAROL. Didn't walk from town, did you?

BRIAN. Erm... no... Cab dropped us off... I was having a look around.

CAROL. At what?

PHILLIP. Stood in't street taking pictures he was. Didn't half shit you up, didn't I?

JANET. It's that bleeding hood.

BRIAN. I thought he was going to mug me.

SONIA. He probably was.

CAROL. Don't carry that camera about round here... They'll slit your throat for less.

SONIA. Your Reece would for starters.

CAROL. Leave him out of it, alright?

SONIA. Touchy subject, is it, Carol?

CAROL. Don't push it, Sonia, alright?

SONIA. Why, what you gonna do?

BRIAN. Auntie Shei looks well.

SONIA *goes and gets another lager from the fridge. Followed by* PHILLIP.

CAROL. Looks beltin', don't she.

BRIAN. Spit of me mam.

JANET. She's a lot steadier on her feet since she had her eyes done.

CAROL. All this with our Frankie has knocked her back a bit though, hasn't it, Janet?

JANET. Yeah. He was always her favourite.

CAROL. First nephew, wasn't he.

JANET. 'I was next!' She keeps saying. 'It should be me' –

SONIA *snaps off the ring on the can.*

SONIA. I'll fuckin' drink to that!

SONIA clinks cans with PHILLIP.

PHILLIP. Nice one.

The door opens and AUNTIE SHEILA and SAMANTHA come in. SAMANTHA has the baby in her arms.

SAMANTHA. Hiya, Brian.

BRIAN stands and gives her a hug and a kiss.

God!... Two kisses as well! What you after!

She laughs nervously. So does BRIAN.

BRIAN. I hear congratulations are in order... This her then?

SAMANTHA. Yeah... Whitney Louise...

She passes the baby straight over to BRIAN, who has no choice but to take it. SAMANTHA lights up a cigarette.

Saw you on the internet.

AUNTIE SHEILA. He knows.

SAMANTHA. What was Elton John like?

AUNTIE SHEILA. Ignore her, Brian, she's celebrity-obsessed. Them and puzzle mazes. I don't know what's worse.

BRIAN looks down at the baby. JANET goes over to the baby.

BRIAN. Hello there...

JANET. Hello, Whitney.

SAMANTHA. Say hello, Whitney... Say hello to Brian.

AUNTIE SHEILA. Ahhh...

BRIAN. Hello, there...

AUNTIE SHEILA. Been here before she has, I'm telling you... Old eyes she's got!

SONIA. Not the kid as well!

SONIA scrunches up her can and tosses it into the night. She heads over to the fridge and gets another.

SAMANTHA. Ahhh... She's looking at the clown. Yeeees. Like your, isn't it, babe?

SAMANTHA *indicates the clown monitor.*

JANET. I got her a laughing policeman one as well.

SAMANTHA. Tickles her it does. Press the laughing button, Mam.

AUNTIE SHEILA *kisses the baby.*

AUNTIE SHEILA. Hang on, sweetheart, Nana put it on.

AUNTIE SHEILA *picks up the monitor. She looks at the lights as they move across and starts to fiddle with it.*

BRIAN. I don't think babies like me...

AUNTIE SHEILA *accidently turns up the sound on the monitor. The room is suddenly filled with* FRANKIE's *terrible death-rattling breath.*

Panicked and embarrassed, she tries to turn it off. Instead she turns it even louder. CAROL *tries to help, so does* PHILLIP. *Eventually they manage it.*

Silence.

AUNTIE SHEILA *gets up and walks over to the door. She is upset and tries to hide it. She looks out into the rain. Takes a handkerchief from her sleeve and blows her nose. She lights a cigarette.*

Pause.

AUNTIE SHEILA. Always seems to piss it down come Bonfire Night these days...

BRIAN. How long's he sounded like that?

JANET. Last couple of days...

BRIAN. What the doctor say?

AUNTIE SHEILA. Don't need a doctor to tell you what that is.

JANET. Said... everything was going... alright.

AUNTIE SHEILA. Alright? What's that supposed to mean?

JANET. I don't know, Auntie Sheila... He only checks him over and goes...

CAROL. It's how it's going to be now, Auntie Shei.

AUNTIE SHEILA. Should be in hospital, he should... Not in this place. They can't do anything for him here.

SONIA. What're they gonna do for him there?

AUNTIE SHEILA. I'll have a word with him.

SONIA. He wants to stay at home.

AUNTIE SHEILA. Council's regenerating us all soon. Might as well pack it up now.

SONIA. He doesn't want to be re-fuckin'-generated! Alright?

AUNTIE SHEILA. They'll be pulling the bleeding lot down round his ears.

SONIA. He wants to stay I said, are you fuckin' deaf or what!

AUNTIE SHEILA. Don't you swear at me like that, you rude little mare. I'm not your mother.

SONIA. Thank fuck for that.

CAROL. Ignore her, Auntie Sheila.

AUNTIE SHEILA. He'll be a lot more comfortable in hospital. They're prepared for things there... they've got everythin' to hand.

SONIA. Can you not get it into your thick head...

BRIAN. She's only thinking of Frankie, Sonia. Maybe it's for the best now.

SONIA *looks at* BRIAN.

SONIA. Brian... If he moves now he thinks – he's not fuckin' goin' alright? So why don't you all just piss off and mind your own business!

AUNTIE SHEILA. It is my business. He's my nephew.

SONIA. Just fuck off!

BRIAN. Sonia!

AUNTIE SHEILA. You wouldn't talk to me like that if your mother was alive.

SONIA. She'd be saying the same thing!

AUNTIE SHEILA. What would you know? When did you ever listen to her? Nothing but bleeding trouble you were to that woman!

SONIA. What?

AUNTIE SHEILA. Old before her time she was, with you.

SONIA. Shut it now!

AUNTIE SHEILA. Don't like the truth, do you!

SONIA *heads for* AUNTIE SHEILA. *She is cut off by* JANET.

JANET. Not now, Auntie Sheila...

SONIA. You fuckin'old witch!

AUNTIE SHEILA. Put her in an early grave, you did. With all your carryings-on.

SONIA. What did you say?

JANET. Auntie Sheila!

SONIA *is very upset and begins to pace about.*

SONIA. Don't you say that about my mam, you, you fuckin' old cunt!

AUNTIE SHEILA. There she is!... The old Sonia. You see that, Brian...

SONIA. You don't fuckin know owt, you! You fuckin'...

BRIAN. Sonia!

AUNTIE SHEILA. Never far from the surface, is she.

SONIA. She fuckin' hated you... She hated you!

AUNTIE SHEILA. She was never out of my house crying. One problem after another it was with you. Ask our Samantha.

SONIA. She hated that gormnless twat an' all.

SAMANTHA. Least I weren't a fuckin' crackhead!

PHILLIP. Oi, no need for that!

BRIAN. Will you all just pack it in!

AUNTIE SHEILA. Evil you are, Sonia, evil. Your mam knew it and rued the day she never had you aborted...

SONIA *angrily takes a step towards* AUNTIE SHEILA. BRIAN *stands in her way.*

BRIAN. Now that's enough, the pair of you!

SONIA. And what about your fuckin' husband! Did you know he shoved his cock in anything that moved 'cause he couldn't get owt off you, you frigid dried-up old bitch!

SAMANTHA. Liar!

AUNTIE SHEILA. He was a better person than you'll ever be!

SONIA. Yeah? Then how come he never stopped trying to shove his finger up me mam all his life, the fuckin' old pervert!

SONIA *runs out of the back door.*

JANET. Sonia!

JANET *runs out after her.*

(*Voice-over.*) Sonia!

Long pause.

AUNTIE SHEILA. I did nothing to deserve that... No respect for anyone, that girl...

SAMANTHA. Twisted, she is.

AUNTIE SHEILA. To say that about the two people I loved most in this world... And that poor lad lay upstairs...

BRIAN. I don't think she meant anything by it, Auntie Shei. She's upset. It's natural.

CAROL. Got a short fuse, always has. Take no notice.

AUNTIE SHEILA. The language she came out with... Bet you a pound to a penny, she's back on that crack again.

PHILLIP. She's not.

BRIAN *brings over a tray of tea. He gives a cup to* AUNTIE SHEILA.

BRIAN. Here you go.

AUNTIE SHEILA. Ta.

JANET *comes to the kitchen door. She hops in on one leg.*

CAROL. She gone home?

AUNTIE SHEILA. Back to the scruff house she comes from.

BRIAN. Come on now, Auntie Sheila…

JANET. She's in that house opposite. Pass us that brush from under the sink, Brian. My shoe's covered in shit.

BRIAN *fetches the brush and gives it to* SONIA.

BRIAN. Give's it here.

JANET. Oh, ta…

She leans against him and takes off the shoe and hands it to him.

BRIAN. She alright?

JANET. She'll be fine…

AUNTIE SHEILA. Oh, don't you worry about that hard-faced little mare. Piss in the sea this, for her.

There's a knock at the front door.

CAROL. That'll be the nurse.

CAROL *goes out.*

AUNTIE SHEILA. If your father were alive to hear what she said to me… I tell you now, she'd know about it.

JANET. I'm not having a go, Auntie Sheila, but you pushed all the wrong buttons with her today…

AUNTIE SHEILA. Oh, I like that!

SAMANTHA. It's not me mam's fault your sister's a bleeding nutter!

AUNTIE SHEILA. Am I not allowed to show a little concern for me own nephew without being attacked for it?

JANET. No one said that.

AUNTIE SHEILA. Having my husband's name dragged through the mud by the likes of her! Now you stand there and accuse me.

JANET. I never...

AUNTIE SHEILA. I'm shocked to hear that from you, Janet.

SAMANTHA. She ought to be locked up.

JANET. All I'm asking is that you think about how she's feeling at the moment.

AUNTIE SHEILA. That's been the problem all her bloody life. She's had everyone walking round her on eggshells. I told your mum as much. She wouldn't have it. Let her get away with murder.

SAMANTHA. She wouldn't have dared say that if Frankie were up and about.

JANET. Well he isn't, is he?

Pause.

BRIAN. I'll go and see how she is.

AUNTIE SHEILA. You see? Sonia, Sonia, Sonia... You're wasting your time, Brian. She'll throw it back in your face. Took your mam a while to realise it, but realise it she did.

BRIAN *heads out of the back door.*

Scene Four

SONIA *stands in a room of a derelict house. She looks out of the window.*

BRIAN (*voice-over*). Sonia! Son! You in here?

SONIA. Up here – mind the shit...

BRIAN *appears at the bottom of the stairs and makes his way up.*

What d'you want?

BRIAN. Had to get out of that house.

SONIA. Is that old twat still there?

BRIAN. Yeah...

BRIAN *sits next to her.*

SONIA. You've dyed your hair.

BRIAN. I move in grey-free circles.

SONIA. Bumming circles more like.

BRIAN *smiles.*

Pause.

I didn't start any of that, you know?

BRIAN. Never said you did.

SONIA. Was her... She came in looking for a scrap.

BRIAN. She's concerned.

SONIA. I'm telling you now, she starts again. I don't care how old she is, I'm gonna fuckin' deck her.

BRIAN. I think she means well.

SONIA. I've had it up to here with everyone meaning well... Why don't they let him get on with it, the way he wants to...

BRIAN. They just want to make things... alright for him, you know?... Make him comfortable and that...

SONIA. He's happy the way he is. They keep pushin' and pushin' him with things...

BRIAN. Everyone wants what's best...

SONIA. Just come in and took over without asking... He's the one that's gonna fuckin'... go, in' he? All of a sudden they know what's best for everyone? Well not this time – I won't fuckin' let 'em.

Pause.

Saw you earlier today, taking your pictures, you lying bastard. 'Only been here a couple of hours, Jan' –

BRIAN *laughs at being found out.*

BRIAN. Where?

SONIA. Nansen Street... I was having a root round in one of the houses.

BRIAN. Why didn't you say owt?

SONIA. I was going to but... didn't want to disturb you...

BRIAN. You daft cow.

SONIA. Like takin' pictures, don't you?

BRIAN. It's alright...

SONIA. Don't fuckin' 'alright' me... you know what I mean... I was watching.

BRIAN *smiles.*

I used to think it was a load of bollocks... you and your pictures. You know that?

BRIAN. You told me often enough.

SONIA. Couldn't see what the fuckin' point was... Until today in that street...

BRIAN. And?

SONIA. I'd love that, me.

BRIAN. I'll buy you a camera...

SONIA. I don't mean it like that... I mean you've got something, haven't you?

BRIAN *looks at her, unsure.*

You know… something you do – Oh fuck off – I don't fuckin' know.

BRIAN. Go on I'm listening.

SONIA (*unsure*). Watchin' you, right… I've never seen you like that before.

Beat.

The way you were looking about at everything. Sometimes you just stood there and watched… Dead still. Took your time and that… just looked…

Beat.

I've never looked at owt that long in my life…

Pause.

She lights a cigarette.

I'd like to though, Bri. And I think I will. I definitely think I will.

BRIAN. Good.

He takes a couple of drags off her fag.

SONIA. I didn't tell anyone I'd seen you.

BRIAN. Ta… I'm in the doghouse as it is, for not staying at home.

SONIA. Jan were looking forward to that.

BRIAN. She knows I never stay at the house.

SONIA. She thought you might this time, what with our Frankie…

BRIAN. I suppose he had something to say about it?

SONIA. He thought, you know… what with everything going on and all…

BRIAN. I haven't stayed here since college.

SONIA. Not sayin' owt, me… I'm not saying you're as stuck-up as Carol, but it were noted you never stopped at home any more.

BRIAN. What d'you mean, 'noted'?

SONIA. Not for me to say…

BRIAN (*irritated*). You know… That's what I hate about
coming back here… your life isn't your own.

SONIA. It isn't.

BRIAN. 'It was noted' – Once, I came down for a day, and
didn't visit! Big fuckin' deal! Noted! I'm a grown man, I
don't have to answer to anyone!

SONIA. Yeah, alright, keep your hair on… You know he didn't
like it.

BRIAN. He should have said something.

SONIA. That's our Frankie all over though, in't it.

BRIAN. Is it?

SONIA. You think it's passed him by… but he don't miss a
fuckin' trick. He's always been quick like that.

BRIAN. I don't know to tell you the truth. Everyone keeps
saying he's this that and the other and… I don't know – is he?

SONIA *is unsure what he's talking about*.

SONIA. Orr, don't you start goin' all fuckin' heavy on me
now… not now, Bri, me head's fuckin' rockin' as it.

BRIAN. I'm not even sure I want to be here, Son. If Phillip
hadn't met me in the street, I'd have been off back to
London.

SONIA. Without seeing Frankie?…

BRIAN. Yeah.

Beat.

SONIA. I thought I were hard-faced but that takes the fuckin'
biscuit, that does. He's dying.

BRIAN. I know…

Pause. They look at each other.

SONIA. Don't start fuckin' crying.

BRIAN. I'm not. I don't do this stuff very well.

SONIA. Who does?

BRIAN. I was ready for me mam and dad… You expect it, don't you?

SONIA. Dad didn't, he were on a bus.

BRIAN. You know what I mean.

SONIA. Yeah… one of us in't it… It's like everything's fuckin' shifted… gone skewiff.

BRIAN. I don't know him… I haven't known him for years. It's like, he's a stranger to me. How am I supposed to feel? 'Cause at the moment… I don't feel anything.

Pause.

SONIA. I went up to see him the other week. He were just standing there, lookin' out the window, into the street. He must have just farted 'cause it smelt fuckin' rank in there… rank… I gagged… tried to hide it but… He looked round at me… and everything was different… I don't know how or why… it were just different. Not real, you know? He knew what I was thinking. Knew I'd smelt it… smelt him… I felt I'd betrayed him somehow. He didn't say owt just turned back to the window.

I just stood there… I thought, they're fuckin' manky, they are, no point getting 'em cleaned… they'll be pulling the place down soon enough – I'm trying not to think of the smell, what it is – why it smells the way it does – How he looked at me.

Then I see all his clothes in piles on the floor. Socks, jumpers, shirts, trousers. A couple of suits hanging up on the wardrobe… shoes. He'd been sorting 'em out. He's sat here and said, I don't need this lot. That's me done. I thought… Fuck me, Frankie, is this it? You bowin' out in a pair of fuckin' jim-jams from BHS… But it were his face, Bri… when he turned and looked at me… It was like seeing someone for't first time. It was dead weird.

He was my brother, Frankie… I'd known him all me life. All the months he'd been ill. Coming up the stairs to ask him what he wanted for his tea. But then, suddenly at that moment, in that room… I didn't know him.

Pause.

BRIAN. Are you alright?

SONIA. I've not even got a black fuckin' skirt for't funeral.

Blackout.

ACT TWO

Scene One

Lights up in the kitchen area. PHILLIP *is still messing about with the camera.* BRIAN *walks in from the yard.* PHILLIP *puts the camera down.*

PHILLIP. She still in there?

BRIAN. No, she got off home. Where is everyone?

PHILLIP. Janet's up with the nurse and Carol. The Addams Family are in the parlour watching telly...

BRIAN gets himself a glass of water.

Pause.

She's not on owt, you know... Been clean for ages.

BRIAN. I know.

PHILLIP. She wouldn't go back to all that. She promised our Frankie.

BRIAN. Yeah?

PHILLIP. Pulled her back from the brink he did.

BRIAN. Did he?...

PHILLIP. I mean, she's always been a fuckin' mental case, hasn't she? Even when we were little.

BRIAN. She'll be fine.

PHILLIP. Very highly strung, me mam used to say.

BRIAN stands uncomfortably.

BRIAN. I think... maybe I'll stay over tonight.

PHILLIP. Yeah?... Go and get your head down then... Be just like old times, us lot all being here.

BRIAN. Yeah.

Pause.

PHILLIP. Want a brew?

BRIAN. Erm… Alright, go on then. If you're making one.

PHILLIP *goes and fills the kettle.*

PHILLIP. Lager in't fridge if you want?

BRIAN. Tea's fine.

PHILLIP *potters about the kitchen getting the tea things together, watched by* BRIAN.

PHILLIP. Can't make me own mind up now… Tea or lager… D'you smoke weed?

BRIAN. No, thanks.

PHILLIP. I could have all three I suppose.

BRIAN *takes a seat at the table and starts to put the camera away in its case.*

BRIAN. Does Frankie let you smoke in the house?

PHILLIP. No. I'll have a cup of tea and a biscuit. Pissing down out there.

PHILLIP *opens a cupboard.*

Want a biscuit with your tea?

BRIAN. Yeah… alright.

PHILLIP. We've got… Bourbons, Rich Tea, Milk-Chocolate Digestive, Custard Creams, HobNobs, Penguins… There's a packet of Wagon Wheels but they're Jan's.

BRIAN. Big selection.

PHILLIP *gives* BRIAN *a nod and a wink.*

PHILLIP. I've gotta mate.

BRIAN. I'll leave it up to you.

PHILLIP. Milk-Chocolate Digestives it is then.

He pulls out the packet and takes them over to the table.

Man United of the biscuit world these are.

BRIAN *takes a biscuit. They both sit and munch.*

BRIAN. Get to Old Trafford much?

PHILLIP. Naa, can't be arsed.

BRIAN. You used to be United mad.

PHILLIP. Can't be arsed any more. Watch 'em on't box and that… Costs a fuckin' fortune now anyway. Got kiddies to support.

BRIAN. They alright, are they? Littluns?

PHILLIP. Yeah… sound.

BRIAN. Two weren't it?

PHILLIP. Three… Kyle, Connor and Barry. Kyle's not mine but he were a baby when I met Karen, so's good as.

BRIAN. Right.

PHILLIP. I know him better than I know Barry and Connor. Funny that, in't it?

The kettle whistles. PHILLIP *gets up and makes the tea.*

We split up couple of years ago. Kids live in Prestatyn with her.

BRIAN. I remember hearing something.

PHILLIP. She were a right toerag.

BRIAN. Did I meet her?

PHILLIP. Must have done. Tall, blonde… Welsh accent… Bit of a slapper.

Pause.

PHILLIP *brings the tea things over and they help themselves.*

I'd have thought you'd have gone for a Bourbon or a Custard Cream.

BRIAN. No.

PHILLIP. Our Carol does.

Pause.

BRIAN. You back here now then?

PHILLIP. All over't shop really, since me split... I've been back here since Frankie's been ill. Company for our Jan.

BRIAN. She here as well?

PHILLIP. Back and forwards between her flat and here. Depending on how our Frankie is.

Pause.

She's mainly here though, now...

Pause.

D'you still have any mates up here?

BRIAN. Naa... Lost touch when I went to college.

PHILLIP. Didn't have many before that though, did you? Not bezzies...

BRIAN. A couple.

PHILLIP. 'Cause me and Frankie was trying to think who was still round here, who'd remember you and we couldn't.

BRIAN. Long time ago.

PHILLIP. He said you didn't have any. Nobby No Mates, he called you.

BRIAN. Well, he doesn't know everything, does he.

Pause.

PHILLIP. That daft lad's still here.

BRIAN. Who?

PHILLIP *waves an imaginary scarf over his head.*

PHILLIP. 'United! United! United for the cup!' Bobble hat. Bit slow, wore a green gaberdine... Never went to a match in his life.

BRIAN *twigs.*

BRIAN. He wasn't me mate.

PHILLIP. Weren't he?

BRIAN. No.

PHILLIP. I thought he was.

BRIAN. He didn't have any mates.

PHILLIP. Frankie said he was your mate.

BRIAN. Did he?

PHILLIP. Kenneth! That's his name... He's the only one left in his street now. Says 'I'm still in it' on his front door... Writing's dead neat for a mong... better than mine.

BRIAN. He lived with his mam, didn't he?

PHILLIP. She's been dead for years now.

BRIAN. I never saw his dad.

PHILLIP. The dad never came out the house. Used to shout at us from an upstairs window. 'Leave him alone! Leave him alone!' Dead white he was.

BRIAN. Yeah?

PHILLIP. They're all dead round here now, who you'd remember...

PHILLIP *glances down at the monitor. He catches* BRIAN*'s eye.*

Pause.

Bad all this, innit? Can't believe it me.

BRIAN. Yeah.

PHILLIP. ...Dead fuckin' gaunt he is. It dropped off him.

BRIAN. Carol said...

PHILLIP. It's good having her about. Glad her and Frankie made up.

BRIAN. Yeah.

PHILLIP. She's sound our Carol. Have you been round her house? Dead smart it is. She's got an home-cinema centre, surround-sound and everything.

Long pause.

I don't think he ever liked me much...

BRIAN. Who?

PHILLIP *nods his head at the smiley clown.*

PHILLIP. We're brothers and that but... Doesn't mean you have to like someone, does it?

BRIAN. Give over. Course he likes you.

PHILLIP. Thinks I'm a loser.

BRIAN. He said that to you?

PHILLIP. And a lot more besides. He's had us all up there. One by one. Telling us things.

BRIAN. How d'you mean?

PHILLIP. What he thinks about us and that. He wants you up there and all.

BRIAN. You should have told him to sod off and mind his own bloody business.

PHILLIP. You can't say that. It's not as if it's some smeghead from roun't corner is it. It's our Frankie.

Beat.

BRIAN. I know what he thinks about me.

PHILLIP. No, he always liked you. Not sure what he thinks at the moment like. But he were always dead proud of what you did. Never stopped telling people about you.

Pause.

Have you been in't front room? Your photograph books are still on't coffee table. He always showed 'em off to people when they came round... He couldn't make head nor fuckin' tail of 'em mind... but, you know...

CAROL *comes into the room.*

I were just saying, Carol, our Frankie were dead proud of what Brian did.

CAROL. Course he is… Pass us me coat.

PHILLIP *retrieves* CAROL's *coat from the back of his chair.*

BRIAN. D'you want a cup of tea, Carol?

CAROL *starts to put on her coat.*

CAROL. No, you're alright, my cab'll be here in a minute.

BRIAN. Your Peter not picking you up?

CAROL. Him? Won't let me drive my own car round here, let alone his precious bleeding Jag.

PHILLIP. Shit scared of it round here, he is.

CAROL. We've an account with a car firm in Didsbury. Peter's got a stake in it.

PHILLIP. Branched out all over, hasn't he, Carol?

CAROL. Yeah… Car lots, cabs – even got an Indian restaurant…

BRIAN. I'm impressed.

CAROL. So's he. Full of himself he is.…

AUNTIE SHEILA *comes in with* SAMANTHA *and the baby.*

AUNTIE SHEILA. We'll get off then.

CAROL. Alright, Auntie Shei.

CAROL *starts to help* AUNTIE SHEILA *on with her coat.* SAMANTHA *shoves the baby at* PHILLIP *and puts her coat on.*

AUNTIE SHEILA. Your cab not here yet?

CAROL. On its way. Phillip'll walk you home.

AUNTIE SHEILA. That's one mugger I don't have to worry about then.

PHILLIP. Who's gonna walk me back?

AUNTIE SHEILA. Have you been up to see him yet, Brian?

BRIAN. Not yet…

AUNTIE SHEILA. 'Cause I know he wants a word.

PHILLIP. I told him.

BRIAN. It's a bit late, Auntie Sheila…

AUNTIE SHEILA. He wants a proper word, with you.

SAMANTHA. We've all had things to settle, haven't we, Mam?

PHILLIP. It's like I said… Clear the air and that.

BRIAN. There's nothing's to clear.

SAMANTHA. Well, you'll be best judge of that, won't you?

AUNTIE SHEILA. You need to get things off your chest at times like this, Brian. Make your peace. You want nothing to linger…

BRIAN. Right.

CAROL, AUNTIE SHEILA, PHILLIP *and* SAMANTHA *all look at each other.*

AUNTIE SHEILA. We've all been up. Not just family, friends an' all.

CAROL. He'll go and see him when he's ready, won't you, Brian?

BRIAN. Yeah.

SAMANTHA. You don't want to leave it too long, does he, Mam, or they'll be regrets. And you won't want to live with regrets. Not good for you or the departed eh, Mam?

She takes a drag off her cigarette.

Leaves 'em restless, doesn't it?

BRIAN. I'll pop up.

Pause.

AUNTIE SHEILA. Alright, cocker… it's lovely to see you, come round and have your tea. Pity about the circumstances but…

She shrugs her shoulders and gives him a hug and a kiss.

BRIAN. I'll see you later Auntie Shei. Taraa, Samantha.

SAMANTHA. See you, Bri.

AUNTIE SHEILA, SAMANTHA *and* PHILLIP *still holding the baby, leave.*

PHILLIP (*voice-over*). Get hold of this will you…

SAMANTHA (*voice-over*). I'll just smoke this first.

CAROL *takes some cups to the sink and starts to wash them up.*

BRIAN. Nothing changes, does it?

CAROL. No.

BRIAN. How you doing?

CAROL. Oh, you know… alright. Can't complain. Husband's a dickhead and me son's a delinquent. Got a nice house though. So it could be worst.

BRIAN *smiles.*

BRIAN. How was it with Frankie? Coming back here and everything?

CAROL. Relatively painless considering we haven't spoke for years.

BRIAN. Took up where you left off, did you?

CAROL. No… nothing like that. You can't can you? Someone hurts you like that… Best just to forget it and move on. No point trying to explain things.

BRIAN. They don't like change.

CAROL. Not with me they didn't. Different for you. You were the clever one, left here to go to college you. Me? I left for a mid-Victorian detached in Didsbury Village.

They both smile.

BRIAN. Fifteen years is a long time to hold that against you.

CAROL. He never liked Peter much, Frankie. Could barely bring himself to look at him, let alone speak. Tell a lie, we come round once to see me mam and our Frankie were sat over there in his chair. He looked up and said 'Diana and Dodo are dead'… No, it were Peter more that anything else. I couldn't see it at the time. (*Smiles.*) Blinded by love I suppose. See it now though. Especially in the mornings when I wake up. I look over at him and I think… still bastard breathing then…

She laughs and BRIAN *smiles.*

Pause.

BRIAN. Do you know what he wants to say to me?

CAROL. Doesn't matter, Brian. Just let him talk.

BRIAN. You know us… We'll just start arguing. We always do.

CAROL. No you won't. Not now. (*Pause.*) Are you scared?

BRIAN. Of Frankie?… No. I'm feeling really awkward about all this though.

CAROL. What?

BRIAN. This going up to see him business. It's all a bit…

CAROL. It's only Frankie.

BRIAN. I know, but it feels like… he's gonna hear my confession or something…

CAROL. He just wants to talk, that's all.

BRIAN. It isn't just that though, is it? A chat… It's not like before… Not that we ever talked much then.

CAROL. That's probably why he wants to see you now…

BRIAN. You know to be honest… I find it all a bit embarrassing.

CAROL. What?

BRIAN. This… this whole… situation. Oh fuck… Now there's a confession. How terrible is that?… That's fuckin' dreadful. (*Laughs.*) What a thing to say… I'm finding my brother's dying an embarrassment.

CAROL. It's the shock of it all.

BRIAN. No, it's true… I don't want to talk to him… If I'm honest, I just want him to fuckin' hurry up and get it over with and not involve me! I don't need this. I just want to get away from it…

We hear a car sounding its horn.

And on that momentous confession – there's your taxi.

CAROL. Oh, Brian…

She moves towards the door, she turns and looks at him.

Just go up there, get it over with, and forget it. You know as well as I do, it's a load of old bollocks… But it keeps everyone happy and it'll cost you nowt. It's him that needs to do it. It's not about us any more, love.

She goes, leaving BRIAN *standing in the middle of the kitchen.*

Blackout.

Scene Two

Kitchen. JANET *is sat drinking tea and smoking. A* NURSE *in uniform stands stirring a cup of tea. The* NURSE *heads out of the room as* BRIAN *comes in.*

JANET. You stayed then?

BRIAN. It was late.

JANET. Some tea in the pot if you want.

BRIAN *gets himself a cup.*

BRIAN. Can't you sleep?

JANET. I heard talking.

He nods to the baby monitor.

BRIAN. He was… doing a lot of coughing… I went in to see if he was alright.

JANET. The nurse said you were with him.

Pause.

BRIAN. He didn't say much.

JANET. No? You know Frankie… time and place for everything.

BRIAN. From the way everyone was going on about it, I were expecting a bit of a lecture.

JANET. He's normally quite chatty of a night-time.

BRIAN. Must be me then.

Pause.

He was watching a video about the SAS.

JANET. That'll be it. It's a box set someone give him. He wants to finish it.

BRIAN. Right. He kept nodding off… so I just sat there.

JANET. He doesn't sleep if he can help it. Scares him, see, sleep… in the circumstances.

She yawns.

BRIAN. Go to bed, you look knackered.

JANET. I'm alright.

BRIAN. Phillip says you're here all the time now.

JANET. I don't mind.

BRIAN. Don't take it all on yourself.

JANET. I'd rather be here than stuck in me flat watching telly every night.

BRIAN. D'you not go to Bingo any more?

JANET. Bastard kids burnt it down. And the library.

BRIAN. No?

JANET. Only two bleeding things I enjoyed doing.

BRIAN. We spent half our lives in that library, us two.

JANET. Council replaced it with a walk-in mobile... That went in the cuts. Now we've got an Estonian lad on a mountain bike with saddlebags.

BRIAN *laughs*.

I'm not kiddin'... His names Jaaghup.

Pause.

He's dead nice... tickles me when he talks.

BRIAN. Fancy him?

JANET. I'm old enough to be his mam.

BRIAN. So?

JANET. Not all cradle-snatchers like you, you know.

BRIAN. They appreciate the experience.

JANET. Dirty bleeder... You still knocking about with that kid then?

BRIAN. She's twenty, her name's Melissa and no I'm not.

JANET. Frankie said it wouldn't last.

BRIAN. Did he.

JANET. Said she definitely weren't a runner. Knew it the moment he saw her.

BRIAN. He would.

JANET. Out of your league, he said.

BRIAN. Yeah, 'cause he'd know that...

Pause.

No one in your life then?

JANET. It took me six years to get rid of the last silly bugger.

BRIAN. So?

JANET. I can't be doing with all that crap any more.

Pause.

BRIAN. Funny, Frankie never settled down.

JANET. He's not gay.

BRIAN. I never said he was.

JANET. You don't have to say owt, you.

BRIAN *smiles*.

Plenty of women been through that front door. He were with Joan Haynes for years.

BRIAN. Confirmed bachelor then.

JANET. I know what you're saying.

BRIAN (*laughing*). What? I just said he was a confirmed bachelor.

JANET. I'll knock that bleeding smirk off your face in a minute. You're terrible, you. You'll bring it back on yourself saying things like that.

Pause.

BRIAN. I can only ever remember him making her cry.

JANET. She's were always very emotional, Joan. He couldn't do owt wrong in her eyes. Besotted she was. Still is. Comes over and sits with him for hours. Reads to him.

BRIAN. Yeah?

JANET. Historical novels.

Pause.

She's been married. He were in the army so she travelled a bit. Aldershot near you?

BRIAN. Not far.

JANET. He knocked her about. She's got a discoloured eye now... Left one.

BRIAN. She were never a looker.

JANET. Got a lovely reading voice though. You can hear her from down here sometimes.

Pause.

BRIAN. He said he wants to be cremated...

JANET *looks at him.*

…Frankie…

Pause.

JANET (*surprised*). He said that, to you – I mean he talked about it… that…

BRIAN. Yeah.

JANET. I thought you said he didn't say owt. What's that if it's not saying owt.

BRIAN. It's about all he did say.

JANET *looks at the smiling clown.*

Pause.

Then he wants the ashes scattered in Chimney Pot Park.

Beat.

JANET. We loved Chimney Pot Park when we were kids. D'you remember?

BRIAN. Yeah.

JANET. It were like playing on the roofs of Salford.

She lights a cigarette.

Do the council do that?

BRIAN. We'll have to do it.

JANET. I mean… do they allow it?

BRIAN. Who's going to tell 'em?

Pause

JANET. It's as good as anywhere else I suppose.

BRIAN. Yeah.

JANET. Mam and Dad are in the Garden of Remembrance at Agecroft… I've never been. Have you?

BRIAN. No.

JANET. You don't with ashes though, do you.

Scene Three

BRIAN *is busy in the kitchen. There are various pots and pans steaming away on the stove.* BRIAN *barely stops running about the kitchen. Within the space of this scene, the dinner must be on the table and everyone sat ready to eat.* BRIAN *looks in the oven and checks the meat cooking there.* PHILLIP *is pulling out cutlery from a drawer.*

PHILLIP. How many of us?

BRIAN. Seven.

PHILLIP. Seven? How d'you make that out.

BRIAN. Because there's seven of us. Me, Auntie Sheila, Samantha, Sonia, Janet, Carol and you.

PHILLIP. Me!… I forgot about me.

He starts to slowly place the sets of cutlery on the side, as he picks them out of the drawer. BRIAN *watches him.*

Me. Sonia, Carol, Auntie Sheila, Samantha, our Janet… our Carol…

For a moment he's unsure.

BRIAN. Me.

PHILLIP. I said me.

BRIAN. No. Me.

PHILLIP. You.

He picks them up and carries them over to the table. BRIAN *watches him.*

I used to do a Sunday roast for my lads. Loved it they did.

Beat.

Just chicken pieces, like… They never liked the look of a chicken.

Pause.

BRIAN. Do you get to see your kids much?

PHILLIP. Haven't seem 'em for a year. They're a bit funny with
me now, you know. Only to be expected really. It's money
and that. Never seem to have it at the right time. I send 'em
what I can, mind. I'd starve before I'd see them wantin' like.
Don't even buy fags or owt...

BRIAN. If it's cash you need –

PHILLIP. You're alright, our kid.

BRIAN. For the fare and that –

PHILLIP. Naa, thanks for offering though, appreciate it.

BRIAN. Prestatyn's only an hour or so on the train?

PHILLIP. I know. It's not just that though. It's all the fuckin'
argy-bargy with her... Every time I've been over there. It's
always the fuckin' same. She just kicks off at me – slagging
me off an' that in't front of the kids.

Beat.

They're better off without seeing all that, aren't they, eh? It
upsets them and... well, that does my fuckin' head in. I
always end up leave 'em crying and that's no fuckin' life for
'em is it? Naa, better off without me.

BRIAN *is taken aback by this. Though he doesn't know how
to deal with it.*

BRIAN. Are they 'eck... You shouldn't say that.

PHILLIP. I love 'em to bits though. Fuckin' love 'em... Life
though innit?

SONIA *comes in.*

SONIA. Hiya!

BRIAN. Alright, Son.

SONIA. Starvin', what're you cooking?

BRIAN. Roast lamb, vegetables.

PHILLIP. You can't go wrong with a roast dinner, our kid.

SONIA (*conspiratorially to* BRIAN). What's he doing?

BRIAN. Laying the table.

SONIO Did you colour-code it for him.

PHILLIP. I heard that.

SONIA (*to* BRIAN). D'you need a hand?

BRIAN. Have a look at the sprouts and the carrots, see how they're doing.

SONIA *starts testing the vegetables.*

PHILLIP. We're having mange tout as well.

SONIA. Mange tout? Nice.

Beat.

D'you eat it or drink it?

BRIAN *ignores her.*

Are these 'em, then? Mange tout – That French for peas in a pod? Do you chuck 'em?

BRIAN. You eat them whole they're a type of –

SONIA. Yeah, alright, we've all seen *MasterChef*.

CAROL *comes in with a bottle of wine.*

CAROL. How's it going?

PHILLIP. There's seven of us.

She looks at the pans.

CAROL. Oh, mange tout, how lovely –

SONIA *rolls her eyes.*

I've brought some wine – red – I don't know what it's like. It's from Waitrose so it should be quite palatable.

BRIAN. Great.

PHILLIP. I can't stick wine, me.

SONIA. We've some lager in't fridge, our kid. Don't know what it's like mind but it's from't Spar so should be 'kin' well tasty.

PHILLIP *laughs.* SONIA *goes over and offers him a fag.*

Do you want a fag, SpongeBob?

PHILLIP *takes one.*

BRIAN. Sonia, give your gob a rest and go and fetch us in the dinner plates from the front room.

SONIA *heads out.*

Sorry, she said she were going to behave today.

PHILLIP. She's in a good mood.

CAROL. Couldn't care less. Shall we have a drink?

BRIAN. Go on then.

CAROL *starts to open the wine.*

PHILLIP. I can't remember the last time us lot sat round a table for dinner.

CAROL. Nor can I... We would have been kids.

BRIAN. Must have been just before I went to college.

PHILLIP. What's that then?

BRIAN. Easily thirty-odd years ago.

CAROL. No.

BRIAN. Must be, 'cause me mam was still alive.

CAROL. We didn't really though did we – sit round together.

PHILLIP. Well we weren't the Waltons, put it that way.

CAROL *wanders over to the table.*

CAROL. Me dad sat here. Glaring at us. Me mam would be stood in the kitchen smoking.

PHILLIP. She could never eat what she'd just cooked, she always said that.

CAROL. By the time she was ready, me dad had scoffed the lot.

They laugh.

PHILLIP. Frankie always had it on his lap.

CAROL. He did, didn't he. I'd forgotten that.

PHILLIP. Frankie! Our Frankie – eight, there's eight of us for dinner... What should we do about Frankie?

BRIAN. He can't come down, Phillip.

CAROL looks over at BRIAN.

CAROL. We'll take him up a tray or something later, cock. I don't think he'll fancy it though, Phillip. Not now, love.

PHILLIP. We can't leave him out.

BRIAN. Go up and ask him if you like… But I think he's asleep.

PHILLIP. Back in a minute.

He exits, meeting SONIA *as she comes in.*

SONIA. Watch it!

She comes into the kitchen carrying a stack of plates and a bottle of Warninks Advocaat circa 1972.

None of this stuff matches. You know that, don't you.

BRIAN. Doesn't matter.

SONIA. More chips on 'em than Harry Ramsden's.

BRIAN. Just stick it on the table.

SONIA. I'll give 'em a wash first. It's mingin' that cupboard.

She heads over to the sink and starts to run the water.

Covered in ratshit and God knows what else.

Found a bottle of Advocaat though. Never been opened by the looks of it.

BRIAN. How old has that got to be?

SONIA. It keeps, don't it? Twenty per cent proof this stuff.

The doorbell rings.

CAROL. I'll get it.

CAROL heads out of the room.

BRIAN. Hey, have a word with Phillip about going to see his kids.

SONIA. No point. He won't go.

BRIAN. He's got rights.

SONIA. Rights cost money, mate. Rights is queuing up in some shitty legal-aid office on the precinct full of fuckin' immigrants on't cadge.

BRIAN. Sonia –

SONIA. He can barely write his own fuckin' name let alone fill out a bunch of bastard forms. It's not that he's lazy or owt, it's just – all beyond him.

AUNTIE SHEILA *comes in with* SONIA *and* SAMANTHA.

JANET. Hiya, I'm back!

JANET *has carrier bags. She heads straight into the kitchen and starts to unpack.* AUNTIE SHEILA *takes off her coat.*

SONIA. He's made his mind up about Prestatyn.

AUNTIE SHEILA. Who's gone there?

BRIAN. No one. Our Phillip's kids are there.

AUNTIE SHEILA. At the Jam Butty Camp?

JANET. Where's this Advocaat come from?

SONIA. Front-room cupboard.

AUNTIE SHEILA. Your mother'd be turning in her grave from the shame.

BRIAN. No, Auntie Sheila, they live there, with their mother. She's Welsh.

AUNTIE SHEILA. Ohhh. Welsh, was she? That figures.

Beat.

I never could stick Rhyl.

CAROL. Cup of tea, Auntie Sheila?

AUNTIE SHEILA. Did you say Advocaat, Janet? You got any lemonade there as well?

JANET. Yeah.

AUNTIE SHEILA. I'll have a snowball then. It's not Christmas but what the 'eck...

JANET *starts to make a snowball.* BRIAN *is making gravy.* CAROL *is putting out the vegetables into serving dishes.* AUNTIE SHEILA *lights a cigarette.*

Beat.

Your mother loved North Wales. Waited all year round for that one week, she did. Your dad was convinced she was having a fling with the donkey man off the beach. Where was that place you always used to go to?

BRIAN/CAROL/SONIA/JANET. Sunny Vale.

AUNTIE SHEILA. Aye, that's it. Sunny Vale. Always pissed down. Bit too near Prestatyn for my liking.

SAMANTHA. I always wanted to go to the Jam Butty Camp, me.

AUNTIE SHEILA. Ringworm Junction that place. Besides, you couldn't have gone 'cause we weren't poor in that way.

She looks over at BRIAN.

What have you cooked for me dinner, love.

SONIA. Jam butties.

AUNTIE SHEILA. You ought to be on the radio with jokes like that.

BRIAN. Sonia, give us a hand, will you.

SONIA *goes over and starts to help.* JANET *starts to rearrange the table settings.*

JANET. Our Frankie been alright?

CAROL. Phillip's up there with him. He went to ask if he wanted to eat.

JANET. I wish he'd stop offering him food. He'll go bang on't turn. He knows he doesn't want to eat. It's driving him mad.

CAROL. I know but… Well, he just wants to do something.

AUNTIE SHEILA. If he wants to do something he ought to get over to Prestatyn and get his bleeding kids back before they go all Welsh.

JANET *comes over with the drink*. AUNTIE SHEILA *takes a sip*.

Oh, lovely – All I need now is me Christmas tree and Ken Dodd.

PHILLIP *comes back in*. BRIAN *takes the meat over to the table*. CAROL *starts to brings over the vegetables*.

JANET. Is he alright?

PHILLIP. Out of it. Doing a lot of moving about though. Janet, d'you think he's alright?

SAMANTHA. That'll be the pain.

SONIA. He's not in pain. He's got tablets for that.

SAMANTHA. Yeah. But do they work when you're asleep?

AUNTIE SHEILA. Course they do, you big daft lummox.

BRIAN. Should we all sit down? Auntie Sheila, you sit at the top as you're the eldest member of the family – Phillip, why don't you sit in me dad's old place.

PHILLIP. Alright.

AUNTIE SHEILA. Oh, what a treat!

Lights up. People sit looking at the food in front of them. PHILLIP, SONIA, JANET, SAMANTHA and AUNTIE SHEILA look unsure. They quietly nibble at the food on their forks. SONIA and CAROL tuck in as BRIAN pulls the cork from another bottle of wine. He fills CAROL's glass.

AUNTIE SHEILA pours herself a drink from the Warninks bottle which is now half-empty. She is slightly pissed. JANET watches her.

JANET. Do you want some lemonade with that snowball, Auntie Sheila?

AUNTIE SHEILA. I'm getting quite a taste for it on its own actually. Do you like Advocaat, Brian?

BRIAN. Not really my tipple, Auntie Sheila.

AUNTIE SHEILA. You ought to try it. Slips down a treat. Could you pass the gravy, Janet.

JANET *passes the gravy.*

JANET. Lovely, Brian.

BRIAN. Thanks.

AUNTIE SHEILA (*without conviction*). Very nice…

She surreptitiously has a smell of the gravy.

SAMANTHA. I'll have a bit of that when you've finished, Mam.

BRIAN. Some more lamb, Auntie Sheila?

AUNTIE SHEILA. I'm alright, thanks, cock. I'll finish what I've got on me plate first.

AUNTIE SHEILA *nibbles a bit of meat and takes a huge slug of Advocaat to wash it down.* PHILLIP *is just moving his food about his plate.*

BRIAN. How did you and Peter get involved in an Indian restaurant?

As the rest of this conversation takes place, AUNTIE SHEILA *starts to get rid of all her lamb onto* SAMANTHA*'s plate.*

CAROL. We always went there to eat. Then one day we just got talking to Akbar, that's the owner, and before we knew it, we were partners. It's very well designed – one of these new places, none of that flock wallpaper and whiny music. Sort of Indian nouvelle cuisine.

SONIA. They used to call it famine over there.

AUNTIE SHEILA *slips more food on* SAMANTHA*'s plate.* SAMANTHA *tries to protest silently by trying to push it back. They begin fighting to keep it off their plates.* JANET *is looking daggers at both of them.*

SAMANTHA (*mouthing*). I don't want it.

CAROL. Ignore her. It's very popular and you can tell the food's good 'cause we get a lot of Asian clients in as well and they're not going to eat rubbish, are they? Better connoisseurs of their own cuisine than we are, wouldn't you think?

PHILLIP. You don't do chips, do you?

CAROL. It's not that sort of Indian restaurant.

SONIA. The Taj Mahal sells savaloys.

CAROL. We've got one of the best Indian chefs in Lancashire. Used to work in a big hotel in Bombay. Came over here when the Balti scene took off.

PHILLIP. That's a con that. Balti. Just curry in a little wok.

CAROL. I'd like to get more involved, you know – more hands-on. I've got a box set of Madhur Jaffrey – but they're quite a close-knit family and not too keen on outside interference. I respect that though, it's in their culture and you have to respect that. Bobby explained it all – that's the chef from Bombay – we call him Bobby. His real name's Brablebinder-something or other. Bobby's less of a mouthful, begins with a 'B' and it makes him laugh, so it can't be racist, can it?

BRIAN *catches what is going on between* AUNTIE SHEILA *and* SAMANTHA.

BRIAN. Sorry, Carol – is there something wrong, Auntie Sheila?

AUNTIE SHEILA *has been caught in the act.*

AUNTIE SHEILA. It's our Samantha… She's not keen on lamb.

SAMANTHA *is gobsmacked by this statement.*

SAMANTHA. It weren't me, it were her, Brian.

AUNTIE SHEILA. Samantha!

SAMANTHA. She were sticking hers on my plate. I can barely keep me own down.

BRIAN. It's okay just to leave it, Auntie Sheila. Really…

AUNTIE SHEILA. No, I think it's lovely – Bit on the bloody side.

BRIAN. There's some darker meat here if you'd like.

AUNTIE SHEILA. You're alright, cock. I'll just eat me mash.

PHILLIP. Is it done properly, our kid?

BRIAN. It's meant to be rare.

PHILLIP. Yeah? 'Cause I can't hold mine down to shear it!

SONIA, SAMANTHA *and* PHILLIP *laugh.*

Just pulling your leg.

BRIAN. Just leave what you don't want.

SAMANTHA. What's on the sprouts?

BRIAN. Sesame seeds.

SAMANTHA. Oh…

Beat.

Can I leave them as well?

AUNTIE SHEILA *looks like she's chewing a wasp.*

AUNTIE SHEILA. I'm sorry, love – Is that garlic on the mash potato?

BRIAN. Yes.

JANET. Just try it.

AUNTIE SHEILA. I am. It's not new to me. I tried it before on an excursion to Pickmere.

SAMANTHA. You didn't like the look of it then, did you, Mam?

AUNTIE SHEILA. Not on me Sunday roast. Though I'm not a fussy eater – Am I, Janet?

She looks to JANET.

I can eat owt she chucks at me – but when it comes to garlic… Well, there's a time and a place for it, isn't there.

PHILLIP. It's on the lamb an' all, in't it?

BRIAN. Yeah.

PHILLIP. Not for me that. I like lamb to taste like –

SONIA. Bernard Matthews…

PHILLIP. Hey, they're alright, them. You can't knock one of them if you're cooking for yourself.

JANET. I think you're all being bloody rude. Our Brian's gone out of his way to make us this dinner and you sit there complaining? I for one am enjoying it, Brian.

AUNTIE SHEILA. Oh, you bleedin' fibber, Janet. You haven't touched them Brussels.

SAMANTHA. Or your green beans.

BRIAN. Mange tout.

She looks at BRIAN *to confirm what he's said.*

SAMANTHA. Right –

She looks back to JANET.

Or your mange, either!

BRIAN. It really doesn't matter.

JANET. I've had more than you have.

AUNTIE SHEILA *starts poking about at her plate.*

AUNTIE SHEILA. I ate the carrots, the cabbage and a bit of a sprout. I didn't know I was under surveillance.

PHILLIP. I was alright with the sprouts, me.

JANET. Brian just thought it'd be nice for us to sit round as a family for a change. The least you could have done was look liked you were enjoying it.

AUNTIE SHEILA. What have I done now? My Samantha has allergies to certain types of cooked meats. She could've broken out in God knows what if she'd have carried on chewing. How appetising would that have looked!

JANET. Oh, don't be ridiculous, Auntie Sheila. There's nothing wrong with Samantha. There never has been.

SAMANTHA. Corned beef gives me hives!

BRIAN. There's ice cream for pudding?

SAMANTHA. I can't go near fresh-salmon paste, can I, Mam?

AUNTIE SHEILA. Get us me fags, Samantha. I've lost all sense of an appetite with this lot. In fact – get me coat, we're going.

AUNTIE SHEILA *gets up and heads for her coat.* BRIAN *stands and tries to placate her.*

BRIAN. Oh, come on, Auntie Shei, no one's having a go at you. Sit down...

AUNTIE SHEILA. I shan't stay where I'm not wanted.

SONIA. See you then.

JANET. Oh, sit down, Auntie Sheila.

AUNTIE SHEILA. No thank you very much. It's been made quite clear ever since that poor boy took ill, we've not been welcome in this house.

JANET. Now you're talking rubbish.

AUNTIE SHEILA. Am I, Janet? Am I? It's not just me saying it. Other people have noticed how you lot have kept us out.

PHILLIP. You're talking bollocks now, Auntie Sheila.

AUNTIE SHEILA. The evidence is there. You don't have to be CSI Salford to see it. I've been made to feel unwelcome in this house since day one. Kept out of any decisions about him –

JANET. It's nowt to do with you. Besides, it's what he wanted.

AUNTIE SHEILA. What Frankie wanted or you, Janet? He wouldn't have kept me away.

JANET. Where's all this coming from?

AUNTIE SHEILA. This is all your doing, this. I've been like a mother to him all his life. More than a mother in fact.

JANET. What's that supposed to mean?

AUNTIE SHEILA. Well our Sylvia was never there for him, was she? Too busy dealing with the rest of you or chucking her money down the drain at Bingo to have any time left for Frankie. He never got a bleeding look-in, that lad. He were always shunned.

BRIAN. Auntie Shei, I don't think this is the time –

AUNTIE SHEILA. Time? Time isn't what he's got any more, is it? So I'll say me piece if you don't mind, Lord bleeding Snowdon!

CAROL. Let's all just calm down and have a drink.

AUNTIE SHEILA. That's your answer to everything, is it, Carol – 'Have a drink'? Well it might work for you in a broken-down marriage in Didsbury, but I believe in speaking my mind.

BRIAN. Auntie Sheila –

PHILLIP (*to* AUNTIE SHEILA). That's bang out of order!

CAROL. It's alright, Phillip. You can say what you like to me, Auntie Sheila. I don't give rat's arse.

AUNTIE SHEILA. You never did. You've always been a hard-faced mare. You only ever come back here when someone's dying. Even then you have to be dragged back. Then you're off like a shot before they're cold in the ground. Why Frankie wanted you back here is beyond my comprehension.

CAROL. That's it, isn't it? You never did like the fact that me and Frankie were close. It always stuck in your craw, didn't it? You were happy when we fell out, were overjoyed when he stopped speaking to me.

AUNTIE SHEILA. He saw you for what you were!

CAROL. I bet he did. And I bet you helped him see it and all, didn't you? I bet you stoked them fires and kept 'em stoked for years. You nasty, shit-stirring old cow!

SONIA, *enjoying the scene, zips her mouth.*

BRIAN. That's enough! Now pack it in, all of you! Now just sit down!

AUNTIE SHEILA. Ah… fuck off, the bastard lot of you!

AUNTIE SHEILA *storms off.*

Samantha, don't forget the baby!

Beat.

SAMANTHA. It's just the Warninks talking.

Scene Four

Night. One week later. SONIA *stands by the back door. She looks as though she dressed hurriedly. Tracksuit bottoms over a faded nightdress. Trainers on her feet. Her hair is dishevelled. She smokes and drinks from a can of lager.* CAROL *comes in, starts to take off her coat, she too looks as though she dressed in a hurry.* SONIA *turns and looks at her.*

CAROL. How's he doing?

SONIA *doesn't say anything.*

Sonia!…

SONIA. They're all upstairs with him… Doctor's just left.

CAROL. What did he say?

SONIA. Could be any time…

CAROL *sits down on a chair, she's in shock. She opens her bag and searches for her cigarettes. She is trying to disguise the fact that she's crying. She lights one up. She tries desperately not to show* SONIA *she's upset. She goes over to the counter and takes some kitchen roll.*

CAROL. Has everyone been told?… Auntie Sheila?

SONIA. She's up there.

Pause.

CAROL *looks uncertain about what she should do.* SONIA *watches her.*

You'd better get up, if you want to see him…

CAROL. Have you been?

SONIA. No point. Nowt to see… He's out of it.

CAROL. Yeah…

She stands and starts to stub her cigarette out nervously. SONIA *watches her.*

(*Reluctantly.*) I'll go up then.

SONIA. D'you not want to go?

CAROL. I thought I did… I suppose I'm expected.

She goes and gets herself a glass of water. She drinks it and looks at SONIA.

SONIA. You don't have to if you don't want to.

CAROL. No... I will... I think I should...

SONIA. Suit yourself... I don't think he knows owt.

CAROL. Maybe...

SONIA. I know I wouldn't want a bunch of fuckin' people, hanging about starin' at me...

CAROL. What else d'you do?

Pause.

CAROL *makes to go.*

SONIA. They keep telling him to let go.

CAROL *turns to her.*

CAROL. Yeah?

SONIA. You know... not fight it... Die... 'You can go now, Frankie, let go now...'

She almost breaks down.

They keep saying...

CAROL. Well...

SONIA. Why say something like that?

CAROL. Look, Sonia, it's not the...

SONIA. I mean, if I were laying there and someone said that to me, I'd think, 'No, you fuck off and die, you cunt!'... Let go?... Like he's got a fuckin' choice...

CAROL. I suppose it's natural... to want to... you know... They say it's the spirit... and that... It's like when they wouldn't tell us how long he had, 'cause some people have a natural fighting instinct... They just can't tell... But if a person's in pain and that... I can understand why families don't want them to struggle... Me mam was... (*Catches herself.*) Well... she didn't linger.

SONIA. Didn't she.

CAROL. No...

SONIA. 'Cause I wouldn't fuckin' know, would I?

An uncomfortably long silence.

CAROL. I don't want us to be like this any more, Sonia...

SONIA. Don't even go there, Carol... I'm not kicking off,
alright? Just don't start your fuckin' yacking! 'Cause I'm not
interested... Not now... not tonight. After tonight it don't
matter what you say or do, alright? After tonight... After
tonight, I don't care about anything... It's all fuckin' gone,
innit? Frankie, this house, us lot. It's a fuckin' nothing...
history.

She gets a cigarette and lights it.

CAROL. We're still a family, Sonia.

SONIA. Believe that, d'you?... You can stand there and spout
off about fuckin' family after the way you treated us? Auntie
Sheila was right the other week – 'bout – That hurt Frankie,
you know, all that... Hurt him.

CAROL. He hurt me.

SONIA. Funny really, 'cause it were nothing in't scheme of
things, were it, eh?... So you don't invite anyone over,
whatever! You don't call, whatever! Nothing at all when you
think about it. Couldn't give a fuck, me, you know me... But
Frankie... hurt him, didn't it... stupid really... grown man
taking it like that. Were a slight to him. Took it to heart, see...

CAROL. I know... and we talked about it...

SONIA. That's good... you talked, nice one, fair dos and that...
eases things for you, doesn't it? It's good talking, talking's
good. Been a lot of it round here lately... good for everyone.
Never too late they say... D'you think? Never too late? Too
late for fuckin' Frankie, like... No one wants to talk to him
now... They just want him to hurry up... let go, don't hold
on... fuck off!

CAROL. I don't think it's meant like that, Son...

SONIA. I want him to go now... Yeah, I think I do... I think...
Not right to want him to stay, is it? Be wrong, that, now. The

way he is. I wouldn't want that. It's okay to think like that now innit, eh, Carol? D'you think? He can't... Not now... not like this... It's not right...

CAROL can see how upset she is and makes to go towards her. But SONIA backs off a little.

CAROL. Oh, Son –

SONIA. Go on... you'd better go up. You should... He'd like that. He'd like you to be there. Go on, 'cause it's not gonna be long now... It's not, listen...

She goes over to the clown and turns up the volume, we can hear FRANKIE's breathing, very laboured now.

You'd best go up 'cause he won't last much longer... Go on, Carol! Go on! Go upstairs... don't look at me! Just don't see me...

She breaks down and CAROL goes over to her. She stands close but doesn't hold her.

Scene Five

CAROL comes into the kitchen dressed in black. She is carrying a large covered bread tray. Leaning against the kitchen unit are four funeral wreaths. A few cards and some flowers in a vase stand on the table. CAROL puts the bread tray down. CAROL bends down to look at the flowers.

CAROL. When did these come?

PHILLIP comes in carrying four small palettes of lager, which he places on a growing pile on the floor. He wears an ill-fitting black suit, the sleeves have been rolled back. On his feet he wears trainers.

PHILLIP. Last night. Weren't sure if I should have stuck 'em in water or not... so I just left 'em. Look alright, don't they?

CAROL. Yeah, they're fine. We only need 'em for the morning.

BRIAN comes in wearing a smart black suit.

BRIAN. Anything I can do?

CAROL. It's all done. We're just heading back to pick the rest of the stuff up.

BRIAN. Alright.

CAROL. There's more flowers coming at nine, you can sort that for us. We should be back by then, but just in case.

BRIAN. No problem.

CAROL. Oh, and they'll be a bloke called Abdul delivering a load of glasses.

She heads out the door, followed by PHILLIP. BRIAN *wanders over and looks at the cards. He pours himself a glass of whiskey from a bottle on the side, knocks it back, then pours himself another.* JANET *comes in, dressed in black.*

JANET. You're starting early.

BRIAN. I need it. Do you want one?

JANET shakes her head and looks around the room.

JANET. Carol seems to have got everything organised.

BRIAN. Right down to the last chicken leg, no doubt.

JANET. Glad she took over... I was useless last week.

Pause.

She made a start packing up the house as well.

BRIAN. That's quick. Thought we were gonna wait.

JANET. Everyone thought, you know... might as well now. Even Sonia. Is there anything you want to take?

BRIAN. Not really.

JANET. It'll just get chucked otherwise.

BRIAN. Everything?

JANET. Yeah. Phillip doesn't want any of it in the new flat. We said Auntie Sheila can have me mam's dressing table, if that's alright with you?

BRIAN. Yeah... fine.

Beat.

JANET. Nothing at all?

BRIAN. No.

JANET. We'll get rid then.

BRIAN. Are you taking anything?

JANET. No.

Pause.

BRIAN. Odd to think none of this'll be here much longer.

JANET *lights a cigarette.*

JANET. Didn't think you'd have cared less...

BRIAN. It was always here though, weren't it? To come back to... This house. Salford. Frankie.

JANET. I suppose.

BRIAN. I'm surprised he stayed here as long as he did.

JANET. Are you?

BRIAN. He always used to talk about doing things after me mam and dad died... moving on and that.

JANET. Changed his mind. Nothing wrong with that. We all do... It suited him here. Doing what he was doing. He were happy. That's all that matters at the end of the day, in't it? Being where you're happiest.

BRIAN. Was he?

JANET. Yeah... Yeah he was.

Pause.

I can't see his face any more... I keep trying... but I just can't picture it in me head.

BRIAN. Funny to think he's dead. Sounds odd...

JANET *goes over to the kitchen door, opens it and breathes in deeply.*

You alright?

JANET. Yeah… Just… Just hearing other people say it. Hearing you say it… makes it more real, you know… Daft, isn't it?

BRIAN. No.

JANET. He never talked to me about any of this. Funerals and what have you. I didn't even think about him not being here any more. Don't know why… 'cause it were always there in the back of me mind… It was going to happen… but you just didn't ponder on it, not really… There were so much to be getting on with.

BRIAN. Look… I'm sorry I wasn't around more…

JANET turns and looks at him.

JANET. Are you?…

She turns away.

You had your work and that…

BRIAN. I know but…

JANET. I've been that busy with it all, the last couple of months. You think it's just gonna carry on…

BRIAN. Things'll get back to normal before you know it.

JANET. Normal?…

Pause.

D'you know what's normal for me, Brian? The four bleeding walls of my flat. Friday I do a weekly shop on the Precinct. Sit in the same café. Have a corn-beef roll. Buy a paper, then I shut me door for the weekend. Sonia might pop over if she's talking to me, and wants a moan. I hardly see Carol, 'cause she's up her own arse and too grand to invite me over. On the odd occasion I push the boat out and go and see Auntie Sheila. That's it. That's me. That's my bastard normal.

BRIAN. Jan…

JANET.…I just turned round one day and that's all I had. Didn't even see it coming. Right in the middle of an episode of… fuckin'… something or other… Couldn't even remember what day it was… what I'd just eaten, if I'd put a fag out or was I about to light one up… You know me, I don't think about anything at the best of times. But that night, sat there... I realised I had nothing... was never going to... that this was it! I cried... screamed... Screamed and screamed... till there was nothing...

It's a terrible thing to say and I'll bring it back on myself, I know, but, since our Frankie got ill, I've been alive. I've had a purpose, been needed. Now what? Have I to go back to all that...

BRIAN. You don't have to...

JANET. It's easy for you to say... you did something... got out... pissed off to London and got a life.

BRIAN. It's what you wanted too. You make it sound like I did something wrong.

JANET. Well it never bothered you what was happening back here, did it?... You swanned in and swanned out when you felt like it.

BRIAN. Do something...

JANET. It's not as simple as that.

BRIAN. What's stopping you?

JANET. This is all I've ever known.

BRIAN. What's stopping you?

JANET. Me! I'm stopping me! I always have. And now I know it! I know it and it'll never change.

BRIAN. Don't be stupid.

JANET. You're not listening! People like me don't go back and start again!

BRIAN. Why not?

JANET. What's wrong with you! Can you not get it into your head? Are you that far away...

BRIAN. Now you sound like Frankie! You're smarter than that.

JANET. That's right, run him down now he's not here to defend himself.

BRIAN. Have you heard yourself?

JANET. Maybe he was right – Maybe you have forgotten where you're from, with your Midland bleeding Hotel and your posh girlfriends looking down their noses at us…

BRIAN. I thought I'd heard the last of this shit, off him…

JANET. Bring 'em back for a laugh, did you? Your pictures not enough for 'em? Wanted to see the monkeys in the zoo, did they?

BRIAN. Don't give me all that 'lost my fucking roots' bollocks!

JANET. You're out of touch, Brian, you have been for years.

BRIAN (*angry*). With what?… Tell me with what?… This house? Those streets? You lot with your petty fucking squabbling! Who's talking to who? Whose side are you on? He doesn't phone, she's moved there! Have I lost touch with that, have I?

JANET. You know what I'm talking about and so did Frankie. That's why you weren't around when he were ill, 'cause you were too scared of what he had to say!

BRIAN. What did he have to say, Jan?… What? What did he have to say to me? Don't give me Frankie! I've had Frankie up to here!

Beat.

He was my brother and he's dead and I'm really fuckin' sorry for that! I thought… something might come out of all this… Maybe I was gonna get closer to him… get to know him again… anything! He was dying… and I sat with him that night and we watched a stupid, useless… fuckin' programme about the SAS and we had nothing to say to each other. Nothing… I just sat there… He could barely fuckin' look at me… and we said nothing… and now we never will.

JANET *is crying*. BRIAN *stands and watches*.

Blackout.

Scene Six

AUNTIE SHEILA *sits drinking tea at the table with* SONIA
and SAMANTHA. BRIAN *stands in the kitchen.* PHILLIP *is
unpacking the lagers and putting them in the fridge.* CAROL *is
putting cling film round plates.*

A man, MICKEY, *stands by the door drinking from a cup and
saucer.* SONIA *comes in looking very smart in a black jacket,
skirt and blouse. She looks a bit self-conscious. She grabs a
packet of fags from the table, goes over to the kitchen door, taking
a can of lager on the way. She opens the can, then lights up.*

SONIA. Tonnes of flowers out there now.

AUNTIE SHEILA. Some lovely sentiments on them cards,
   Janet. Must make sure you collect them up after.

   AUNTIE SHEILA *and* SAMANTHA *both light up.*

JANET. Yeah.

   Pause.

SAMANTHA. Cath and John said to say they donated money to
   an hospice, rather than send flowers.

AUNTIE SHEILA. Did they...

   Pause.

PHILLIP. There's one in the shape a football.

BRIAN. Who sent that?

PHILLIP. Dunno, just says 'From all the lads on't team.
   Remembered days' –

BRIAN. What team?

AUNTIE SHEILA. That'll be the lads from The Lima Arms. He
   used to play football with 'em years ago.

BRIAN. The Lima Arms?

AUNTIE SHEILA. Ordsall.

MICKEY. Peru Street, to be exact. Salford's first theme pub.
   Full of Inca gods it was. Excuse me.

   He puts down his cup and leaves.

AUNTIE SHEILA. Who's he when he's at home?

PHILLIP. I've never seen him before. Thought you lot knew him.

BRIAN. He just asked for tea in a cup and saucer... So I give him one.

CAROL. He came with flowers.

SONIA. Make sure he doesn't leave with 'em.

AUNTIE SHEILA. He can't get in any of the cars. Them's for family only. You'd better go and tell him, Brian.

JANET. He must have a lift, if he's come here first.

AUNTIE SHEILA. We'll be hard pushed for space as it is.

SAMANTHA. The two lead cars are always for closest family, aren't they, Mam?

PHILLIP. I've made a list.

AUNTIE SHEILA. I've been in this situation before. The moment they see a black saloon, they all pile in. Any decorum flies out the window.

BRIAN. He said he's reading a poem.

CAROL. He is not. There's only two readings and I never asked him.

AUNTIE SHEILA. Go and sort it now, Carol, otherwise they'll all be getting up to do a turn.

CAROL. I'll go and have a word with him.

AUNTIE SHEILA. Gotta be careful these days. There's that many head-the-balls walking the streets.

CAROL *goes out*.

Pause.

SONIA. What time'll the cars be here, Brian?

BRIAN. About half past ten... You alright?

SONIA. Yeah.

PHILLIP. You looking smart, our kid.

JANET. Yeah, looks great, that outfit, Son.

BRIAN. I told you it suits you.

SONIA is unsure how to handle the compliments.

SONIA. Brian took us shopping… It'd give our Frankie a fuckin' shock seeing me in a skirt, wouldn't it?…

She suddenly breaks down and cries. JANET *lowers her head as well.* AUNTIE SHEILA *starts to cry.*

SAMANTHA. Alright, Mam…

AUNTIE SHEILA. It's not right though this, is it, eh?… Not right…

SAMANTHA tries to comfort her. BRIAN *looks out of the window.* PHILLIP *just stands and watches.*

SAMANTHA. Have a little drink.

AUNTIE SHEILA. I'm fine.

SAMANTHA. Got any rum there, Brian.

BRIAN. Yeah.

BRIAN pours her a glass. SAMANTHA *gets up to fetch it.*

SAMANTHA. I think you all need something. Janet?

She proffers the bottle.

JANET. Yeah, ta. Just a small one.

She pours BRIAN *one and* PHILLIP.

SAMANTHA. There you go, lads. Sonia?

SONIA. I'm alright.

SAMANTHA. Bollocks, you're having one.

She takes one over to SONIA.

SONIA. Ta.

She takes another over to AUNTIE SHEILA.

SAMANTHA. Here you are, Mam.

AUNTIE SHEILA takes the drink. SAMANTHA *lights a cigarette for her.* BRIAN *takes some kitchen roll over to* SONIA. CAROL *comes in.*

BRIAN. Sorted?

CAROL. Hilda O'Dwyer's son, Mickey?

AUNTIE SHEILA. She was a good friend of your mam's. Used to go't wash-house together on Hodge Lane.

CAROL. Well, he was a mate of Frankie's apparently.

BRIAN. And was he going to do a reading?

CAROL. No… He just wanted to speak about Frankie. But he understood.

PHILLIP. Loads of people wanted to get up and say something.

AUNTIE SHEILA. Very well respected was Frankie. 'Greatly missed.' That's what most of them cards say. 'Greatly missed.' Shows the measure of a man, that.

Pause.

CAROL. He asked if he could help with the coffin.

AUNTIE SHEILA. We've a full compliment, haven't we?

PHILLIP. Me, our Brian, Jonjon, Burkey, Ernie Barlow and Tony.

AUNTIE SHEILA. You wouldn't get any more round it.

BRIAN. He can take my place…

Beat.

CAROL. Are you sure?

BRIAN. Yeah.

CAROL. I'll go let him know.

AUNTIE SHEILA. We'll have to find space for him in a car now. Ask him if he's got a lift while you're at it.

JANET. Hang on a minute, Carol.

JANET *turns to* BRIAN.

Why don't you want to carry the coffin?

Pause.

BRIAN. I just don't feel comfortable with it.

JANET. It's your brother.

BRIAN. I know, I…

SONIA. Leave it, Janet, if he doesn't want to do it, he doesn't have to.

JANET. I'd just like to know why he's left it till now to tell us.

AUNTIE SHEILA. Frankie would've wanted it.

BRIAN. I'm sorry… I haven't got an excuse other than… I just don't want to carry the coffin.

JANET. Should have said so earlier then.

BRIAN. I just don't feel easy with it …

JANET. There's plenty of people who'd of jumped at the chance.

BRIAN. Well if you'd have asked me, instead of just presuming I was gonna do it.

PHILLIP. She shouldn't have to ask, our kid. That's our brother lying in that coffin. It's about respect and that, innit?

JANET. That's exactly what it's about. That's what all them people out there have come for.

BRIAN. I just felt I'd like to… Look, this isn't the time or the place…

JANET. Bet you won't be putting your hand in your pocket, either now.

BRIAN (*exasperated*). I'll pay for the whole bloody thing if you want.

AUNTIE SHEILA. It's not about money though, is it, Brian. It's about family.

CAROL *comes in. She is now wearing a black coat. She's been crying.*

CAROL. Frankie's here.

Pause.

AUNTIE SHEILA. Come on then, let's not keep him waiting…

AUNTIE SHEILA, SAMANTHA and JANET move to the door, putting on coats. BRIAN puts on his overcoat. PHILLIP takes out a bit of paper.

PHILLIP. Right, erm... Auntie Sheila, Samantha and Janet. Erm, you're in the first car. Sonia, Brian and Carol you're in the second. Everyone else to follow in their own... That leaves, erm...

SONIA (*good-naturedly*). You, you pillock... Come on.

They all head out of the door, leaving BRIAN and CAROL.

BRIAN. I'll lock up.

She turns and leaves. BRIAN closes the back door and turns the key in the lock. He goes over to the windows and pulls them closed. He stops. Looks at the armchair. Slowly, the lights fade to black.

The End.

TO SIR, WITH LOVE

after E.L. Braithwaite

For Miss Snowdon,
Ordsall Board School, Salford 1966/1970

Who taught me to read and showed me
the world beyond my own.

This adaptation of *To Sir, With Love* was first performed at
Royal & Derngate, Northampton (James Dacre, Artistic Director;
Martin Sutherland, Chief Executive), on 10 September 2013
(previews from 7 September). The cast was as follows:

DENHAM	Mykola Allen
MONICA	Harriet Ballard
GILLIAN	Peta Cornish
SEALES	Kerron Darby
RICK	Ansu Kabia
FLORIAN	Matthew Kelly
WESTON	Paul Kemp
PAMELA	Heather Nicol
CLINTY	Nicola Reynolds
COMMUNITY	Ben Ayers, Alana Castle, Sasha
ENSEMBLE	Farmer, George Attwell Gerhards,
	Christian Needle, Cameron Percival,
	Poppy Roberts, Isobel Scanlon

Director	Mark Babych
Designer	Mike Britton
Lighting Designer	Johanna Town
Sound Designer	Ivan Stott
Choreographer	
& Movement Director	Nick Winston
Fight Director	Philip d'Orléans
Associate Director	
& Associate Producer	Neale Birch
Casting Director	Camilla Evans
Deputy Stage Manager	Jo Phipps

Scenery, set painting, properties, costuming, wigs and make-up
by Royal & Derngate workshops and facilitated in-house by
stage-management and technical teams.

Characters

MR LEON FLORIAN, *fifty-five, headmaster*
VIVIENNE CLINTRIDGE 'CLINTY', *thirty-five, teacher*
RICARDO BRAITHWAITE 'RICK', *thirty-one, teacher*
GILLIAN BLANCHARD, *twenty-one, teacher*
HUMPHREY WESTON, *thirty-nine, teacher*

THE SENIOR CLASS
PAMELA DARE, *fourteen*
MONICA PAGE, *fourteen*
DENHAM, *fourteen*
SEALES, *fourteen, mixed-race English-Nigerian*
ESTHER JOSEPH, *fourteen*
ARCHIE, *fourteen*
EDWARD EDWARDS, *fourteen*
JANE PURCELL, *fourteen*
FERNMAN
ROSE
NORA
YOUTH GROUP KIDS

ACT ONE

London 1948

Scene One

The staffroom of a large Victorian school in the East End of London, 1948. The room is untidy, filled with books, odd bits of sports equipment, coats and bags. There is a torn poster from the 1948 Olympics. The mantelpiece is loaded with cups. A door to the side leads off to a toilet. In the centre of the room, a large table covered with newspapers and magazines. Various armchairs are placed around in no particular order. We can hear the sounds of children from the playground. A small coffee table has been turned over. VIVIENNE CLINTRIDGE is on her hands and knees picking up some broken crockery. GILLIAN BLANCHARD is mopping the floor. HUMPHREY WESTON is sat in an armchair, legs hooked over the arm; watching the women clean, he is lighting a pipe.

Enter MR LEON FLORIAN. *In the background we can hear children shouting an un-cherubic version of 'We are the Ovaltineys'.*

MR FLORIAN. I've just been informed. Was it ugly?

WESTON. Let's say I don't think we'll be seeing our esteemed colleague amongst these hallowed halls of enlightenment again.

MR FLORIAN. Is he still around? Maybe I could talk to him.

CLINTY. It's gone quite beyond that, I'm afraid.

GILLIAN. And he seemed such a quiet sort of chap.

WESTON. He'll have reached divisional office by now. Demanding a more salubrious relocation. Listen to those obnoxious little toads!

We can hear the senior class shouting 'The Ovaltineys' theme.

WESTON. Bloody Eviltineys more like!

CLINTY. He seemed perfectly fine this morning. Did you upset him, Weston?

WESTON. Me? I'm shocked you should even think that way, Clinty. I barely said a word to the man. He walked in. Sat in that chair and the next thing I know, he went completely doolally tap. Ranting and raving like a madman.

GILLIAN. I offered him a coffee.

WESTON. That'd be it then. It's your fault. He drinks tea. 'White, weak, half-sugared.' Very particular was our Mr Hackman. If you get my drift.

MR FLORIAN. Really, Mr Weston –

WESTON. Let's face it, Headmaster. The man just wasn't man enough to deal with that class. Christ! The Waffen SS would be hard pushed!

MR FLORIAN. Mr Weston, I know it's your free period after break but could you –

WESTON. No, I could not. It's bad enough dealing with my own little monsters without taking on board their delinquent elder siblings.

CLINTY. That's the Dunkirk spirit, Weston.

WESTON. I wouldn't touch them with a six-foot pole or a Yugoslav for that matter.

CLINTY. I'll bring them over into mine. They won't mess with me.

MR FLORIAN. Thank you so much, Miss Clintridge. It'll just be for the first period, then I'll take over for the rest of the day. I'd take them myself now, only I've a meeting with the education office.

WESTON. More bad news on the horizon?

MR FLORIAN. I certainly hope not, Mr Weston. But they do like to keep abreast of the way we work here.

WESTON. Not going to be too happy with the Hackman episode then, are they?

MR FLORIAN. It's nothing that doesn't happen at any other school in the country.

GILLIAN *heads off to the toilet through the door by the fireplace.*

WESTON. Only it happens here with such alarming regularity.

CLINTY. Do get to your point, Weston.

WESTON. I'm merely saying that if there were more discipline in the classroom, we'd have firmer control over the children, which in turn would put a halt to the hysterical happenings of this morning repeating themselves.

CLINTY. Spare the rod, spoil the child?

WESTON. Well, at least we'd all know exactly where we stood. Them as well as us. It's just as important for them to understand the parameters.

MR FLORIAN. You know my thoughts on corporal punishment, Mr Weston.

WESTON. Yes, Headmaster. But when it comes to running a classroom there has to be some rules.

MR FLORIAN (*good-naturedly*). Ahh, rules. But to what purpose, Mr Weston. To what end? Who gains more from rules you or the children? To rule, Mr Weston. You want to rule in your classroom? Do you want to be king of all you survey?

WESTON. No, Headmaster, I'm merely pointing out that –

MR FLORIAN. We must be careful of rules; rules have a way of ruling. These children are surrounded by rules, their whole –

There is a knock on the door.

Enter! Their whole lives, from the –

The door opens and standing there is RICARDO BRAITHWAITE, *a black, thirty-one-year-old West Indian. He's dressed smartly in his demob suit. Everyone turns and stares at him.*

Good heavens, Mr Braithwaite. I'd quite forgotten about you in all the excitement. Come in, come in, my dear fellow. Everyone, this is Mr Braithwaite. He's come to take a look at us – the school that is – with the prospect of joining our ranks if we pass muster.

All smile encouragingly to him. All except WESTON.

WESTON. Another sheep to the slaughter. Or should that be a black sheep?

No one says anything. The comment hangs in the air until the silence is broken by the school bell. Everyone starts to head out of the door.

MR FLORIAN. Always the way, I'm afraid, Braithwaite. Little matter! You can meet them all properly at lunch. Meanwhile, I too must abandon you. But do have a wander about the place. I'll join you just as soon as I can, then maybe we can have a chat about what you think of us. If indeed we are your cup of tea – no pressure. No pressure at all. Though I might add we suddenly find ourselves bereft of another member of staff – again. Rather careless I know, but these things happen. But as I said, no pressure. Tea in the urn! Cheerio!

MR FLORIAN *heads out of the door. Leaving* RICK *alone in the staffroom. He looks about the room. He walks over to the window and looks out. He goes over to the table and flicks a few pages of a paper. He just stands there not knowing what to do with himself. We hear a toilet flush.* GILLIAN *comes in and jumps when she sees* RICK.

GILLIAN. Arrrh!… I'm sorry you startled me –

RICK *smiles and proffers his hand.*

RICK. Ricardo Braithwaite.

She takes it and shakes it rather too enthusiastically.

GILLIAN. Gillian, I'm Gillian Blanchard. Lovely to meet you.

RICK *has to pull his hand away gently.*

Sorry…

Pause. They look at each other. He smiles.

RICK. I'm here to look at the school.

GILLIAN. Ah – you're from the divisional office, come to check up on us.

RICK looks confused.

RICK. No, I might be joining the staff.

GILLIAN. Oh, I see – Gosh, that was quick.

RICK. What was?

GILLIAN. You replacing our Mr Hackman. He's only been gone an hour.

RICK. I'm not here to replace anyone.

GILLIAN. Oh, hell – Of course you're not. That would be quick – and far too efficient. Maybe I should just come back in again.

She smiles.

Would you like a cup of tea?

RICK. Yes. Please.

GILLIAN proceeds to pour tea from a tea urn into a cup.

GILLIAN. Milk and sugar?

RICK. One sugar. No milk.

GILLIAN. It might be a bit stewed. There are some biscuits in that Oxo tin over there, if you fancy.

He walks over to the tin.

It's usually well stocked from what the girls in domestic science knock out. I'm afraid the taste varies from batch to batch and year to year – In fact, don't have a biscuit.

RICK. No?

GILLIAN. I think they were made by first years and they haven't quite grasped the concept of hygiene.

She passes him the tea.

Do sit down.

RICK. What happened?

GILLIAN. Sorry?

RICK. To your Mr Hackman?

GILLIAN. Oh, unable to handle the kids – so they say or rather Weston says. You may have seen him earlier – Weston that is – he's maths – with the beard.

RICK *smiles*.

RICK. Are the children difficult to manage?

GILLIAN. Hard to say really, I've only been here a couple of weeks myself. So I'm not the right person to ask. They seem okay.

Beat.

It is different; this school. You do know that? About the school – the headmaster?

RICK. I don't know anything.

GILLIAN. There's no corporal punishment for starters. Any form of punishment for that matter, and the children are encouraged to speak up for themselves.

RICK. Really?

GILLIAN. They write their own reports – on us and the school... Student councils, that sort of thing.

RICK. That sounds interesting.

GILLIAN. Unfortunately they're not always particularly choosy about what they say and the manner in which they say it. They can be rather alarming reads at times.

RICK. They unnerve you?

GILLIAN. No, not really. They're just so frightfully grown-up, some of them. The girls have a way of looking at me, sort of pityingly, as if they're so much older and wiser than I am. I think they're more interested in my clothes and private life than anything I try to teach them. They're obsessed with knowing if I have a boyfriend or not.

RICK. Maybe it's your youth, they're playing on your inexperience.

GILLIAN. You mean they can smell fresh meat.

RICK. I wouldn't say that.

GILLIAN. I would.

Enter CLINTY.

CLINTY. Hello again, just got to grab a couple of things.

She picks up a piece of newspaper, goes over to a cupboard and takes out a packet of Dr White's sanitary towels. She proceeds to wrap them up in the newspaper.

Sorry, Gillian, could I steal you away to fix a bath, for the Murphy girl. Kids are complaining of the smell again. Won't sit near her.

RICK. What's the matter with the child? Enuretic?

CLINTY *looks at him.*

CLINTY. Good God no! She's been wearing the same sanitary towel for days.

RICK. Oh, I...

RICK *is lost for words.* GILLIAN *inadvertently raises her hand to her mouth.*

CLINTY. Child stinks to high heaven. Fourteen years old and as helpless as an infant. Some mothers ought to be shot.

Beat.

(*Laughing.*) You should see the look on your faces! This is teaching, my dears. Front-line stuff. You're well and truly in the trenches here.

Scene Two

Same day. Staffroom. MR FLORIAN *leans over the staff table looking at a paper.* RICK *comes in.*

MR FLORIAN. Ah, there you are, Braithwaite. Had a good look about the place?

RICK. Yes.

MR FLORIAN. Do you know London at all?

RICK. I took some leave here during the war, so I know it as a tourist. And of course from what I've gleaned from Chaucer and Pepys.

MR FLORIAN. Yeeeeees… Well, I think Samuel Pepys would have a good deal more to add to his diaries, if he'd been here during the blackout! Now that would be a good read!

RICK. Indeed, sir.

MR FLORIAN. Now, before we take the next step, I want to outline how we do things here. You may agree or disagree. Either way I expect you to be honest and say so. That's part of my position on teaching. Honesty – clear and simple. If we can't be honest amongst ourselves, how on earth can we be honest with the children.

RICK. Yes, sir.

MR FLORIAN. Most of our children, have been classified as difficult. Their experiences in their junior schools, positive or negative, they carry over to us. That's five years of rules and regulations. Never having to think for themselves, learning everything by rote and God forbid, if a child can't keep up…

MR FLORIAN *takes* RICK*'s arm and walks him over to the window.*

Look at this place, Mr Braithwaite. All over this country, young minds are being shaped by similar stinking environments. Poverty, unemployment. We can't blame the war, things were just as bad before. How can we expect children who grow up in these conditions, to take seriously, anything we have to teach them. What do they care about arithmetic, when their main concern is whether they'll go

home to a hot meal – any meal for that matter. Us
threatening punishment means nothing to them. It's just
another endurance in a life full of daily endurances.

He turns to RICK.

What I'm trying to do here, is to create an atmosphere where
young people can feel safe, wanted and secure. Free to work,
play and express themselves. For a few hours of their day,
they will be guided by adults who will listen to them, who
care about their opinions, who try to understand without
condemnation. Well, there it is. I can offer you no blueprint
for teaching, it wouldn't work, especially here. You're on
your own. The rest of the staff, myself included, will always
be ready to help and advise if need be.

RICK. I don't know what the department has told you about
me, Headmaster. But I think it only right that you should
know, that I've had no experience of teaching or any form of
training.

MR FLORIAN. Oh, I know. I've seen your file.

RICK. Then you'll know that teaching was not my first choice
of profession.

MR FLORIAN. No; I should have thought that a man with your
outstanding qualifications would have chosen something
quite different for himself. Electronics, wasn't it?

RICK. Yes.

MR FLORIAN. Well, then it's our good fortune that you have
decided to teach for now.

RICK. I'm reading a lot of books on teaching and teaching
methods –

MR FLORIAN. Oh, my dear fellow, you don't want to do that.

RICK. No?

MR FLORIAN. Good heavens, no, I'd rather have you and all
that you've seen and done with your life, than some wet-
behind-the-ears novice with umpteen teaching certificates.
Now then, what is it to be? 'Is Barkis willing?'

RICK. Have you had any thought as to what class I'd be teaching?

MR FLORIAN *thinks for a moment.*

MR FLORIAN. You'll have charge of the top class.

RICK. Your Mr Hackman's class?

MR FLORIAN. Yes, our Mr Hackman. Unfortunately Mr Hackman, though a perfectly adequate teacher, was completely unsuitable for this kind of work.

RICK. Really?

MR FLORIAN. Look, I'm not offering you the booby prize, Mr Braithwaite. They're an important class, they need the influence of a good teacher, particularly as they'll be leaving us shortly. I think you're the man for the job.

Beat.

RICK. Then you can tell Peggotty, that 'Barkis is willing'.

MR FLORIAN. Good man!

The school bell sounds.

RICK. When would you like me to start?

We hear the sounds of excited children and doors slamming.
MR FLORIAN *heads out as* CLINTY *comes in followed by* GILLIAN *and* WESTON.

MR FLORIAN. I'm pleased to announce Mr Braithwaite is going to be joining the staff.

CLINTY. Good for you.

MR FLORIAN. I hope you'll all make him very welcome.

MR FLORIAN *heads out.*

Back in a minute.

GILLIAN. Which class have you got?

RICK. Hackman's.

WESTON. May the Lord God, have mercy on your poor soul.

He goes over to the fireplace and takes out his pipe.

I suppose the old man gave you all the old blather about these poor deprived angels?

CLINTY. Ignore him.

She holds out her hand.

I'm Vivienne Clintridge, domestic science, art and drama. Welcome aboard. It's not too bad here. They might bark but they don't bite. That's pretty good odds in my book. And regardless of anything else you might hear – Weston! – The old man knows exactly what he's doing.

WESTON. You'll be sharing PE duties with me, he did tell you that? There's no negotiation.

RICK. Well –

WESTON. – No, there's no crying off, I saw your lot doing track and field in the Olympics. So I know you can run and chuck things about!

RICK. I was about to say, I'll look forward to it.

Beat.

WESTON. Oh, will you now.

CLINTY. How wonderful to have a new man about the place.

WESTON *gives her a dismissive look and starts to light his pipe.*

WESTON. Careful, Clinty, your psyche is showing.

CLINTY. Always does when I'm close to a real man, Weston. Been in the country long?

GILLIAN. Clinty!

CLINTY. Only asking. Nothing wrong in a bit of background information, is there, Braithwaite?

RICK. Certainly not. I've been here since '39. I came to enlist.

CLINTY. Good for you. What service?

RICK. RAF. I flew fighters.

CLINTY. My brother was RAF Bombers... Didn't make it unfortunately.

RICK. I'm sorry.

CLINTY. Thank you.

WESTON. I didn't know we were that hard up, that we had people of your persuasion in the RAF. Canteen staff, was it?

RICK. I flew Spitfires actually… When I wasn't too busy polishing the mess silver.

GILLIAN. We had men from all over the Empire fighting and dying for us, Mr Weston. If you've forgotten just how big and diverse the Empire is, I suggest you sit in on one of my classes.

WESTON. Getting smaller by the minute, isn't it? I should think by lunchtime we'd have lost most of the Far East.

CLINTY. You didn't serve did you, Weston?

WESTON. Unfortunately, I have flat feet.

CLINTY. And a flat personality to match!

 WESTON *heads out of the room.*

 Glad you joined us, Braithwaite. Look, don't mind Weston, there's one in every staffroom and unfortunately he's ours.

 MR FLORIAN *pops his head around the door.*

MR FLORIAN. Come along, Braithwaite, we'll go and have some lunch.

 The lights fade and we hear King Perry singing 'Going to California'.

Scene Three

Lights up in the school gym. There are a number of BOYS *and* GIRLS *aged fourteen to fifteen. They are jiving to King Perry singing 'Going to California'. Others stand around watching. The dancers are extremely proficient as they exercise energetic moves.* RICK *and* MR FLORIAN *walk into the gym.*

MR FLORIAN. What do you think?

RICK. Erm…

MR FLORIAN. Their idea. Voted for by the student council. They're good, aren't they? Oh, well done, Pamela!

RICK. I'm impressed.

MR FLORIAN. Do you dance?

RICK. Are you asking?

MR FLORIAN *laughs.*

MR FLORIAN. Good heavens, no! I couldn't possibly expect you to keep up with me. Besides, I always lead.

RICK. You said they voted for this?

MR FLORIAN. Yes. Student council. Head boy and girl and their two deputies, all voted in by the other students. They're in on all decision-making here.

RICK. How far are we supposed to take this… student council?

MR FLORIAN. Sorry, not with you?

RICK. Well, what exactly are they allowed to vote for?

MR FLORIAN. Ah, yes. Good point.

RICK *waits for an answer but* MR FLORIAN *has turned back to watch the dancers.*

Oh, well done, Denham. I've never seen you do that before. I shall have to learn that.

He turns to RICK.

You see, Rick, by giving them autonomy in certain areas and including them on aspects of running things they're forced to think, not only of themselves, but what's good for their class, the student body and ultimately the school.

RICK. Democracy in action.

MR FLORIAN. Exactly.

RICK. I see.

MR FLORIAN. I know your worry, Mr Braithwaite. But they can't vote away subjects – interesting idea though, we should put it up for discussion? Are you hungry?

He leads RICK *off while trying to emulate* DENHAM's *dance move.*

Scene Four

We hear Chopin's 'Fantaisie-Impromptu'.

RICK *stands in front of the class. The* KIDS *sit at desks. Looking sullenly at him.*

RICK. Well, I thought that was a most interesting assembly.

Pause.

No one says anything. They just stare silently back at him. He turns and starts to write on the blackboard.

How interesting that the headmaster should use my favourite composer, Frederick Chopin. And John Keats, 'La Belle Dame Sans Merci'. A poem I too learned at school.

The blackboard now has 'John Keats 1795–1821'. Alongside 'Frederick Chopin 1810–1849'. He turns and looks back at the class. They are still staring at him.

Both renowned artists of the Romantic school. Does anybody know anything about the Romantic school?

The KIDS *continue to stare.* RICK *looks uncomfortable and puts down the chalk.*

DENHAM. Is it in Stepney?

RICK (*unsure how to take it*). Erm, no, what I mean is –

DENHAM. Then we wouldn't know anything about it. Would we?

Beat.

RICK. No – Well then...

MONICA PAGE. It's in Bromley-by-Bow. Three Mills – Near the brewery.

DENHAM. Naaah, it ain't.

RICK. Yes. Thank you... Now, the headmaster has told you my name, but it will be some little while before I know all of yours. So in the meantime, if I just point at you, I hope it won't be taken rudely.

MONICA PAGE. It's gotta be on the Whitechapel Road then.

RICK. It doesn't matter.

MONICA PAGE. Then why ask us? I've spent bleeding time thinking about it now, I have.

PAMELA DARE. Me too. I think it's on Brick Lane.

MONICA PAGE. By the synagogue?

PAMELA DARE. That's it.

RICK. It's really nothing that important. Now, I don't know anything about your abilities, so I'll begin from scratch. One by one I'll listen to your reading; so when I call out your name, will you please read anything you like from one of your school books.

RICK looks down at his register.

Erm... Denham?

He looks at the class. DENHAM *reluctantly stands. He's a surly-looking tough.*

DENHAM. Me, sir?

RICK. Could you start, please.

The GIRLS *find him amusing.*

DENHAM. What should I read?

RICK. Anything from one of your school books.

DENHAM. Which one?

MONICA PAGE. He's just said any bleedin' book, dummy!

DENHAM. He didn't ask you!

MONICA PAGE. I'd know what to bleedin' read if he did!

The others all laugh.

RICK. Thank you! Any book you have in your desk, Denham.

DENHAM *picks up the lid of his desk and looks.*

MONICA PAGE. Someone run down the bleedin' library for
him, for God's sake!

RICK. Would you mind your language, please.

More laughter from the others. DENHAM *produces a book.*

DENHAM. I've got this.

He holds up a book.

RICK. That'll do. Please start reading.

DENHAM. 'In… I… g-ot… bod… illy… in… to the… app…
le… baaaarel – barrel.'

RICK. Thank you, Denham. You can sit down now.

MONICA PAGE. That was worth the bleedin' wait.

RICK *looks at her.*

RICK. You seem to have a lot to say for yourself. Who might
you be?

MONICA PAGE. Monica Page, sir. Should I read for you now,
sir?

RICK. If you will, please.

She grabs at the book held by DENHAM.

MONICA PAGE. Gis' that –

DENHAM. Get your own.

RICK. It's *Treasure Island*, Monica. You should have your own
copy.

She reaches into her desk, looks, and pulls out the book.

MONICA PAGE. This it?

RICK *nods his head.*

What page?

DENHAM. Fifty-three.

RICK. It's of no consequence.

MONICA PAGE. Fifty-three. Here we go.

MONICA PAGE *gives a sniff, pushes out her breasts and starts to read. And in a BBC* Watch with Mother *voice, says:*

Are you sitting comfortably? Then I'll begin.

RICK. Yes, thank you, Monica.

MONICA PAGE.
'InIgotbodilyintothebarrelandfoundtherescarceanappleleft'

All the others start to laugh.

Get stuffed, you lot. At least I can read.

RICK. Thank you, Monica. You may sit down now.

MONICA PAGE (*pleased with herself*). I'm good, aren't I, sir?

RICK. Well, you read all the words, but didn't necessarily make any sense of them. A feat I doubt Robert Louis Stephenson himself could ever have imagined.

MONICA PAGE *looks to the class.*

MONICA PAGE. At least I read all the bleedin' words, you toerags.

There is sniggering coming from the back of the class, where some of the BOYS are turning back to look at DENHAM, who is showing something around to them. RICK strides over and snatches the item from one of the BOYS. RICK looks at it. Realises what it is.

DENHAM. Here, that's mine. Give us it back. You can't take that!

MONICA PAGE. Yeah, give it him back, sir.

RICK. If you insist on bringing such disgusting objects into school, you run the risk of having them confiscated.

DENHAM. It's the human body, sir. It's not disgusting, sir.

ROSE. Don't give it him back, sir. It's rude that is.

PAMELA DARE. I'll tell your mum you've got that, Denham.

MONICA PAGE. She's the one gave it to him.

They all laugh.

JANE PURCELL. No, that was 'is granny.

DENHAM. Me gran's the model!

SEALES. Jane Purcell's the model!

More laughter.

JANE PURCELL. Shut it, Seales, you coon!

DENHAM. You'd need more bleedin' ink than that pen's got to cover Purcell's knockers!

All the BOYS and some of the GIRLS laugh.

RICK. Thank you. You'll have this back at the end of the day, Denham. If I see it again in school, I will take it off you and dispose of it once and for all.

DENHAM. D'you find the female form disgusting, sir?

RICK *chooses to ignore this remark. He reads out another name.*

RICK. Seales?

DENHAM. Your dad wants you, Seales.

More sniggering. SEALES holds up his hand.

RICK. If you will please, Seales.

MONICA PAGE. Page fifty-three, wasn't it, sir?

RICK. It doesn't matter.

MONICA PAGE. Fifty-three, Seales.

SEALES. 'In I got… bodily… into the bar… reland… found there s… c… arse… ly s… carse… ly…'

RICK. *Scarcely. Scarcely* – It means few. Less.

SEALES. 'And found… scarcely – an apple left.'

The lights slowly fade. They come up and RICK *is standing looking out of the window. Another* BOY *is reading as badly as the others.*

ARCHIE. 'In I got bodily – '

RICK (*irritated*). Maybe start from another part of the book?

MONICA PAGE. At least get us out of this bleedin' barrel, it's getting a bit crowded in here!

The class start to laugh.

No wonder there's no more bleedin' apples!

RICK. Sit down, please.

RICK walks up and down the aisles.

I take it you would all agree that this book was written in English, your language and that of your ancestors? After listening to you read I'm not so sure whether you are reading badly deliberately, or that you are unable to understand or express yourselves in your own language. However, it may be that I've done you the injustice of selecting the worst readers. Would anyone else like to read for me.

PAMELA DARE *raises her hand.*

And you are?

PAMELA DARE. Pamela Dare, sir.

RICK gestures that she has the floor.

PAMELA *takes out a different book.*

'Oh what can ail thee, knight-at-arms,
Alone and palely loitering?
The sedge has withered from the lake
And no birds sing.

Oh what can ail thee, knight-at-arms,
So haggard and so woe-begone?
The squirrels's granary is full,
And the harvest's done.

> I see a lily on thy brow
> With anguish moist and fever-dew,
> And on thy cheeks a fading rose,
> Fast withereth too.

RICK.
> 'I met a lady in the meads
> Full beautiful-a fairy's child,
> Her hair was long her foot was light,

PAMELA DARE.
> 'And her eyes were wild.'

Beat.

MONICA PAGE. What the bleedin 'ell was that?

RICK. 'La Belle Dame Sans Merci'... Thank you, Miss Dare.

The school bell goes and the KIDS *suddenly become animated as they grab coats and bags and head out of the classroom.*

Scene Five

RICK *sits at his desk. Head in his hands. There's a knock at the door.*

RICK. Come in.

CLINTY *comes in carrying two cups of tea. She places one in front of* RICK.

CLINTY. Thought you might need this.

She perches herself on the edge of his desk.

Well, how'd it go?

RICK *smiles and takes a sip of tea.*

RICK. Oh, not too badly. One of the boys was a bit of a nuisance. Denham, I think it was.

CLINTY. Yes, it would be. Testing the waters. He's the leader.

RICK. I took this pen from him. It's a got a woman and –

He passes it over to her.

CLINTY. I know, turn the pen upside down, the ink runs away revealing her gobstoppers. If only they'd show as much interest in pens that have ink on the inside. By the way, what's your name?

RICK. Braithwaite.

CLINTY. That what your parents called you, Braithwaite? 'Braithwaite, lunch is ready!' I hope you appreciate that I didn't attempt the accent!

RICK smiles.

RICK. Ricky or Rick, you know, short for Ricardo.

CLINTY. Mine's Vivienne, but everyone calls me Clinty.

RICK. Clinty – It suits you. Sharp.

CLINTY. So I've been told.

RICK. I don't think I made much of a first impression on them.

She takes out a pack of cigarettes and lights up. Taking in the writing on the blackboard.

CLINTY. I don't know, Keats and Chopin? They're not going to forget that in a hurry. Did those dates come out of a book or did you have them stored in the old noggin?

RICK. The old noggin, I'm afraid.

CLINTY. Ouch!

RICK. But Clinty, the language they use and the… the smuttiness. I thought by showing them something of myself. My likes –

CLINTY. Nooooo!

RICK. What?

CLINTY. Never, never give of yourself so soon, at least not until they show an interest. Even then be wary or they'll find some way of using it against you.

RICK. You know it was easier trying to shoot down Messerschmitts.

CLINTY. Don't be so hard on yourself. We all know the old man's views and ideas about teaching, but it's us who have to put those theories into practice. And that, my dear, Ricky Ricardo, Braithwaite, is a different kettle of fish.

RICK. But am I expected to ignore it when I hear the way they speak to each other – to me?

CLINTY. Look at it from the kids' point of view, they come from homes where an order is invariably accompanied with a smack across the head. They might use bad language with their friends but they daren't try it at home, they'd get clobbered. So?

She looks at him pointedly.

RICK. So here they say and do anything they like without fear of any repercussions? And we're expected to accept it.

CLINTY. Precisely. So no matter how badly behaved they are, don't show it. Don't lay a finger on them, especially the girls or the next thing you know they'll be screaming high and low that you were interfering with them. But at the same time find some way of letting them know who's boss. We've all had to.

RICK. How did you show them?

CLINTY. I was born around hereabouts and they know it, so I can give as good as I get. It's a matter of finding your own balance... and theirs.

She looks up at the blackboard as she puts out her cigarette.

Keats and ruddy Chopin? Ohh, Ricky, Ricky, Ricky...

She takes up the teacups and heads out.

Scene Six

RICK *stands at the blackboard. He takes a second and begins to clean it off.*

DENHAM. You rubbin' off Chopin and Keats, sir? I thought you liked 'em?

MONICA PAGE. That's why he's rubbin' 'em off!

The KIDS *start to laugh.*

RICK. Our arithmetic lesson will be on weights and measures. As with our reading lesson, I am trying to find out how much you actually know so I can gauge how best to help you. So you can help me by answering questions as fully as you are able. Does anyone know the table weights of avoirdupois?

MONICA PAGE. 'Aver what?

DENHAM. I've had her.

MONICA PAGE. No you haven't, Denham. Ignore him, sir.

DENHAM. I've felt 'em!

NORA. Who hasn't.

MONICA PAGE. Shut it you, you scrubber!

NORA. Takes one to know one.

DENHAM. I've had her an' all!

NORA. In your dreams, Denham.

ARCHIE. In my dreams, actually!

ARCHIE grabs his cheeks and starts to pull on them making a wet, squelching sound. Some of the GIRLS scream out. This has the whole class in an uproar of laughter as other BOYS follow suit.

RICK. Quiet down, please!

The classroom goes quiet as RICK stares them down.

Avoirdupois. It refers to those weights commonly used in grocers' shops and suchlike.

DENHAM. Yeah, I know.

DENHAM *counts them off on his fingers.*

Heavyweight, light-heavy, cruiserweight, middle, light bantam, flyweight, featherweight.

The others are impressed, clap and cheer him. DENHAM stands and takes a bow. He blows on his nails and polishes them on his chest.

RICK. It's Denham, isn't it?

DENHAM (*mock surprise*). You've heard of me?

This has the others in fits.

RICK. Well, Denham, that's one way of applying the table of weights. Are you interested in boxing, Denham?

DENHAM *runs through a few muscleman poses, to the class's delight.*

DENHAM. I believe I can handle myself.

RICK. I see. Well, if you have at least learned to apply the table in that limited respect, it cannot be said that you are altogether stupid, can it, Denham.

There is a chorus of 'Oooooh!' from the class.

MONICA PAGE. I think he's just been rude to you, Denham.

The laughter stops as they all turn to RICK. DENHAM *gives him a dirty look.*

RICK. Is there anyone else who would like to say something about the table of weights?

A BOY *at the back puts his hand up.*

EDWARDS. Tons, hundredweights, quarters, pounds and ounces.

RICK. Yes. That's correct. What's your name?

EDWARDS. Edwards, sir. Edward Edwards.

DENHAM. They named him twice so he wouldn't forget.

RICK. Well, Edward Edwards, did you know that in places like the USA and the West Indies, although they use this same table of weights, they refer, to pounds or tons, but never to stones or hundredweights. So a man would speak of his weight as one hundred and seventy pounds, while here in England it would be twelve stone, two pounds which would put him at cruiserweight, wouldn't it, Denham?

DENHAM (*casual and authoritative*). Welterweight. God, who's the bloody teacher here?

The class laugh.

RICK. Thank you, Denham, welterweight. There are other weights in use. Troy weight is used by jewellers in weighing precious metals like gold, silver and platinum.

ESTHER JOSEPH. Diamonds are a girl's best friend, sir.

DENHAM. She's a Jew, so she should know. Probably got 'em stashed away all over the house.

FERNMAN. Shut it, Denham.

DENHAM. Oh, have I upset your girlfriend?

RICK. What did you mean by that remark, Denham?

DENHAM. What?

RICK. You referred to Miss Joseph as a Jew who would know about diamonds.

DENHAM *has no idea what* RICK *is talking about. He looks to the others.*

DENHAM. It was a joke.

MONICA PAGE. Yeah, it was just a joke.

RICK. Two years ago the war ended. We are now in the process of trying members of the Hitler regime for the systematic murder of men, women and children, whose only crime was that they were Jews. The victims are now being numbered in their millions, do you think that's funny, Denham?

DENHAM (*surly and defensive*). I didn't mean it like that, did I? – I just said –

RICK. That's how it begins, Denham... When people 'just say'. Don't let me hear you 'just say' it again. Any of you.

PAMELA DARE *stands up and runs her fingers through a glass-bead necklace around her neck.*

PAMELA DARE. Pearls is more my line, sir. Much more sophisticated, I think. A single string of pearls.

There is a chorus of 'Woooo!' 'Get her!' from the class.

DENHAM. Why didn't you say so, Pam. I've got a pearl necklace for you right here!

He grabs at his crotch and gives it a rub. Again, pandemonium.

RICK. I said enough!

RICK slams his book down on the desk. Everyone looks up at him.

I find it very interesting and encouraging to discover that you have a sense of humour, especially about something as simple and elementary as weights. As a matter of fact, you seem to find everything quite amusing. You were amused at your inability to read simple passages in your own language, and now you are amused at your own ignorance of weights. It is therefore clear to me that we shall have a delightful time together; you seem to know so very little, and are so easily amused, that I can look forward to a very happy time.

The KIDS are unsure of what RICK has just said. There are a few murmurs of discontent.

MONICA PAGE. Are you allowed to say that to us?

RICK. Say what, Miss Page?

Beat.

MONICA PAGE. That what you just said then.

RICK. Let's turn our attention to measurements, beginning with linear measurement. Do you know the table of linear measurement – Denham.

DENHAM. Don't know what you mean.

RICK. Well, before I explain I'll wait till you've all had your little laugh.

He stands there looking expectantly at them as they glare back at him.

No? Nothing? Not even a giggle?… Well, it's called linear because it deals with lines, inches, feet, furlongs and miles.

Scene Seven

RICK *is gathering up his books and putting them into his bag.* MR FLORIAN *comes in.*

MR FLORIAN. Ahh, good, there you are, Mr Braithwaite. Glad I caught you. Survived your first week. These are yours.

He hands RICK *a sheaf of papers. End-of-the-week reports.* RICK *looks bemused.*

By the children. Reports on you. Other things as well, but mostly about you and your teaching. They do them every week.

RICK. Ah, yes. Miss Blanchard did mention them.

MR FLORIAN. The idea being that if something matters to the child, he will go to great pains to set it down carefully and in great detail.

RICK. I see.

MR FLORIAN. Stands to reason that it'll go towards improving their written English, spelling, construction and style. In turn, we get to see ourselves through the child's eyes… How we are perceived by them. Our behaviour. Whether what we teach is of any interest.

RICK. I…

MR FLORIAN. Yes?

RICK. I'm sorry, I don't quite follow, Headmaster. We're the teachers. They're here to learn from us.

MR FLORIAN. Yes?

RICK. What if they don't like what I teach?

MR FLORIAN. Then examine your methods.

RICK. You won't find a child in the world who doesn't dislike some aspect of schooling.

MR FLORIAN. There are some aspects of schooling I don't particularly like myself but it doesn't stop me from attending.

RICK. But you're the headmaster.

MR FLORIAN. And that makes me what?

RICK. That makes you... What I mean to say is, it's not necessary for you to...

MR FLORIAN. Yes?

RICK. You're here to teach, is what I'm saying. You're... you're the headmaster for starters – You're not here to learn.

MR FLORIAN. Aren't I? I disagree completely with that statement, Braithwaite. There's not a day goes by that I don't continue to grow and learn; from my classes, the other members of staff but particularly from the children. Teaching should be a continuous flow of ideas. We must never stop questioning ourselves and our relationship with the young people in that room. A child might not care much for something, Mr Braithwaite, but it doesn't mean they can't be engaged.

RICK. You think I should tailor my classes, because my class may not like the way I teach?

MR FLORIAN. No, but if they're all alluding to the same thing, we should be confident enough to accept that we might be failing them. Do you think so highly of your teaching that you believe every child is held in rapt attention by your methods?

RICK. Well no, but I believe –

MR FLORIAN. Teaching is hard, Mr Braithwaite. You can't just clock in and out. This isn't a factory, though there are plenty of individuals in the education department would have us think that way.

RICK. I think what I have to teach is important. If some of the kids find it boring, then... well, so be it. This is a school and they are here to learn. It's my job to teach them.

MR FLORIAN. Try to see them as individuals as well. If you can understand their individual needs, that would go a long way to knowing what they require as students.

RICK. I'm limited to a timescale. I barely have time to get through what I have now.

MR FLORIAN. Education has to be organic. We have to find a way to bring something different into the room. If we aren't excited by what we teach, how in God's name can we expect these children to feel inspired by what we have to say to them? It's all common sense, you know.

RICK. Common sense?

MR FLORIAN. Common sense. A simple phrase. An overworked phrase that seems to have lost all meaning in its flippancy of use, but is in fact the answer to so much, when applied in the right circumstances. Have a nice weekend, Braithwaite!

He walks off.

We hear: 'Listen While You Work' by Eric Coates, the theme from Workers' Playtime. *Lights fade and we hear the sound of a bus. Projected on the cyclorama we see London as it journeys through the East End.*

Scene Eight

A bus seat has been placed on stage. RICK *is sitting reading.*
GILLIAN *comes and sits next to him.*

GILLIAN. Morning, Rick.

RICK. Miss Blanchard, good morning.

GILLIAN. Gillian, please.

> *He stands politely and moves along the seat to allow her*
> *more space.*

> Back for more, not put off by your first week, then?

RICK. I'm a glutton for punishment.

GILLIAN. That bad?

RICK. It was a trial by fire. But I was given some fine words of
advice from Clinty.

GILLIAN. Oh, taken you under her wing, has she?

RICK. It was a good place to seek refuge for a little while.

GILLIAN. Well, if you need another wing… Just come and
knock on my door.

RICK. Thank you. I will.

GILLIAN. How were your first reports?

RICK. Apart from the odd comment about having a new
'blackie teacher'… nothing. Certainly nothing that echoed
their behaviour in class.

GILLIAN. How was that?

RICK. Initially completely unresponsive to anything, but in a
strange way…

GILLIAN. Servile?

RICK. Precisely.

GILLIAN. They were just figuring out their strategy. Then they
became more aggressive, verbally challenging?

RICK. Yes. What should I expect next?

GILLIAN. It's hard to say. They've bypassed the silent treatment. With me it was 'Considering you're a bit of a toff, miss, your clothes don't look expensive – my nan's got a blouse just like that.'

RICK *laughs*.

What is it?

RICK. It's just all so far away from where I thought I'd be.

GILLIAN *looks quizzically at him as he continues to laugh*.

GILLIAN. Which was?

RICK. Before the war, I was a communications engineer. I specialised in new electronic technology.

GILLIAN. In England?

RICK. No, America.

GILLIAN. So how have you ended up here?

RICK. It's a long story, but basically it wasn't my ability that disqualified me from any of the jobs I sought…

GILLIAN. Oh.

RICK. Whereas I was perfectly acceptable in Air Force Blue over Germany, it didn't have the same effect when applying for jobs that would place me above white Britons in the workplace.

GILLIAN. I'm so sorry. You must have felt terrible.

RICK. It brought me firmly back down to earth, so to speak.

GILLIAN. Oh, you must feel so angry. I would be. Damn angry.

RICK. Only with myself, for believing the war may have changed people's attitudes. It's hard when ideals die. But I won't allow it to beat me. I know who I am and what I can do and one day I'll get where I need to be.

GILLIAN. Good for you – Sorry, that sounded rather patronising. I mean –

RICK. I know what you mean. Thank you.

He looks out of the window.

This is us.

The sound of the bus stopping as the lights fade.

Scene Nine

Lights up on a darkened set. RICK *and* GILLIAN *walk on. A shadow ballet. The* STUDENTS *are paired off, kissing and groping with the hurried abandon of teenagers. Each couple break apart momentarily as they become aware of* GILLIAN *and* RICK, *but continue as they pass by.*

Scene Ten

The staffroom. RICK *and* GILLIAN *enter.*

CLINTY. Morning, Ricky. Morning, Gillian.

WESTON *sees them and joins them.*

WESTON. Oh, I thought it was you two I saw getting off the bus together. Very cosy.

RICK. We've just witnessed the most – Well… On the stairwell. Some children were –

CLINTY. Weren't doing what children are supposed to do on Monday mornings. We know.

WESTON. I blame the rationing.

GILLIAN. There's nothing on ration down there, I can assure you.

CLINTY. I've seen a lot more than heavy petting in my time. Besides, they're hardly children, Mr Braithwaite. They know more about procreation than we ever did at their age.

WESTON. They probably witness the rutting rituals on a regular basis in the hovels they dwell in. Surely you should know that coming from your neck of the jungle. It's all on show over there, isn't it?

CLINTY. Oh, do shut up, Weston, you bearded buffoon. They're kids, Rick. We can't stop it. They'll only do it somewhere else. At least it's warm down there.

WESTON. And getting warmer by the minute, I shouldn't wonder.

RICK. But surely some decorum – decency –

CLINTY *starts to laugh.*

CLINTY. It's human nature, Rick. You can't fight it. It's inherent in the species. Men and women will look to each other.

WESTON. Although where you're from our four-legged friends haven't been left out of the equation by all accounts.

GILLIAN *and* CLINTY *both look at* WESTON, *slightly horrified.*

GILLIAN. Oh, for goodness' sake, Mr Weston.

WESTON. I subscribe to the *National Geographic*. It's all in there.

CLINTY. I bet that's not all you subscribe to either.

WESTON. Scientific facts. Who am I to refute years of academic research?

GILLIAN. You do come out with the most utter... rot sometimes. Do you spend the whole night thinking up ways to be obnoxious?

WESTON. At last! The worm turns! I'm sorry, my dear, I seemed to have touched a raw nerve. I didn't know you were both – I mean to say that when I saw you both get off the bus together, I merely presumed that it was a happy coincidence.

GILLIAN. If you don't have anything civil to say. Then say nothing at all!

GILLIAN *heads out of the room.*

WESTON. I'd be careful there if I were you, old man.

RICK. I beg your pardon?

WESTON. Our Miss Blanchard. She's cocked a feather in your direction.

RICK. What on earth are you talking about, Weston?

WESTON. I think you've worked some of your black magic on her. I've never seen her so animated. Can't blame her though, strapping young buck like you…

He picks up his briefcase and heads for the door.

Still, no good will come of it. They never do, these things. Not part of nature's way, old man.

WESTON *leaves the room.*

CLINTY. Why don't you knock his bloody block off. No one would blame you.

RICK. That's exactly what he's daring me to do. Believe me, I've heard it all before.

CLINTY. He's right about one thing though.

RICK. And that is?

CLINTY. Gillian. She likes you.

RICK. And I her.

CLINTY (*exasperated*). Oh, Chopin and bloody Keats and he still hasn't got a clue! I said she likes you, likes you!

RICK. I find that hard to believe. It's such a short time… we hardly know each other.

CLINTY. Time's got nothing to do with it. It never has. It's an instant reaction. And believe me, she's had one.

RICK. Oh.

CLINTY. Oh? Oh? Is that all you've got to say, you silly man?

She leans in conspiratorially.

Listen, lose the Keats – I've got a copy of *Lady Chatterley's Lover* hot off the press.

RICK. Isn't that book illegal?

CLINTY. Nothing's illegal in this country, Rick, just as long as you don't do it in front of the vicar or Queen Mary.

The school bell goes.

Scene Eleven

RICK *stands with his back to the class copying from a book onto the blackboard. The class are copying what he is writing. There is a lot of whispering going on.*

RICK. Can you keep the noise down, please. You can't possibly be able to concentrate with that racket.

He carries on writing. He slides the board along and starts to rub out some of his previous work. There is a chorus of groans.

MONICA PAGE. Sir! I haven't finished that one yet!

PAMELA DARE. Me neither, sir.

DENHAM. You can't expect us to write it as quickly as you, sir.

RICK. As I said before, if you spent more time concentrating instead of chatting, you'd have got it finished. Those of you who haven't been able to finish, stay in over lunch and copy it down at your own leisure.

SEALES. That's not fair, sir.

RICK. Life isn't fair, Seales.

PAMELA DARE. Sir, I'm just missing massive chunks.

RICK. Now, quietly put away your exercise books.

There is a clatter of desk lids and general noise.

I said quietly.

He takes a book down from a bookshelf.

I'm now going to read to you a poem by Rudyard Kipling. Some of you may know his work from *The Jungle Book* –

DENHAM. You'd know that one, Seales!

There is laughter from the KIDS.

RICK. Or the *Just So* stories. My personnel favourite is 'How the Elephant got his Trunk'.

He looks to see if there is any reaction.

'How the Leopard got his Spots'? 'How the Camel got his Hump'?

MONICA PAGE. I'll be gettin' the bleedin' hump in a minute if I have to hear another bleedin' poem.

RICK *ignores her.*

RICK. The poem I'm about to read is called 'If'. A poem that continues to provoke debate amongst scholars of literature, as to its relevance on the life we live today. Whether its sentiments can be applied in the modern world. 'If' by Rudyard Kipling.

He clears his throat.

'If you can keep your head when all about you
Are losing theirs and blaming it on you,
If you can trust yourself when all men doubt you
But make allowances for their doubting too;

DENHAM *gives* MONICA PAGE *a nod.*

If you can wait but not be tired by waiting
Or lied about, don't deal in lies.'

MONICA PAGE *picks up her desk lid and lets it drop with a loud bang. It makes* RICK *spin round to see what the noise was.*

MONICA PAGE. Sorry, sir, it's this bleedin' lid. It's broke, sir.

RICK. You're meant to be listening. Not opening your desk.

He returns to the poem.

    'If you can meet with triumph and disaster
    And treat those two imposters just the same;'

DENHAM *looks over at* FERNMAN.

DENHAM (*whisper*). Fernman...

He indicates his desk lid. FERNMAN *acknowledges him.*

RICK.

    'Or watch the things you gave your life to broken – '

FERNMAN *drops the lid of his desk.*

RICK *looks up.*

Monica!

MONICA PAGE. It weren't my bleedin' fault, it was him.

FERNMAN. Sorry, sir, I just reached in for my ruler and the bloody thing fell down.

MONICA PAGE. Nearly took his bleedin' fingers off, didn't it?

RICK *ignores the sudden and deliberate use of curse words.*

RICK. Then I'll have a word about getting them fixed.

MONICA PAGE. Well, it's about bleedin' time if you ask me.

PAMELA DARE. Mines the bleedin' same, sir.

She lets hers drop with a bang.

DENHAM. And mine, sir.

He lets his drop.

RICK. Thank you, you can stop now.

ROSE. Mine's on its last bloody legs too, sir.

Soon the whole class are demonstrating their lid defects.

NORA. Mine's been like this since the bleedin' juniors.

She lets it drop again.

MONICA PAGE. It's a bloody cheek if you ask me. How do they expect you to work on these bleedin things, if they're all bleedin' knackered?

DENHAM. It's a bleedin' disgrace.

MONICA PAGE. I've a good mind to bleedin' report this to the bloody education people. You can't get a bleedin' education working on a bleedin' death trap like this. I could be crippled for bleedin' life, I could.

RICK. I said that's enough!

MONICA PAGE (*mock shock*). Bleedin'ell –

The class stop dropping the lids and turn to RICK.

RICK. What did you just say?

MONICA PAGE. What, sir? Me, sir?

RICK (*controlled*). You swore. You're always swearing. Does it make you feel any bigger or more intelligent to use such words in front of me? Am I supposed to feel shocked?

MONICA PAGE. Weren't just me!

RICK. I don't care. It is you I'm addressing. Tell me, is this the way you speak to your mother and father? Do you all address each other in this manner in your home. 'Here's your bleedin' tea, Dad.' 'Where's my bloody dinner?' 'Where's that bleedin' Monica?'

The other KIDS *are sniggering.*

Is that the way in which you communicate to each other?

MONICA PAGE. No, it's not!

RICK. Then why do you think I should put up with it in my classroom!

She looks about at the class. No one says anything. She turns back to look at RICK.

MONICA PAGE (*flat and vicious*). Because you're not my bleedin' dad!

The school bell rings and the KIDS *all jump up and head for the door.* RICK *sits down at his desk, as* MONICA PAGE, *looking triumphantly at him, is led out by the others.*

As they exit we can hear: 'That put the black bastard in his place.' 'Cheeky bloody coon.' 'How dare he talk about my bleedin' parents like that?' 'Bloody monkey.' 'Good job he didn't try that on me.' 'You showed him there, Monica!'

Scene Twelve

The staffroom. RICK *is slumped in a chair. The others are sat about.* CLINTY *is laughing out loud.*

CLINTY. But Ricky, Kipling?! I thought we'd decided to abandon the nineteenth century?

RICK. I think the poem still has some points to make about the way we conduct ourselves as individuals.

CLINTY. Only if your name's Rupert and you want to go charging across the Somme, all colours flying!

GILLIAN. I think they reeled you in, Rick –

CLINTY. Hook, line and sinker, boyo.

GILLIAN. Did you get angry? Please, say you didn't?

RICK. I didn't show it.

CLINTY. Good. Thank heavens for small mercies. You're getting there, Rick.

RICK. Am I? It doesn't feel that way.

CLINTY. It's harder with your kids, Rick; there they are, about to leave and join the real world and already they're completely jaded. Don't be too hard on them. They mean no harm, really; they're not too bad when you get to know them.

RICK. How am I supposed to get to know them, if all they do is resist any efforts I make to help them?

WESTON *peers over his newspaper.*

WESTON. Why on earth does he need to know them?

GILLIAN. Really, Mr Weston, I think you should take a look at whether you're suited to working in a school like this.

WESTON. I didn't say the beggars shouldn't be educated. Lord knows you've got to have a basic education to work on a factory floor, these days. I just don't see what becoming their best friend will bring you – apart from possibly head lice and ringworm.

CLINTY. Bring back those dark satanic mills, eh, Weston?

WESTON. At least you'd be able to get a decent ruddy shirt off ration.

CLINTY. You carry on the way you're going, Rick.

GILLIAN. Yes, you're doing a splendid job. Don't be too downhearted.

RICK. Oh, I intend to.

WESTON. I thought you emancipated johnnies were all against Kipling, anyhow. Imperial prop of Empire and all that.

RICK. I happen to think Kipling's work goes beyond Imperial politics.

CLINTY. He was a writer of his time and of his class.

WESTON. Not you as well –

RICK. Precisely, Clinty, and that's no reason to discount and condemn everything he wrote.

Beat.

WESTON (*feigning boredom*). Oh, God, I feel like slamming my own 'bleedin'' desktop down.

RICK. I'm a product of the British Empire.

WESTON (*mock surprise*). You know, if you hadn't of pointed that out, old chap –

RICK. My ancestors' slavery was a product of it. This area where these children and their families have lived and made a living for generations, is a product of it too. The Empire will have far-reaching consequences on this nation, long after it ceases to exist.

WESTON. What's that got to do with this lot? Waste of ruddy time if you ask me. Teach 'em the basics and send 'em off.

RICK. I happen to believe its history is pertinent to their development. How they see themselves as citizens of this country and its relationship with the people of its dominions. It's imperative that they understand all aspects of what made them and this wonderful country. Especially the Imperial props.

The school bell sounds and RICK *stands to leave.*

'Take up the White Man's burden –

CLINTY *and* GILLIAN *start to laugh.*

Send forth the best ye breed –
Go bind your sons to exile
To serve your captive's need;'

WESTON. Are you taking the mickey?

RICK *heads for the door.*

RICK.
'To wait in heavy harness
On fluttered folk and wild –
Your new sort sullen peoples,
Half devil and half child.'

He exits to a cheer and a round of applause. Everyone laughing except WESTON.

WESTON (*flustered*). Well… There's no need to ruddy well encourage him!

This sends the WOMEN *into further fits of giggling.*

Scene Thirteen

RICK *enters the classroom. The room is filled with smoke. The* KIDS *are standing about joking and laughing.*

RICK. What the hell is going on here!

He pushes through the throng of KIDS *and looks at the fireplace.*

What is that?

SEALES. It's a ladies' whatsit. You know, sir… a thingamabob.

DENHAM. When they've got an oil leak down below in the engine room, sir.

DENHAM *points down to his crotch.* RICK *is disgusted by what he sees.*

There is sniggering behind him. He turns on the kids, fuming.

RICK. All of you boys out of the room now.

DENHAM. We haven't done anything.

RICK. Out, now!

The BOYS, *shocked at his anger, head off. The* GIRLS *start to follow.*

You girls stay behind.

The GIRLS *stop.*

Stand over there, all of you.

In the little while that I've been here I have become more and more dismayed at your general behaviour. Neither your deportment or grooming leaves me with any doubt that you care very much about your reputations, as you allow yourselves to be mauled about in public, like cheap dockside tarts. But this! I never thought I would meet women who were so lacking in dignity and self-respect, that they would permit themselves to be used in this disgusting manner.

ESTHER JOSEPH. But, sir –

RICK. I'm talking! There are certain things which decent women keep private at all times. Only a filthy slut would have dared to do this thing, and those of you who stood by and encouraged her are just as bad. I want that object removed and the windows open to clear away the stench.

The GIRLS *pick up the waste bin and scuttle out of the room.* RICK *opens his briefcase and starts to shove books into them. He begins to empty his desk.* MR FLORIAN *enters.*

MR FLORIAN. Ah, Mr Braithwaite –

RICK. That's it! No more! I'm tired of their utter disrespect, the utter contempt... How am I supposed to engage with these monsters! Monsters, yes. That's exactly what they are. I'm sorry if that offends you, sir. But I've had enough! There isn't a spark of common decency in any of them. Everything they say or do is... is coloured with viciousness and filth. Why? If it's not because I'm black, then why? Do they want me to be another Hackman?

MR FLORIAN. You will be if you walk out on them now. You'll just be turning your back on them like most other adults in their lives.

RICK. I can only be their teacher.

MR FLORIAN. We have to be much more than that.

RICK. Is it my fault they're growing up in slums?

MR FLORIAN. No it isn't. And that's not what I'm saying.

RICK. Then what are you saying? That I should just grin and bear it? I've been walking into that room every day for months now and –

MR FLORIAN. And you still haven't a clue who they are.

RICK. I've tried... I am trying desperately to understand them. But you expect me to throw everything I've ever learned, about how one conducts oneself, out of the window? There has to be some form of mutual respect in the classroom.

MR FLORIAN. No. You walk into that room and you already see yourself as being morally and intellectually superior to them. Don't you think they see that you're teaching?

RICK. I'm their teacher!

MR FLORIAN. It doesn't mean anything. If you walk in there wearing your cloak of authority, demanding respect because you think you're something special, then they will fight back. I'm glad they fight back. At least it shows they still have some fight left in them.

RICK. I just... I don't understand what it is you want me to do? I go in there and I feel that I'm failing every day. Failing them, and that's not what I want. I just end up spewing out facts and figures and it means nothing – to them and to me!

MR FLORIAN. It's not just you, the whole system's rotten. We need a bloody revolution, followed by an equally bloody civil war! We need to be radical. There's too much at risk for the future. For the way we want society to develop. It must start now. Here. With you and those children in your classroom.

RICK (*despondent*). I know nothing. Nothing about them. About teaching! I haven't a clue really, have I? I haven't got a bloody clue about any of this! And these useless bloody things! Have taught me nothing!

RICK o*pens his briefcase and shakes out his books.*

MR FLORIAN. Let's burn the bloody books! Burn, foul and vicious lies! Burn in the bottomless pits of hell! Oh, Mr Braithwaite, this is your Damascene moment! Feel it! Enjoy it! Bask in its light!

RICK *picks up his books and tosses them into the fire. Smoke starts to rise. He starts to whoop and dance about the room.*

I told you, Rick, there are no blueprints to this job. Now you will rise phoenix-like from the ashes. You are reborn, no longer a virgin. You will go forth and communicate. The shackles of established teaching methods lay broken at your feet.

RICK. How can I possibly speak to them, when I don't know them.

MR FLORIAN. Well, now it's time to find out!

RICK. You know something? They don't know me either.

MR FLORIAN. Exactly!

RICK. Ohh, but they're going to! I know how to conduct myself! How to behave civilly to people.

MR FLORIAN. Yes!

RICK. How to show respect, where respect is due.

CLINTY comes in.

MR FLORIAN. See! He walks!

There's smoke coming from the smouldering books.

CLINTY. What's all this smoke?

MR FLORIAN. We have a Pope!

RICK. No more 'bleedin'' and 'bloody', no more banging desks. And silence! I'll have that too. Silence on demand. They've pushed me about as far as I'm willing to go. Now I'll do a bit of pushing of my own!

He heads out of the room. MR FLORIAN *collapses happily onto the sofa.*

Beat.

MR FLORIAN. Rick seems to be settling in nicely?

ACT TWO

Scene One

RICK *stands in front of the class.*

RICK. Good morning, class. As your teacher, I think it right and
proper that I should let you know something of my plans for
you.

*He looks about the class. They say nothing but stare back at
him.*

My… my purpose in being here is to teach you and I shall do
my best to make it as interesting as possible in what little
time we have left together. If at any time I say something
which you do not understand or with which you do not
agree, I would be pleased if you would let me know.

Beat.

I'm going to, with your help, restructure the work we do here
together. I want us to discuss your future. About what
happens after you leave us this summer. Your hopes, dreams,
the practicalities of looking for employment. From now you
will be treated, not as children, but as young men and
women.

As he says 'women' he looks directly at the GIRLS, *who all
look rather sheepish.*

Both by me and each other.

Suddenly, MONICA PAGE *bursts in and sits down in her
seat. She pulls out a textbook and lets her desk slam back
down. Everyone looks at her. Then back to* RICK, *waiting for
him to explode.* RICK *casually walks over to the door.*

For instance, there are really two ways in which a person
may enter a room –

He opens the door.

One is in a controlled, dignified manner, the other is as if someone has planted a heavy foot in your backside. Miss Page has just shown us the second way; I'm sure she will now give us a demonstration of the first.

Everyone looks at MONICA PAGE.

Well, Miss Page?

MONICA PAGE, *unsure, gets up and walks to the door, opens it and steps out closing it behind her. Moments later the door opens and she comes back through gently closing the door behind her and goes back to her seat.*

Thank you, Miss Page. As from today there will be certain courtesies that will be observed at all times in this classroom. Myself you will address as Mr Braithwaite or sir – the choice is yours. The young ladies will be addressed as miss and the young men will be addressed by their surnames.

SEALES. Why should we call them miss, when we know them… sir.

RICK. Is there any young lady here you consider unworthy of courtesies, Seales?

All the GIRLS *turn to look at* SEALES *as if daring him to say anything.* SEALES *is unnerved by them.*

SEALES. Erm, no, sir…

The GIRLS *turn back to* RICK.

RICK. I've already made clear my pertinent points to the ladies last week. I will add that in the future they must show themselves both worthy and appreciative of the courtesies we men will show them. As Seales said, we know you. We shall want to feel proud to know you, and just how proud we shall feel will depend entirely on you. Now, gentlemen, there is nothing weak and unmanly about clean hands and faces, and shoes that are polished. A real man never needs to prove himself in the way he dresses or cuts his hair. Being a real man has nothing to do with muscle, fists and knifes. You have it in you to be a fine class, the best this school has ever known. But it is entirely up to you now. I am here to help, but ultimately the responsibility is on you. Now, are there any questions?

MONICA PAGE *puts up her hand.*

RICK. Yes, Miss Page?

MONICA PAGE. What about Mr Weston, sir? He's never tidy and he's always picking his nose when he thinks you're not watching him.

RICK. Mr Weston is a teacher, Miss Page, and we shall not discuss him.

There is a murmur of discontent.

I am your teacher, and I'm the one you should criticise if I fail to maintain the standards I demand of you.

The school bell goes. But the KIDS *continue to sit. Neither* RICK *nor they know quite why there hasn't been the sudden rush for the door.*

Beat.

That'll be all for now. Thank you for listening.

They slowly rise and begin to gather up their things and head out of the door. As the door closes, RICK *slumps back into his chair. A look of surprise on his face. As the lights fade we hear 'Hole in the Wall' by Albina Jones.*

Scene Two

The KIDS *are jiving away, watched by* GILLIAN. RICK *comes in and joins her.*

GILLIAN. I was never very good at this. I think it has something to do with a middle-class upbringing and an abject fear of showing my knickers in public.

RICK. And that's precisely what I want to ask you about.

GILLIAN. Flashing my unmentionables?

RICK. Could I ask a favour of you, Gillian?

GILLIAN. Ask away.

RICK. I told the girls in my class that you'd give them some tips on deportment, how to dress well and make-up.

GILLIAN. You said what?

RICK. It's one area of expertise I don't have, I'm afraid.

GILLIAN. What on earth are you talking about?

RICK. Let's get out of here.

They head into the corridor and walk towards the staffroom.

They want to start looking their best.

GILLIAN. And they said this to you? Apropos of nothing?

RICK. Well, not quite. You see... I told them they all looked and acted like dockside tarts.

GILLIAN. You said what?

RICK. It's a long story, but in short, they asked me how they were supposed to look. And I gave you as an example.

GILLIAN *starts to laugh.*

GILLIAN. Very well, count me in. They couldn't do any worse, I suppose. At least my sojourn at an expensive finishing school won't have been a complete waste of time.

RICK. Thank you, Gillian. You've saved my neck.

GILLIAN. How's it all going?

RICK. Well – I think. I'm trying to look at things differently...
My approach. I feel they're beginning to trust me a little.

GILLIAN. Really?

RICK. Well, they're speaking to me.

GILLIAN. That's always a good sign.

RICK. More importantly, I'm getting to know them a little more.

GILLIAN. But that's wonderful, Rick.

RICK. It's just Denham.

GILLIAN. It's always Denham.

RICK. He's antagonistic. He's the one pulling all the strings. I
don't think he's bullying them. That's just it, they all seem to
like and support each other in an odd way. But Denham...
he's the natural leader of the group and for some reason he's
resistant to me.

GILLIAN. Resistant to the charms of Rick Braithwaite? How
dare he.

RICK. They're good kids, Gillian. I didn't see it at first. Some
of them have a real thirst for knowledge. But their
expectations in life are so low.

GILLIAN. What else would you expect, growing up here?

RICK. It's not just that. It's as if... I don't know... They don't
have any dreams. It's assumed these kids are incapable of
achieving anything. The terrible thing is they believe it
themselves.

GILLIAN. There are lots of people from similar backgrounds
who've done very well for themselves, in all walks of life.

RICK. I bet they weren't encouraged to think that way in
school. We have to change that. We have to change the way
we communicate with them.

GILLIAN. Rick, I talk to these kids every day.

RICK. We don't – we don't, Gillian, we walk in and we start
laying down the law of learning. Life is a struggle. That's what

we should be telling them. You have to struggle for what you
want. But they need to believe that things are possible.

GILLIAN. We're worlds apart from them. No matter how much
we care.

RICK. We're not.

GILLIAN. Oh, Rick –

RICK. The only thing these kids lack, that we had, is ambition.
They need to be aware that there are possibilities. We
shouldn't encourage them to sit back and be content with
mundane lives working in a shop or on the docks or on the
market –

GILLIAN. What's wrong with that, if they're happy?

RICK. Nothing. Nothing at all. I just want them to know that
there are other choices. Yes, we teach them how to read,
write and count, but… It has to be more than that. There has
to be much more to teaching than that. They have to
understand that life is important – their lives are important,
that their contribution to life will be equally important. We
have to tell them about the world that exists out there. A
world and opportunities that are there for everyone.

GILLIAN. And from what you've experienced – are they there
for everyone?

RICK. Yes. I believe they are. I have to believe they are for my
own sake as well as theirs.

GILLIAN. It's a lovely idea. But most of them won't go further
than the end of their streets.

RICK. Fine. Then I'll walk to the end of the street with them
and tell them what else there is to see around the corner.

GILLIAN. I see Mr Florian's made a convert.

Beat.

RICK. It's just common sense.

GILLIAN. What?

RICK. Nothing, just something someone said to me once.

Scene Three

RICK *stands at the front of the class. There is a large object under a dust sheet beside him. The* KIDS *are intrigued by it. Suddenly, with a dramatic flourish, he pulls off the cover. Hanging from a stand is a laboratory skeleton. Some of the* GIRLS *and a couple of the* BOYS *scream. Then they start laughing and making fun of it.*

DENHAM. Cor blimey, he's gone and brought his dinner in.

All, apart from DENHAM, *are dressed smarter and are more groomed.* RICK *accepts the laughter and the jokes.*

RICK. Alright, if you would all just settle down.

DENHAM. That your girlfriend, sir?

The others laugh. RICK *smiles good-naturedly.*

RICK. Certainly not, Denham. As you should all know by now I wouldn't take out a lady so inappropriately dressed.

All except DENHAM *laugh.*

MONICA PAGE. That's funny that, sir, I didn't know youse could make jokes that I could laugh at.

PAMELA DARE. Why shouldn't he?

RICK. Is there anything you'd like to ask me about this skeleton?

DENHAM. Was she tasty?

RICK. She? Why do you presume it's a woman, Denham?

DENHAM. It ain't got nothin' between its legs, has it!

RICK. And nor would it, Denham. The penis is an organ and not a bone. It would have rotted away long ago. But you're right, this is the skeleton of a female.

PAMELA DARE. How can you tell, sir?

DENHAM. It won't shut up talking!

There is good-natured laughter.

RICK. Because the female pelvis is wider, for childbirth. The male is much narrower.

MONICA PAGE. My mum's must be huge, sir, there's ten of us!

More laughter.

EDWARDS. Blimey, I'm surprised she can keep anything in at that rate.

They all laugh.

DENHAM. What colour was she then?

PAMELA DARE. Denham!

RICK. No, Miss Dare. Denham has a point. How can we tell what race a skeleton is? Well, race is best identified by the skull. Caucasians have angled, gently sloping eye sockets and triangular nasal cavities. The Negro has a much more rectangular eye socket and a smaller, squatter nasal cavity. Asians typically have an oval-shaped nasal cavity and wider eye sockets.

DENHAM. What's she, then?

RICK. She was white.

DENHAM. Oh, right, then she can't be your girlfriend then, eh. Then again, it could be Seales' mum!

SEALES. Shut it.

DENHAM. You gonna shut it for me?

SEALES *says nothing.*

PAMELA DARE. I think she looks sad, sir.

DENHAM. What d'you expect, she ain't eaten for years!

MONICA PAGE. I think she should be in the ground. Proper burial. Decent like. It's not right, sir.

SEALES. Then how could we learn about skeletons and that, Miss Page?

RICK. A good point... Did you know doctors and surgeons used to have grave robbers steal bodies so that they could study and discover more about human anatomy?

SEALES. Like Burke and Hare, sir?

RICK. Exactly.

The class are fascinated.

MONICA PAGE. That's not right.

RICK. Do you know something else I know about this woman?

He produces a pipe from his pocket and sticks it in the skeleton's mouth.

She smoked a pipe.

They all start to laugh. RICK *too.*

It's true. Look here.

He points to her teeth.

You see here, this gap between the upper and lower plates. How the teeth are worn down. That is through the constant use of a pipe being placed in that position. She probably smoked from a very early age. Like you.

There are murmurs of awe at this information as various KIDS *examine the gap.*

So tell me. What do we know about this woman, so far?

PAMELA DARE. She was white.

SEALES. Of child-bearing age, sir.

RICK. What about her social standing?

MONICA PAGE. Her what, sir?

RICK. Was she a toff?

MONICA PAGE. Not smoking a blee–… I mean a pipe, sir.

SEALES. And she's small, sir. That's caused through not eating well, sir.

RICK. Correct, Seales. Bad dietary habits. Anything else?

DENHAM. She's bald.

The KIDS *laugh loudly.*

RICK. And…

Beat.

PAMELA DARE. She's one of us, isn't she, sir?

The KIDS *stop laughing and look to* PAMELA.

RICK. Yes, Miss Dare. One of you. Or rather how one of you ladies may have been over a hundred years ago.

The GIRLS *go quiet.*

This skeleton came from the London Hospital, just down the road. She was probably a native of this area. She's in her teens. From her size we can see she was probably malnourished. She has poor teeth. She smoked a pipe, which also tells us that she wasn't ever going to be having tea with Queen Victoria. We'll never know how she ended up like this. Maybe she was a derelict.

MONICA PAGE. I wonder what she looked like. You know, with skin and that? What colour her hair was?

SEALES. What do you think her name was, sir?

DENHAM. How the hell does he know, you berk.

RICK. We'll never know. But it was quite common for people of her period to use the names of members of the Royal Family.

PAMELA DARE. Yeah! My grandmother was named Victoria, sir. Like the Queen.

MONICA PAGE. My granddad was called Edward, sir.

RICK. After Queen Victoria's eldest son. Edward Prince of Wales. Who later became?

MONICA PAGE. King Edward the seventh, sir. He came to the East End, sir, my granddad saw him.

Beat.

DENHAM. My gran was called Albert.

RICK *ignores* DENHAM.

RICK. So you see, from merely looking at this one skeleton, we can learn not only about our own anatomy, but discover so much about our past and our social history as well.

PAMELA DARE. What do you think she wore, sir?

RICK. Well, why don't you take out your copies of *Oliver Twist*.

There is a chorus of moans from the KIDS.

I was about to say – and just look at the illustrations.

Excitedly they all open their desks and grab their books.

They're exactly the kind of clothes this young lady and you would probably have worn.

PAMELA DARE. I'd have loved to wear a big dress like that, sir.

RICK. I'm sure you would have looked very elegant in it, Miss Dare.

PAMELA DARE. Do you think so, sir, really?

RICK. I'm sure.

SEALES. I'd of liked a top hat like the Artful Dodger, sir.

The other KIDS *laugh.*

RICK. You should go along to the Victoria and Albert museum. They have a wonderful display of costumes there.

MONICA PAGE. Us, sir?

PAMELA DARE. Go to a museum on our own?

RICK. But why wouldn't you? It's not very far. South Kensington.

DENHAM. It wouldn't happen. We don't go to places like that.

PAMELA DARE. Couldn't you take us, sir?

RICK is unsure how to respond to this.

SEALES. Yeah, sir. We could go with you.

The others except DENHAM *join in the plea.* RICK *looks at them.*

DENHAM. Well, sir? Are you gonna take us then?

RICK looks at them.

RICK. Well, I could certainly put it to the headmaster. It's worth a try. He can only say no.

The KIDS *cheer.* DENHAM *gives* RICK *a dirty look.*

DENHAM. One other thing.

RICK. Yes, Denham.

DENHAM. Regarding clothes and that. We've got this book at home and it's got blacks in it dancing about with nothing on. My gran says they're all 'bare-arsed where they come from'. Are your parents like that?

All the KIDS *look at* RICK *as he is challenged to respond by* DENHAM.

RICK. I think what your Granny Albert is referring to, Denham –

The other KIDS *laugh at this joke.*

RICK *smiles.*

Is that some people in very hot climates prefer to wear next to nothing. Which may seem odd to us and our customs but is perfectly natural to them. As for my parents? Well, they both studied at Cambridge, so I would have thought it rather chilly to be wandering about its precincts totally naked. Besides, my family come from British Guyana where the custom is to be fully clothed at all times, unless of course you're in the bath.

The other KIDS *laugh at this. The school bell goes and the kids head out in high spirits.* GILLIAN *heads into the classroom.*

GILLIAN. They're happy about something.

RICK. I want to take them on a trip.

GILLIAN. Really, where?

RICK. The V&A, to see the costume exhibition.

They enter the staffroom.

Scene Four

The staffroom.

WESTON *is sitting reading the paper.*

CLINTY *is sitting drinking tea and reading and smoking a cigarette.*

GILLIAN. Goodness, are you sure you want to do that?

CLINTY. Do what?

RICK. Take my children on a field trip.

WESTON. Good God, have you brought your family over here already?

As usual RICK *ignores him.*

RICK. What do you think, Clinty?

CLINTY. I don't think the old man will allow it. But I think it's a great idea.

RICK. Good for you, Clinty.

WESTON. You want to lead the great unwashed into the real world? Don't we have to give a year's notice for something like that? So they can screw everything down.

RICK. I think it would be interesting for them to see some of the things we've been talking about in class.

WESTON. God protect us from reformers. I swear this is missionary zeal in reverse! Leave them alone, man, we like our working class as they are. Two world wars have already given them strange notions of equality as it is.

CLINTY. Oh, do shut up, Weston. Where're you thinking of taking them, Rick?

RICK. The Victoria and Albert museum.

WESTON. All of them?

RICK. All of them, Weston. Fancy joining us?

WESTON. Rather tear off my own testicles, old boy.

CLINTY. I think they'll have a wonderful time, Rick.

WESTON. Are you going to be able to manage them?

RICK. I manage them here, don't I?

WESTON. I dare say you do. But this will be very different. Like taking the Mongol hordes to the Ballets Russes.

RICK. That's a wonderful idea, Weston – the ballet, I hadn't thought of that. Maybe if this trip goes well.

WESTON. You're doomed. There's going to be rape and pillage the likes of which have not been seen in London since the Vikings! Lock up your daughters and your livestock, here comes Green Slade School!

MR FLORIAN *comes in.*

RICK. Headmaster, just the man I want to see. I wondered if it would be possible for me to take my class on a field trip.

MR FLORIAN *looks at* RICK.

MR FLORIAN. Outside the school?

RICK (*puzzled*). Yes.

MR FLORIAN. With your class?

RICK. Yes.

MR FLORIAN. How far are we talking?

RICK. South Kensington.

MR FLORIAN (*dramatically horrified*). 'But there be dragons there, Rick!'

RICK *smiles.*

I wouldn't advise it, Rick. I'm not saying never. You're settling in nicely but taking them across London on your own is another matter altogether.

RICK. I'd like to try nonetheless.

MR FLORIAN. I'll tell you what, if you can persuade another member of staff to accompany you –

GILLIAN (*enthusiastically*). I'll go.

Everyone turns to her. CLINTY *smiles enigmatically and slips* RICK *a sly wink.*

MR FLORIAN….I'll say yes.

RICK. Would you, Gillian?

GILLIAN. Yes. I'd love to.

MR FLORIAN. There it is then. Permission granted. Good luck and Godspeed. Just get me a list of names and the date you intend to travel on and we'll hit the school funds for tickets and tuck!

WESTON. The Geneva Convention applies to all prisoners.

MR FLORIAN heads out of the room.

CLINTY. Well done, Rick. Now, plan it carefully down to the minutest detail. Logistical ramifications and all that. Leave nothing to chance. Think of yourself as General Eisenhower on D-Day.

WESTON. Let's just hope it's not Dunkirk.

The lights slowly fade as Vera Lynn sings 'White Cliffs of Dover'.

Scene Five

Victoria and Albert Museum.

Interiors of the V&A are projected on the stage.

RICK *enters wearing a rain mac. He is followed by* GILLIAN *and the* KIDS. *The class have really pushed the boat out on dressing for the occasion – all, that is, except* DENHAM. *They all look very excited a little bit nervous and awed.*

MONICA PAGE. God, it's full of toff kids, isn't it, sir?

RICK. You have every right to be here as well, Monica.

PAMELA DARE. I haven't heard anyone talkin' like me, sir.

RICK. So what? You're all well behaved and well turned-out all of you. My goodness but you all look very smart. I'm very proud to be here with you today. You make me look good.

They all smile at this acknowledgement of their efforts.

PAMELA DARE. You look very smart and handsome too, sir.

RICK. Thank you, Pamela.

PAMELA DARE. I feel a bit scared here, sir. Could I walk about with you.

RICK. There's no need for any of you to feel intimidated.

SEALES. It's a public museum, Miss Dare. Isn't it, sir?

RICK. That's right. Okay, quiet a moment, please; you all have paper and pencils. I want you to go and explore. Note down what you find especially interesting so we might talk about it later back at school. If in the event we become separated, we'll meet back here at 12 p.m.

DENHAM. What if I don't find anything interesting, sir?

RICK *takes a moment.*

RICK. Then you won't have to write anything down, will you, Denham?

DENHAM. I'll be bored.

RICK. Yes, you will, won't you. Now, just be aware that other people are here enjoying the museum as well as you. So let's respect that and keep the noise down to a minimum. Well, what are you waiting for? Go, enjoy yourselves.

The class scatters excitedly about the stage. Images of the exhibits are projected. Not only the costumes but exhibits from all over the world.

GILLIAN. Do you think that's wise, letting them wander off like that?

RICK. I shouldn't think they'll get into too much trouble.

GILLIAN. They like you, Rick. You're good with them.

RICK. They're growing on me.

GILLIAN. I think Pamela Dare has a real crush on you.

RICK *laughs.*

RICK. For heaven's sake, Gillian.

GILLIAN. She's no child, Rick. She's almost a woman. It's quite common. I dare say a few of my juniors are taken with me – I hope they are – I should be very disappointed if they weren't.

She smiles.

But Pamela, I would definitely say, has fallen in love with you.

RICK. It had never even crossed my mind.

GILLIAN. Of course it hadn't. I had a crush on my art teacher at school, for years. And believe me I played out every romantic scenario in the book. You know, he never so much as gave me a second glance.

RICK. But I haven't done anything to encourage it – I mean –

GILLIAN. You didn't need to. Look at the rest of the men we have in school. Mr Florian, Weston. Then along comes Mr Rick Braithwaite. Kind, generous, smartly dressed, big, broad and handsome.

RICK. Really, Gillian.

GILLIAN. You've shown her respect. I can hear it when she talks about you. 'Sir said this.' 'Sir said that.' Just be patient with her, Rick, she's only just finding out she's a woman. You're turning out to be her ideal man.

RICK. It just never occurred –

GILLIAN. I feel sorry for any other man who comes along and doesn't live up to your standards. They won't stand a chance with her. Do you know something else, Rick?

RICK. What's that?

GILLIAN *moves closer to him.*

GILLIAN (*smiling*). I completely agree with her.

RICK. Oh?

GILLIAN. In fact, I find myself to be a little bit jealous.

There is a moment when it looks as though they are about to kiss. Suddenly they become aware that SEALES is standing there watching them.

RICK. Yes, Seales?

SEALES. I was just wondering if I could ask you something, sir.

RICK. Yes, Seales.

SEALES *looks at* GILLIAN, *she takes the hint.*

GILLIAN. I'll just go and see how the others are getting on.

She walks off.

RICK. What is it you wanted to ask me?

SEALES. I... I was watching you, sir, with Miss Blanchard, sir.

RICK. Yes.

Pause.

SEALES *looks as if he's about to change his mind as to what he is about to ask.*

What is it, Seales?

SEALES. Do you think that it's okay... For a black man and a white woman to be together, sir?

RICK *did not expect this.*

RICK. I... don't understand what you mean, Seales...

SEALES. It don't matter, sir...

He turns to go back to the others.

RICK (*unsure where this is leading*). Your mother's white, isn't she, Seales?

SEALES. Yes, sir. My dad's from Nigeria, sir.

RICK. Then I'm not sure what you want to know, Seales.

SEALES. It's what people say, sir. About me mum, sir.

RICK. Your parents' relationship has nothing to do with anyone else but them. Has someone said something in school to you?

SEALES. No, sir... Me mum's gone into hospital, sir. Some woman in the next bed saw me and my dad when we went to visit her, sir... She said it was unnatural – inhuman, that it made her want to throw up.

RICK *is angry and unsure what to say.*

RICK. Do you think it's unnatural for two human beings to love each other, Seales?

SEALES. No, sir.

RICK. Then that's all that matters. The world is full of such narrow-minded, bigoted people, Seales. They seem to have already forgotten that we fought a world war to bring an end to such philosophies. You can fall in love with whoever you damn well please and if anyone says anything to the contrary, you tell them to go to hell!

SEALES. Yes, sir.

RICK. Women like your mother are very special, Seales. Always remember that. They put up with a lot. Your father is a very lucky man to have found her.

SEALES. Thank you, sir, I think he knows that.

RICK. Good for him. Now, go on, off you go and join the others.

GILLIAN *comes back over. They both stand looking slightly embarrassed.*

GILLIAN. What's the matter, Rick?

RICK. Nothing.

GILLIAN. Was it because of what I said? I'm sorry, I just wanted to –

RICK. You don't have to explain anything.

GILLIAN. I do have a tendency to run off at the mouth. Just jump in, it was stupid of me – Sorry – Oh, I have spoilt it now... Don't be angry with me –

RICK. Far from it. I'm glad you brought it up.

GILLIAN. Let's just pretend that I didn't say anything.

RICK. I don't want to do that either.

GILLIAN. Really? Nor do I.

RICK. But you know this kind of thing isn't easy.

GILLIAN. I think I know what I'm letting myself in for.

RICK. Do you?

GILLIAN. Does it matter?

RICK. You see, I've been in this situation before.

GILLIAN. Then I shan't feel so alone.

RICK. I hope not... Come on, we'd better go and find those kids.

Scene Six

The gym.

The BOYS *come running on in their gym kits, pushing a wooden vaulting horse. They stand around as* DENHAM *ties* ARCHIE*'s arm up in a sling.* FERNMAN *stands by the door.*

ARCHIE. Oh, come on, Denham, this isn't fair.

DENHAM. Shut it! No one asked your opinion.

SEALES. He's right, though, Denham. You could hurt him.

DENHAM. Remember whose side you're on, Seales. That goes for the rest of you and all. I'm gonna teach that wog a lesson he won't forget. He's got it coming.

FERNMAN. He's here!

They all line up as RICK *comes in. He has removed his shirt and is wearing a vest.*

RICK. Okay, let's start up with a bit of running on the spot.

DENHAM. Please, sir, could we do some boxing, sir? We never do any with Mr Weston, sir. He always makes us do the vaulting.

RICK. Very well, get the gloves and sort yourself out into pairs.

DENHAM. My partner's hurt his hand, sir?

DENHAM *points out* ARCHIE's *arm.*

Will you have a go with me, sir.

RICK. You can wait and have a bout with Potter or one of the others.

DENHAM. They'll be knackered, sir. I don't mind having a knock-about with you.

ARCHIE. Go on, sir, take him on!

FERNHAM. Yeah, there's nothing of him, sir!

RICK. No, Denham, you'll have to skip it for today.

DENHAM. You're not scared of me, are you, sir?

DENHAM *looks at the others. The others look at* RICK, *as if he chickened out. Even the ones who were against the fight initially.* RICK *realises he can't not fight* DENHAM *now.*

RICK. Very well, Denham. Put your gloves back on.

DENHAM *smiles at* POTTER *who slips the gloves back onto* DENHAM's *hands.*

DENHAM *turns and starts to dance over to* RICK, *who has taken a defensive position. They act out a few moves.* DENHAM *shows how he outclasses* RICK *with a few body blows. The rest of the lads are egging on both boxers.* DENHAM *lets* RICK *have another series of blows to the upper body. Again* RICK *reels backwards.*

SEALES. Come on, sir, go after him!

Suddenly, DENHAM *hits* RICK *squarely in the mouth.*

ARCHIE. Keep your guard up, sir!

RICK *has blood coming from his mouth. He looks at it and heads back to* DENHAM. DENHAM *attempts another volley of blows, but leaves himself open and* RICK *seizes the opportunity and sends a punch right in the stomach.* DENHAM *drops to the ground immediately, coughing.*

FERNMAN. Bleedin' 'ell!

SEALES. He's Joe Louis! The Black Bomber himself!

RICK. Potter, help him up. Seales, collect up the gloves. You others start running on the spot.

The others suddenly jump to the running on the spot. RICK slips the gloves off his hands and goes over to DENHAM.

Come along, Denham, you must have taken plenty of punches like that. I just got in a lucky shot.

DENHAM. No it wasn't, you're good. You got me good and proper.

RICK. Take yourself off to the washroom and soak your head. You'll feel much better afterwards.

DENHAM. Yes, thank you, sir.

RICK. Fernman, go with him.

Scene Seven

Staffroom.

RICK *is standing talking to* CLINTY. WESTON *is sat in his usual chair reading the newspaper.* GILLIAN *comes in. She goes over and casually puts her arm across* RICK*'s back.* WESTON *sees this and gives his newspaper a shake.*

GILLIAN. Rick, my parents are expecting us at the weekend.

RICK. Lovely, I look forward to it.

CLINTY. Are you going to Pangbourne?

GILLIAN. Yes, for his sins. My parents want to meet him.

WESTON. I'd like to be a fly on the wall at that little powwow.

Everyone ignores him.

CLINTY. You'll love it, Rick, it's charming. Take some good walking shoes – Take him up on the downs, Gillian. Get some good clean air into his lungs.

There is a knock at the door.

WESTON. Enter!

SEALES *come in and stands by the door.*

Speak!

SEALES. Excuse me, sir, but Miss Dare and Miss Page were wondering if they could have the netball.

RICK. Yes, of course, Seales.

RICK *goes over to the cupboard and pulls out the ball and throws it over to* SEALES.

There you go.

SEALES *catches it and leaves.*

SEALES. Thanks, sir.

WESTON. Miss Dare? Miss Page? Good lord, Braithwaite, I hope you don't expect us all to address them like that? There's no Brownie points in it, you know?

RICK. What you do in your classroom is not my concern, Weston. But if you come into mine, I expect you to behave as courteously as the young men and women of my class will be to you.

CLINTY. It must be rubbing off on the other kids. Some of mine are calling the girls miss.

WESTON. Damned creepy if you ask me. I won't have it. Good God, you've got to know where you stand with 'em.

RICK. I believe basic manners in the classroom go a long way to making our job a lot easier. Mutual respect is important for the learning process.

WESTON. God, you're beginning to sound like the old man.

RICK. I'll take that as a compliment.

WESTON. Look, Braithwaite, I don't know how they went about it where you're from. Probably taught you too bloody much for your own good. But here, I say stick it on the blackboard and if they don't get it – tough. We're not here to turn out academics. Not in this school anyway.

RICK. Why not? Where 'I came from', Weston, we had half the facilities that you have here. Barely two rooms in the whole school. But what we did have were dedicated teachers who wanted the best for us. Irrespective of colour or class.

The school bell goes.

WESTON. Thank God, saved by the bell – or not in my case. I've got your lot for PE.

The others head out of the door as MR FLORIAN *comes in.* GILLIAN *gives* RICK *a rub on the back as she leaves. This is noticed by* MR FLORIAN.

MR FLORIAN. Do I sense romance in the air, Braithwaite?

RICK *smiles.*

I'm so pleased. You make a lovely couple.

RICK. You think so?

MR FLORIAN. You should think of settling down. Starting a family. Time to put the war behind you.

RICK *starts to laugh. He pours himself some tea.*

Thought any more about what you're going to do about this place?

RICK. No, not really.

MR FLORIAN. The end of the year will be here before you know it.

RICK. It's gone so quickly. I've barely touched on what I was hoping to do.

MR FLORIAN. You're really getting involved with these children, aren't you?

RICK. I suppose we all are, one way or another.

MR FLORIAN. You're more involved than most.

RICK. I think Gillian's pretty serious.

MR FLORIAN. I think she's just passing time. She doesn't know it yet. That may make me sound rather chauvinistic but

I assure you I'm not. Just my experience of teachers. I like Gillian, but I've seen teachers come and go. Not you, you've got a vocation.

RICK. My being here is just an accident. I'm not doing what I'm supposed to be doing.

MR FLORIAN. Aren't you?

RICK (*unsure*). No…

MR FLORIAN. You're a communicator, Rick, and communicators are few and far between. Every child remembers one teacher. No matter what their school experiences may be, there's always one that stands out from the rest. The one they'll remember for the rest of their lives. And whether you like it or not, you're going to be one of them.

RICK. I'm flattered.

MR FLORIAN. I don't flatter. It's a wonderful gift and sad for it not to be used with children. Especially children like ours, who, I think, need it more than most.

There is furious knocking at the door.

Come in.

The door opens and SEALES *stands there looking excited.*

SEALES. Sir, you've got to come quickly, Denham said he's going to kill Mr Weston. He's gonna smack his brains in with a bit of the vaulting horse!

RICK *heads quickly for the door.*

Scene Eight

The classroom.

DENHAM *and the other* BOYS *troop into the classroom still in their gym clothes.* RICK *follows them in. He is carrying the leg of the vaulting horse. The* BOYS *sit at their desks.*

RICK. Now, will somebody please explain to me what happened in the gym?

DENHAM. It was Weston's fault.

RICK. Mr Weston.

DENHAM. He knows Archie can't do the vault. He never does the vault.

EDWARDS. He made him do it, sir.

SEALES. Archie didn't want to, sir. Mr Weston just kept on at him, sir.

DENHAM. Kept saying, 'Come on, boy!' 'Jump, boy!' 'What's wrong with you!'

SEALES. He wouldn't leave off on him, sir. Just kept shouting and shouting at him.

SEALES. It wasn't right what he was doing, sir. Teachers shouldn't behave like that, sir. You know that, sir… Archie… He was crying, sir. You can't do that to someone…

ARCHIE. He just ran at the vault, sir.

SEALES. He didn't stand a chance. He just went flying. Denham just got angry, sir.

RICK. There is no excuse for your shocking conduct in the gym.

They all look shocked.

DENHAM. It was him that started it!

RICK. Mr Weston was the master in charge. Anything that happened in the gym was his responsibility.

DENHAM. But Archie told him he couldn't do it and he made him, sir.

RICK. I'm not concerned with Mr Weston's conduct, but with yours.

DENHAM. I thought Archie had really hurt himself. He was screaming on the floor.

RICK. So you rushed in like a hoodlum with your club to smash and kill, is that it? Suppose this was a knife or a gun, what then?

SEALES. Denham was narked, sir. We all were, seeing Archie on the floor like that, crying.

RICK. You're missing the point. Very soon you'll be at work and a lot of things will happen which will annoy you. Are you going to resort to knives or clubs every time you get upset or are angered?

ARCHIE *comes back in followed by the* GIRLS, *obviously excited by the news.*

Come in. All of you, sit down. How are you feeling now, Archie?

ARCHIE. Better, sir.

RICK. Good lad. Sit yourself down.

ARCHIE. It wasn't Denham's fault, sir.

MONICA PAGE. Course it weren't.

ARCHIE. Mr Weston's always picking on me, sir. He knows I can never get over the vault.

RICK. Denham, you were discourteous to Mr Weston, and I believe you owe him an apology.

This causes consternation amongst the class.

DENHAM (*angry*). Why should I apologise? It was Weston that was in the wrong. You know he was in the wrong – I could see it in your face what you thought.

DENHAM *stands up angrily.*

What's wrong is wrong. That's what you say, isn't it? Or do your rules only apply if you're a teacher?

The whole class look at RICK.

RICK. That was a fair question. Although you will agree it was put a little, shall we say, indelicately?

RICK *smiles and so too does* DENHAM.

Are you truly pleased with the way you behaved with Mr Weston?

DENHAM. No, sir. But I couldn't help it, sir.

RICK. That may be so, Denham. But you agree your actions were wrong.

MONICA PAGE. Then what about Mr Weston apologising, to Archie?

PAMELA DARE. Yeah, what about him, sir?

There is a general consensus from the KIDS.

RICK. My concern is how your actions will be perceived.

SEALES. It's easy for you to talk, sir. Nobody tries to push you around.

RICK *gets up and walks over to where* SEALES *is sitting.*

RICK. I've been pushed around, Seales, I've been pushed until I began to hate people so much that I wanted to hurt them, really hurt them. I think you all know what I'm talking about.

He looks at the class.

I know how it feels to hate. But the one thing I learned is to try always to be bigger than the people who hurt me.

RICK *realises the class has gone quiet and are listening to him. He walks to the front of the class.*

The point, Denham, is whether you are really growing up and learning to stand on your own feet. In this instance, you lost your temper and behaved in an inappropriate manner to your teacher. Do you think you're man enough to accept you were wrong and go and apologise to him?

Beat.

Everyone looks at DENHAM.

DENHAM. Yes, sir.

Beat.

RICK. It's always difficult to apologise, especially to someone you feel justified in disliking. Remember you're not doing it for Mr Weston's sake, but your own.

DENHAM *stands up.*

DENHAM. Is he in the staffroom, sir?

SEALES *stands up too.*

SEALES. Sir, I think if Denham's big enough to apologise, I am too.

The other BOYS *stand up as well.*

RICK. Very well, gentlemen. You'll find Mr Weston in the staffroom.

The BOYS *all troop out behind* DENHAM.

RICK *sits looking at the* GIRLS *and* ARCHIE. *We can see the* BOYS *walk to the staffroom. Knock and go in.*

MONICA PAGE. I'm not saying anything me, sir. No, sir.

RICK. Good.

Beat.

MONICA PAGE. Nothing.

RICK. I'm glad.

MONICA PAGE. But... from what I gathered happened down there, there were – what's it me dad's lawyer said... Extenin...

RICK. Extenuating circumstances?

MONICA PAGE. That's it, sir. Extenuating circumstances in this case.

RICK. Yes, Miss Page. You're right, there were.

MONICA *is quite pleased with herself.*

MONICA PAGE. I could be a brief, me.

RICK. There's absolutely no reason why you couldn't take up the law, Miss Page. If you worked hard.

MONICA PAGE. I'd be dead good at that me, an' all. Hang 'im, hang 'im and hang 'im, an' all! No messin' about with me.

The GIRLS *start laughing, as the* BOYS *come back. This time followed by* WESTON.

WESTON. Mr Braithwaite, I wondered if I may address your class.

RICK nods agreement and WESTON *comes over and stands by the desk. The other* BOYS *all sit down.*

These boys have just apologised for the incident in the gym. I just wanted all of you to know that I too am sorry. As your teacher you were my responsibility and anything that happens is down to me and me alone. I think one way or another we were all a bit silly, but the sooner we forget about the whole incident the better.

He looks over at ARCHIE.

How are you feeling, Archie?

ARCHIE. Much better, sir.

WESTON. Good, good.

He nods to RICK *and heads out of the class.*

Beat.

MONICA PAGE. I'm sorry, sir, but… bleedin' 'ell!

They all start laughing. RICK *tries to hide the grin crossing his face.*

MR FLORIAN *appears at the door. He calls* RICK *outside.* RICK *leaves and returns moments later. He looks shocked. He looks over at* SEALES.

RICK. Seales, why don't you get your things together. Mr Florian is outside. He wants a word with you. You're needed at home.

SEALES *stands up.*

SEALES. What is it, sir?

RICK. Maybe you should go along and see Mr Florian.

SEALES. It's me mum, innit, sir?

RICK *doesn't know what to say.*

Is she dead?

RICK. I'm sorry, Seales...

SEALES *suddenly starts to cry. It's a howl of pain. The other* KIDS *look on visibly shocked. A couple of the* GIRLS *start to cry as well.* RICK *goes over to* SEALES *and stands by his desk. He reaches out and puts his hand on his back.* SEALES *suddenly throws his arms around* RICK'*s waist.*

Scene Nine

The staffroom.

We hear the sound of rain. RICK *stands looking out of the window.*

CLINTY *comes in.*

CLINTY. You're in early?

RICK. So are you.

CLINTY. Early bird and all that.

RICK. Do you want some tea?

She nods. He pours her a cup.

CLINTY. Hey, how did your weekend with the prospective in-laws go? Did he take you out shooting? He's a very good shot, I seem to remember –

RICK. We didn't get that far.

CLINTY. Oh?

RICK *says nothing but just looks at her.*

That good, eh? Is it something you want to talk about?

RICK. I decided to cut the weekend short by about... Oh, the weekend.

CLINTY. Oh, Rick, what happened?

RICK. Let's just say Gillian's father decided it best to lay his cards on the table from the off, and leave it at that.

CLINTY. I'm sorry to hear about Seales' mother. Poor little blighter.

RICK. Mmmm, I felt so useless... I've spent so much time trying to get close to them, then something like this happens and I'm... What could I do...

CLINTY. You were there for him. That's all that matters. That's what's important.

RICK. What's going to happen to him now? He's the eldest of six, for God's sake. His father's just lost his job... I'm not cut out for this. The old man thinks I have some kind of aptitude for teaching.

CLINTY. And he's right.

RICK. You think?

CLINTY. I know. You care about these kids. Really care. That's why you're worried about Seales. I'm not saying we don't, but most of us see four o'clock come round with a sense of relief. Not you. It bothers you what comes afterwards for these kids.

RICK. But I... I don't know if I want this... I didn't think for a minute it was going to be like this. I've applied for some electronics jobs.

CLINTY. Well, I for one would be sorry to see you go.

The door opens and GILLIAN *comes in.* CLINTY *stands and heads for the door.*

Morning, Gillian, I'm off to set up my stall. We're making bread-and-butter pudding today. Should be quite a ghastly experience. I'll save you a bit.

She heads out.

GILLIAN. I thought you were going to ring me when you got back?

RICK. Sorry, it seemed every telephone box I tried was out of order.

GILLIAN. I spoke to my father. He told me everything he'd said to you.

RICK. Did he?

GILLIAN. I can't tell you how angry I am with him.

RICK. Not angry enough to come back to London with me?

GILLIAN. How could I leave it like that? Will I still see you tonight? I've booked a table.

RICK. Yes.

He leaves.

Scene Ten

RICK *is looking for papers on his desk.*

MONICA PAGE. Please, sir.

RICK. Yes, Miss Page.

MONICA PAGE. Seales' mum, sir. She's being buried tomorrow morning, sir.

RICK. Is she?

MONICA PAGE. We were wondering, sir. If we could have a whip-round to buy a wreath.

RICK. I think that would be a wonderful gesture, Miss Page. I think Seales would be very moved and grateful. May I be allowed to contribute as well?

MONICA PAGE. Course you can, sir. Come on, you lot, get your money out.

The other KIDS *start to hand* MONICA PAGE *their contributions.* RICK *hands her his.*

PAMELA DARE. My auntie's got a flower stall, sir. She said she'll do us up something lovely. Not cheap mind.

RICK. That's very kind of her.

PAMELA DARE. Mrs Seales used to do her washing for her, see.

DENHAM. She did ours and all, sir. She worked at the washhouse for years. Everyone knew her.

RICK. I'm sure the family will be very touched. Who will take the wreath round to the house?

MONICA PAGE stops what she's doing and they all look at RICK.

MONICA PAGE. The flowers, sir? Take the flowers?

RICK. Yes, who'll take them to the house?

MONICA PAGE (*apologetically*). We can't take them, sir.

RICK. What do you mean, Miss Page? Why can't you take them?

MONICA PAGE looks about the class for help in explaining.

MONICA PAGE. It's what people would say if they saw us going into a coloured person's house. You know... one of us girls, sir.

RICK. What they would say?

Suddenly the penny drops. RICK is struck dumb. He can't bring himself to speak. He looks at them. He's appalled, embarrassed and disappointed. He sits down in his chair. There is a pause of forty seconds, as he continues to look at them. He is unable to say anything. He looks out towards the window. The KIDS look at each other and at RICK but say nothing.

MONICA PAGE. Sir, I don't think you understood. We've got nothing against Seales. We like him. Honest we do, but if one of us girls was seen going to his house, into a coloured's... you can't imagine the things people would say... We'd be accused of all sorts.

RICK. Thank you for making that so clear, Miss Page. Does the same thing apply to the boys as well? Would it affect your honour in any way?

The BOYS *can't bring themselves to look at* RICK.

Very well –

PAMELA DARE *stands up*.

PAMELA DARE. I'll take them, sir.

RICK. Aren't you afraid of what might be said of you, Miss Dare?

PAMELA DARE. No, sir, gossips don't worry me. Besides I've known Larry – Seales, since we were in the infants together.

RICK. Thank you, Miss Dare. I'll see you there tomorrow.

The bell rings.

You'd better go.

The KIDS *head off looking embarrassed and subdued.* MR FLORIAN *comes in as they go out.*

MR FLORIAN. They're usually full of beans coming out of here. What on earth's happened?

RICK. My kids won't deliver a funeral wreath to the Seales' house, because of what people might think of them. Going into a coloured person's home.

MR FLORIAN. Oh, my dear fellow –

RICK. It's a wreath, for God's sake! The boy's mother's dead! Can there be no compassion even in death?

MR FLORIAN. This bears no reflection on you, Rick.

RICK. Doesn't it? What in God's name have I been doing all these months then? Have I been wasting my time? Have I taught them nothing... I thought they liked me – I thought they'd begun to respect me, but this?

MR FLORIAN. They do respect you. The very fact that they stood there and told you, shows they don't agree with it. And that's down to you and the relationship you have with them. They're as appalled as you are.

RICK. Are they?

MR FLORIAN. Yes. But they have to live here and unfortunately that is how many people think. You can't stamp out prejudice overnight. But you've got a classroom full of young people that you're sending out into the world. They've learned from you. You've taught them to think differently. That's how we beat the bigotry, class by class. Year after year.

Scene Eleven

Street.

RICK *and* GILLIAN *walk onto the stage.*

GILLIAN. I'm sorry, we should never have gone there.

RICK. We had to eat somewhere.

Beat.

GILLIAN. Why didn't you say something, Rick? Why did you just sit there and take it?

RICK. I suppose you're referring to the waiter?

GILLIAN (*angry*). Who else would I be referring to?

She brings her voice back down.

RICK. What was I supposed to do, hit him? Did you want a scene in that place?

GILLIAN. Yes, I wanted a scene. I wanted the biggest scene you could have come up with!

RICK. What good would that have done?

GILLIAN. I don't know and I don't care. But I wanted you to do something. You should have hit him. Beat him hard.

RICK. It wouldn't help, it never does.

GILLIAN. Why not? Just who do you think you are, Jesus Christ? You just sat there all good and patient. Were you afraid? Is that it? Were you afraid of that damned little waiter, that wretched little peasant of a waiter?

RICK. Beating people up doesn't solve anything.

GILLIAN. Doesn't it? Well, what does?

RICK. I thought you knew me a little better than that, Gillian.

GILLIAN. You've been taking it and taking it, don't you think it's time you showed a bit of spirit?

RICK. What is it, Gillian?

GILLIAN. Why is it always someone else fighting your fight? Everyone stands up for you against Weston –

RICK. I don't need them to.

GILLIAN. And me, Rick, was I meant to stand up for you tonight? Or was I suppose to sit and watch that disgusting, bigoted little man humiliate you because of your colour? You should have given him a good slap across the face.

She makes to move off. RICK *grabs her arm and turns her.*

RICK. And is that what I should have done to your father?

GILLIAN. Let go of me.

RICK. No, you're going to listen. You think it's perfectly acceptable to beat up a waiter because of his obvious racism. But when it comes to a nice middle-class gentleman, like your father, you expect me to sit there and take it?

GILLIAN. That's not what I'm saying.

RICK. At least the waiter was honest. He didn't hide his disgust at my colour with phony sugar-coated platitudes of sympathy.

He mimics GILLIAN's *middle-class father.*

'You're a very nice chap, Rick, charming, intelligent – but you're a Negro.' 'Have you considered your children, Rick? What will happen to them? They won't belong anywhere, Rick.' Well pardon me, Mr Blanchard, for lumbering you with a couple of piccaninnies to play with on the village green!

GILLIAN. That's not what he –

RICK. That's exactly what he meant! Don't you think I wanted to smash his face in too? Don't you think I wanted to wring his scrawny little neck!

GILLIAN. Stop it, Rick, you're making it all sound so ugly!

RICK. It is ugly, Gillian, and it'll get uglier!

GILLIAN. I don't want to hear it!

RICK. The looks of disgust, the snide remarks, people spitting at you in the street. This is what a relationship with me, means! Your family turns their back on you. Friends stop calling.

GILLIAN. No –

RICK. Yes. All that and more! Much more!

They both calm down.

GILLIAN. I never thought...

RICK (*incredulous*). Didn't you know that such things happened?

GILLIAN. I'd heard and read about it, but... My parents were... It's as if I suddenly didn't know who they were. I never imagined it happening to me.

RICK. It needn't happen again.

GILLIAN. What do you mean? Is that what you want, Rick?

RICK. No. Of course it isn't. But I have to be sure that you do.

GILLIAN. I think I'm in love with you. But I'm afraid now. Everything seemed alright before, now it's all so frightening. I just don't understand how you take it so calmly. Don't you mind?

RICK. I do mind. But I've learnt how to mind and still live.

GILLIAN. I don't know if I'm going to be strong enough.

RICK. No, I don't know if you are either.

She runs off, leaving RICK *alone.*

Scene Twelve

The street.

RICK *stands alone. He is joined by* MR FLORIAN, *who walks on carrying a funeral wreath.*

MR FLORIAN. Thought you might need some company.

RICK. Thank you, sir.

> PAMELA DARE *enters carrying the wreath.*

> Hello, Miss Dare. It's good to see you here.

> *Suddenly all the other* KIDS *walk onto the stage and join them.* RICK *says nothing but just looks at them proudly.*

DENHAM. It's traditional to walk behind the hearse for a few streets, sir.

RICK. Thank you, Mr Denham.

MONICA PAGE. Here it comes now, sir.

PAMELA DARE. We just fall in behind it, sir.

MONICA PAGE. There's Seales. He's looking at us.

> *A few of the* KIDS *give little embarrassed waves.*

DENHAM. Come on, sir.

> MR FLORIAN *smiles at* RICK.

MR FLORIAN. Class by class, year after year.

> *They all start to walk slowly off the stage.*

Scene Thirteen

The staffroom.

Late afternoon. The room is decorated with paper lanterns.
WESTON is sitting snoozing in his chair. RICK is standing by
the pigeonholes cleaning his out, dropping the rubbish into a
waste-paper basket he holds. We can hear the excited cries of
the KIDS in the playground. CLINTY is sitting, looking
exhausted.

CLINTY. Well at least that's over for another year.

RICK. You must be exhausted, Clinty. I've never seen such a
collection of cakes.

WESTON. You must be teaching them something, old girl,
because they didn't taste half bad either.

CLINTY. End of term. Everything comes together as if by magic.

WESTON. What about you, Braithwaite, how was it for you?

RICK. I must admit. I really quite enjoyed it.

RICK pulls out a letter. He looks at the address. He puts
down the waste basket and opens the letter. RICK reads the
letter.

My God!

CLINTY. What is it?

RICK. My birthday has come early this year. I've been offered
a job with an electronics company. In Birmingham.

CLINTY. But Rick, that's wonderful! Well done. You know my
thoughts on the matter, but I'm very pleased for you.

RICK. I don't believe it.

WESTON. You mean you're buggering off?

RICK. It would seem that way.

WESTON. But you can't!

Everybody looks at WESTON, surprised.

You make those delinquents almost agreeable to teach, for
God's sake. What are we going to do with the next lot if
you're not here?

CLINTY. You hardly make anyone welcome, Weston.

WESTON. Oh, don't mind me. That's just my way. I'm rude and bigoted to everyone. Even my parents disliked me. They said so often. You can't possibly want to go to Birmingham.

RICK. Why?

WESTON. Well, well there's that extraordinarily awful accent for starters.

GILLIAN comes in.

CLINTY. Guess what, Rick's got a new job.

GILLIAN. Really?

She looks at RICK.

RICK. Yes.

GILLIAN. That's wonderful, Rick. I'm really very pleased for you.

RICK. Thank you, Gillian.

GILLIAN. Good luck.

She picks up her bag and heads out.

Have a lovely summer, all of you.

CLINTY. Aren't you stopping for the seniors' dance?

GILLIAN. No, I can't. Bye, bye…

She glances at RICK as she leaves.

WESTON. You know, it's a bit rum if you ask me. Abandoning ship like this mid-ocean.

CLINTY. We're hardly the *Titanic*, Weston.

WESTON. I'm surprised at you, Rick. Waste of a good teacher.

CLINTY and RICK look surprised. WESTON has called RICK by his first name. They find it amusing but cover their smiles.

RICK. I'm sorry you feel that way, erm…

RICK looks at WESTON questioningly. All eyes are on WESTON.

WESTON....Humphrey...

RICK. Well, Humphrey, I shall miss you too.

There is a knock at the door.

WESTON. Enter!

PAMELA DARE *comes into the room. She is dressed up and looks wonderful.*

Yes, Miss Dare. What can we do for you this fine day?

PAMELA DARE. I've brought some invitations for our dance, sir. Do you think I could hand them out?

WESTON. But of course.

PAMELA DARE *comes in and starts to hand out the invitations.*

RICK. You're looking lovely today, Miss Dare.

PAMELA DARE. Thank you, sir.

She hands them out. She goes over to WESTON *and gives one to him.*

WESTON. Me?

PAMELA DARE. Yes, sir...

WESTON. You're inviting me?

PAMELA DARE. If you want to come, sir.

WESTON. Erm, I'd be delighted...

RICK *goes over to the door and opens it for her. Just as he's closing it –*

PAMELA DARE. Oh, sir.

RICK. Yes, Miss Dare?

PAMELA DARE. Will you have a dance with me tonight?

RICK. Of course, Miss Dare. I'd be honoured. But no jiving – I'm getting too old for that.

She smiles.

PAMELA DARE. Okay, sir, I'll bring in a special record for you. Promise?

RICK. Yes, Miss Dare. I promise.

PAMELA DARE. And, sir.

RICK. Yes?

PAMELA DARE. Will you call me Pamela, just for this evening?

RICK. Of course, Pamela.

> PAMELA DARE *smiles widely.*

PAMELA DARE. Thank you.

> *She walks off.*

CLINTY. You've just given that young girl the best leaving present ever!

WESTON. I've been invited to the party.

> *They look at* WESTON *and start laughing.*

> *We hear Bill More singing 'We're Going to Rock' as the lights fade.*

Scene Fourteen

The gym.

The gymnasium has been decorated for the party. The KIDS *are all dressed up and dancing.* MR FLORIAN *is having a go as only old people dancing to modern music can, to the delight of the* KIDS. WESTON *is acting as DJ. He yanks off the record to a chorus of groans.*

WESTON. Erm, the next record I am about to play for you is called 'It Takes a Long Tall Brown-skin Gal' by the Four Blues.

> *He pops on the record and everyone starts to dance again.*

CLINTY. I think Humphrey's found a new calling.

RICK. I think you may be right.

CLINTY. Listen, Rick, tell me if I'm sticking my big nose in but I spoke to Gillian. She told me everything that happened. You know she's not coming back next term?

RICK. You're sticking your big nose in.

CLINTY. Right.

RICK. Look, Clinty, what happened, happened for the best. It could have been a lot worse further along down the line.

MR FLORIAN *comes over, wiping his brow.*

MR FLORIAN. I somehow manage to impress them with my terpsichorean knowledge every year.

CLINTY. You certainly do, Headmaster!

MR FLORIAN. The trick is to keep up with them. Every year without fail, I nip down to my local ballroom and learn the latest steps.

RICK. You're very good, sir.

MR FLORIAN. And you both know how to flatter an old man.

They laugh.

Clinty tells me you're going to be leaving us.

RICK. I've been offered a position, sir.

MR FLORIAN. It's what you wanted, I believe?

RICK. Yes, sir. Very much so.

MR FLORIAN. Well, you deserve it, Braithwaite. But I'll hate to lose you.

PAMELA DARE *comes over to them.*

WESTON *changes the record again with a scratch.*

WESTON. The next dance is a ladies' excuse-me foxtrot. 'In the Still of the Night'. By Cole Porter.

RICK. I think this is our dance, Pamela.

PAMELA DARE. I think it is, sir.

They dance elegantly around the floor. Other dancers stop to watch. PAMELA DARE *is in seventh heaven as she allows*

RICK *to glide her about the floor. As the music stops everyone claps.*

RICK. Thank you, Pamela.

PAMELA DARE. Thank you, sir.

DENHAM starts to clap his hands to gain attention.

DENHAM. Hello, could I have your attention, please. Mr Weston, sir. The music.

WESTON turns off the music.

Thank you. Erm, I'd like to say a few words on behalf of the senior year.

The others gather around DENHAM. DENHAM takes out a prepared speech.

I know you others have taught us as well. But this is for sir –

MONICA PAGE. Mr Braithwaite, dummy.

The others giggle.

RICK. Sir will do, Denham.

DENHAM. We just wanted to say how grateful we are for all you've done for us in the short time you've been our teacher. We know it hasn't been a bed of roses for you, what with one thing and another. And we could have given you an easier time at first. But if we had you wouldn't have loved us as much as you do now!

They all laugh.

We think we're much better people for having had you as our teacher. And we liked the way you treated us as adults and the way you spoke and did things… We… we…

He looks up at RICK and at the rest of the class. He screws up the speech.

We just wanted to say, thank you, sir… For me… I don't know what you did, sir… and it might well sound stupid to anyone else… but you made me feel like I've been somewhere, you know? These last months and that. Somewhere I'd like to go back to one day… I think if I have kids – if any of us have kids – we'd like them to be taught by a man like you, sir. Because I think they'd be safe in your hands.

DENHAM *looks at* SEALES. SEALES *walks over to* RICK *and hands him a present wrapped in ribbon.* RICK *takes it.*

RICK. Thank you, Seales.

He opens the card.

MONICA PAGE. Read it out, sir.

RICK. 'To sir with love…'

He doesn't get any further. He knows if he attempts to say another thing he'll end up in pieces. The KIDS *sense it and start clapping. Everyone else joins in.* RICK *turns and heads for the classroom.* WESTON *starts to sing 'For He's a Jolly Good Fellow'.*

WESTON.
    'For he's a jolly good fellow!
    For he's a jolly good fellow!'

All the others join in the song.

ALL.
    'For he's a jolly good fellow.
    And so say all of us.
    And so say all of us.
    And so say all of us.'

The light fades in the gym.

Lights up in the classroom.

RICK *stands by his desk listening to the singing. He opens the present. It's a silver frame. He takes out the letter from his inside pocket.*

    'For he's a jolly good fellow!
    For he's a jolly good fellow!
    For he's a jolly good fellow.
    And so say all of us.
    And so say all of us.
    And so say all of us.'

He tears it up as the lights begin to fade.

The End.

www.nickhernbooks.co.uk

 facebook.com/nickhernbooks

 twitter.com/nickhernbooks